Russell

GUIDES FOR THE PERPLEXED

Guides for the Perplexed are clear, concise, and accessible introductions to thinkers, writers, and subjects that students and readers can find especially challenging. Concentrating specifically on what it is that makes the subject difficult to grasp, these books explain and explore key themes and ideas, guiding the reader toward a thorough understanding of demanding material.

A GUIDE FOR THE PERPLEXED

Russell

JOHN ONGLEY AND ROSALIND CAREY

B L O O M S B U R Y

LONDON · NEW DELHI · NEW YORK · SYDNEY

Bloomsbury Academic
An imprint of Bloomsbury Publishing Plc

50 Bedford Square
London
WC1B 3DP
UK

175 Fifth Avenue
New York
NY 10010
USA

www.bloomsbury.com

First published 2013

British Library Cataloguing-in-Publication Data
A catalogue record for this book is available from the British Library.

ISBN: HB: 978-0-8264-9753-6
PB: 978-0-8264-9754-3

Library of Congress Cataloging-in-Publication Data
Ongley, John.
Russell: a guide for the perplexed/John Ongley and Rosalind Carey.
pages cm – (Guides for the perplexed)
Includes bibliographical references and index.
ISBN 978-0-8264-9753-6 (hardback) – ISBN 978-0-8264-9754-3 (paperback) –
ISBN 978-1-4411-9123-6 (epub) 1. Russell, Bertrand, 1872–1970. I. Carey, Rosalind.
II. Title.
B1649.R94O54 2013
192–dc23
2012020365

Typeset by Deanta Global Publishing Services, Chennai, India
Printed and bound in India

CONTENTS

PREFACE

This book is a guide to some of Bertrand Russell's more difficult philosophical works and ideas. Russell's most important and at the same time most difficult work is *Principia Mathematica*, the monumental three-volume opus cowritten with Alfred North Whitehead. These volumes present in elaborate detail his ground-breaking logical analysis of the foundations of mathematics. Written almost entirely in logical notation, it is difficult in the extreme to work through and understand.

Russell wrote an informal guide to *Principia Mathematica*—one without logical symbolism, and, he says, one "offering a minimum of difficulty to the reader." This is his *Introduction to Mathematical Philosophy*. Though concise and beautifully written, it is itself not always easy to understand. This guide's first aim is to help the reader master Russell's informal *Introduction*, then, having mastering that, to understand *Principia Mathematica*. This will enable the reader to also understand Russell's earlier masterpiece on the foundations of mathematics, *Principles of Mathematics*.

Russell also had a larger philosophy—one not just about logic and mathematics, but about the world more broadly, one that sought to understand the nature of the universe and the way that we know it. This philosophy especially includes Russell's metaphysics, his theory of knowledge, and his theory of language, which are the subjects of his following works: "Philosophy of Logical Atomism," *Analysis of Mind*, *Analysis of Matter*, *Inquiry into Meaning and Truth*, and *Human Knowledge*. Because his ideas on these subjects are spread out over many works and evolve over time, we take a different approach in covering them and present each subject as it occurs in Russell's early, middle, and late work. Here, we aim to give the reader a broad understanding of Russell's larger philosophy and to see the evolution of his thought as a whole.

We are grateful to Dr Ray Perkins Jr, professor of philosophy at Plymouth State University, for advise and support, Jay Barksdale, reference librarian at the New York Public Library, for exceptional assistance over a very long period of time, and Douglas Ferguson and Dr Stefan Andersson for generosity in making available to us affordable copies of the many volumes of Russell's *Collected Papers*.

CHAPTER ONE

Introduction

Bertrand Russell (1872–1970) was arguably the greatest philosopher of the twentieth century and the greatest logician since Aristotle. He wrote original philosophy on dozens of subjects, but his most important work was in logic, mathematical philosophy, and analytic philosophy. Russell is responsible more than anyone else for the creation and development of the modern logic of relations—the single greatest advance in logic since Aristotle. He then used the new logic as the basis of his mathematical philosophy called *logicism*.

Logicism is the view that all mathematical concepts can be defined in terms of logical concepts and that all mathematical truths can be deduced from logical truths to show that mathematics is nothing but logic. In his work on logicism, Russell developed forms of analysis in order to analyze quantifiers in logic and numbers and classes in mathematics, but he was soon using them to analyze points in space, instants of time, matter, mind, morality, knowledge, and language itself in what was the beginning of analytic philosophy.

This first chapter introduces Russell's work in logic, logicism, and analysis, and then introduces his broader inquiries of analytic philosophy in metaphysics, knowledge, and meaning. Subsequent chapters treat each subject in detail. However, all of Russell's technical philosophy revolves around his logicism. Because Russell's mathematical philosophy is the key to the rest of his work, and because it is the most difficult part of it, we begin this chapter with a discussion of logicism, then keep circling back to it, relating it to the rest, until it seems to the reader that it is the easiest thing in the world to understand.

1 Logic and logicism: Basic concepts

Let's start with some basic logical concepts. A sentence is a group of words that express a meaning that is a complete thought. A declarative sentence expresses a meaning that is either true or false. A proposition is the meaning expressed by a declarative sentence such as the true proposition "The earth is round" or the false one "The earth is flat." So propositions are either true or false. The declarative sentences that express them are also said to be true or false.

Subjects and predicates follow. The subject of a proposition is who or what the proposition is about. "The earth is flat" is about the earth. So the earth is the subject of that proposition. The predicate is what is said about, or attributed to, the subject. Here, the proposition attributes flatness to the earth, so "___ is flat" is the predicate. Logicians write predicates using blank spaces, or more usually, variables like x, y, or z to indicate where the subject goes in relation to the predicate. Bertrand Russell called predicates *propositional functions*. In this book, we use the terms interchangeably.

The predicate "x is flat" is a *one-place predicate*, because it only has one place where a subject can go—it attributes a property to one thing. Two-place predicates are *relations* like that in "Indiana is flatter than Ohio." Here, the subjects are "Indiana" and "Ohio" and the predicate is "x is flatter than y." (In grammar, the first is the subject and the second is the object; in logic, they are both subjects.) Common two-place relations in mathematics are $x = y$, $x > y$, and $x < y$. There are also three-place relations like that in "Ohio is between Indiana and Pennsylvania," where the predicate is "x is between y and z," which is often used in geometry. There are also four-place relations, and so on.

Before Russell's logic of relations, logic consisted principally of the Aristotelian logic of one-place predicates. This simple logic can analyze sentences that use one-place predicates to attribute properties to objects like "Tom is tall" or "The sky is blue." It can also analyze slightly more complex sentences like "All humans are animals" (if someone is human, that person is an animal) and "Some humans are thoughtful" (at least one person is both human and thoughtful) and from these two sentences infer that "Some animals are thoughtful." You can't get too far with such a simple logic and you certainly can't analyze many mathematical or scientific statements with it.

It was Russell's first great achievement to develop the more powerful logic of relations to describe concepts such as "x is taller than y" used in propositions like "Tom is taller than Bob," which you can't say with a one-place predicate like "x is tall." This allowed Russell to describe propositions containing two-place mathematical relations like $x = y$ or "$x > y$" (needed for arithmetic and algebra), three-place relations like "x is between a and b" (needed for geometry), and the like. With it, all of the concepts of pure mathematics can be expressed, which can't be done with the logic that came before it.

Russell's logic includes set theory. This is because his logic contains predicates and every predicate defines a set. For example, the predicate "x is human" defines the set of all things that can replace the x to make "x is human" a true proposition, namely, the class of humans. The *comprehension axiom* is the assumption that every predicate defines a class. It is an assumption of Russell's logic. Thus, Russell's logic contains sets and a theory of sets, as well as one-place predicates and two-place relations. Russell refers to sets as "classes" and set theory as "the theory of classes." We will use both ways of speaking indifferently and without distinction.

2 The emergence of logicism

After the logic of relations, Russell's greatest achievement is his theory of logicism—the view that mathematics is just logic, so that all mathematical concepts can be defined with logical concepts and all mathematical truths derived from logical truths. Russell's logic and his logicist philosophy were first fully described in his 1903 *Principles of Mathematics*. The actual derivation of mathematics from logic, to prove that all mathematics can be derived from logic, occurs in the three-volume 1910–13 *Principia Mathematica* that Russell wrote with Alfred North Whitehead. Russell also presents logicism simply and informally in the 1919 *Introduction to Mathematical Philosophy*.

Logicism comes down to is this: In the nineteenth century, mathematicians had shown that all of classical mathematics can be defined in terms of, and derived from, arithmetic. Most importantly, Richard Dedekind had shown in 1872 that the real numbers can be defined in terms of rational numbers. Then rational numbers were defined in terms of natural numbers, thus demonstrating that the real numbers can be derived from natural numbers. The next step was taken when Giuseppe Peano, based on work by Dedekind, showed in 1890 that arithmetic can be reduced to five axioms and three undefined terms.

To reduce mathematics to logic, one then simply has to define Peano's three concepts with logical concepts, thus expressing Peano's axioms logically, and then derive the axioms from logical truths, thus showing that Peano's axioms, and all the mathematics based on them, are logical truths. Russell starts by defining natural numbers logically as classes of classes. Specifically, a natural number is the class of all classes containing the same number of things, so that the number 1 is the class of all singletons (classes with one member), 2 is the class of all couples, and so on. With this definition, Russell then defines Peano's other two basic concepts logically and derives Peano's axioms from logic.

Put this way, demonstrating logicism is a seemingly simple task. But Russell and Whitehead soon ran into difficulties, namely, contradictions Russell found in the new logic and set theory. The most famous of these is called *Russell's paradox*. Some sets are members of themselves, others are not. The set of things that are not red is itself not red, so it is a member of itself, but the set of red things is not red, so it is not a member of itself. This allows us to construct the predicate "x is not a member of itself," which defines the set of all sets that are not members of themselves. But is the set itself a member of itself? If it is a member of itself, then it isn't. But if it isn't a member of itself, then it is. A contradiction ensues no matter how one answers.

To avoid this and similar paradoxes, Russell's logic, and the logicism based on it, became quite complex, and the ultimate success of this logicism is still a matter of debate. Many believe that it cannot be carried out completely. Others say the final verdict is not yet in. Still others say it can be done. In any case, it is significant and astonishing how much of mathematics Russell and Whitehead demonstrated *can* be reduced to logic. And if one is willing to tolerate a few pesky contradictions here and there, it absolutely can be done.

Russell's original form of logicism, in his 1903 *Principles of Mathematics*, did not attempt to avoid the paradoxes of the new logic, and so did not contain the complex mechanisms Russell later added to his logic to avoid them. It is a straightforward theory, containing all of logicism's basic elements. We present this basic logicism, which we call *naïve logicism*, in Chapter 2. The complex version meant to avoid paradoxes, which occurs in the 1910–13 *Principia Mathematica*, we call *restricted logicism*. We describe that in Chapter 3.

3 Logicism and analysis

As well as founding the logic of relations, developing the theory of logicism, and discovering fundamental contradictions in logic and set theory, Russell more than anyone else founded the twentieth-century movement of analytic philosophy that still dominates philosophy today. Analytic philosophy as practiced by Russell logically analyzes language to say what there is and how we know it. Analysis is a significant part of analytic philosophy and its role in the movement is largely due to Russell. His logical analysis of mathematics is the primary example of analysis.

Notions of analysis vary from one analytic philosopher to another and from one analysis to another by a single philosopher. This last case is true of Russell himself. Most generally, "analysis" for him means beginning with something that is common knowledge and seeking the fundamental concepts and principles it is based on. This is followed by a synthesis that begins with the basic concepts and principles discovered by analysis and uses them to derive the common knowledge with which one began the analysis.

In Russell's own words (*Introduction to Mathematical Philosophy*): "By analyzing we ask . . . what more general ideas and principles can be found, in terms of which what was our starting-point can be defined or deduced" (p. 1). Similarly, in *Principia Mathematica*, he says "There are two opposite tasks which have to be concurrently performed. On the one hand, we have to analyze existing mathematics, with a view to discovering what premises are employed . . . . On the other hand, when we have decided upon our premises, we have to build up again [i.e., synthesize] as much as may seem necessary of the data previously analyzed" (vol. 1, p. v).

Immanuel Kant uses the same concepts of analysis and synthesis to describe his *Prolegomena to Any Future Metaphysics* and *Critique of Pure Reason.* "I offer here," he says in the *Prolegomena*, "a plan which is sketched out after an analytical method, while the *Critique* itself had to be executed in the synthetical style" (p. 8). In the *Prolegomena* we start with science (mathematics and physics) and by *analysis*, he says, "proceed to the ground of its possibility," that is, to its fundamental concepts, while in the *Critique*, "they [the sciences] must be derived ... from [the fundamental] concepts" (p. 24).

Russell's *Introduction to Mathematical Philosophy*, an informal introduction to *Principia*'s logicism, is similarly analytic. About it, he says: "Starting from the natural numbers, we have first defined *cardinal number* and shown how to generalize the conception of number, and have then analyzed the conceptions involved in the definition, until we found ourselves dealing with the fundamentals of logic." About synthesis, he says "In a synthetic, deductive treatment these fundamentals [reached by analysis] come first, and the natural numbers [with which the analysis started] are reached only after a long journey" (p. 195).

And *Principia Mathematica* is a synthesis: it begins with the logical fundamentals found by analysis, and from them deductively builds up the mathematics the analysis started with. As Russell says in *Principia* itself, it is "a deductive system" in which "the preliminary labor of analysis does not appear." Instead, it "merely sets forth the outcome of the analysis . . . making deductions from our premises ... up to the point where we have proved as much as is true in whatever would ordinarily be taken for granted" (vol. 1, p. v).

Russell's *Introduction to Mathematical Philosophy* is thus to *Principia Mathematica* what Kant's *Prolegomena* is to the *Critique of Pure Reason*—an analysis that takes common knowledge and finds its basic principles, which synthesis then uses to demonstrate the knowledge analyzed. The *Introduction to Mathematical Philosophy* and *Prolegomena* also both informally introduce the subjects presented more rigorously in the synthetic works. But Kant seeks to justify knowledge with the principles uncovered by analysis. Russell does not. For him, the logical ideas analysis uncovers are less certain than the arithmetic it analyzes.

For Russell, what we analyze—arithmetic—is certain and *inductively* justifies the fundamental principles found by analysis when synthesis deduces arithmetic from them. (If synthesis shows that logic implies arithmetic, and arithmetic is true, then logic is *probably* true. The argument is inductive.) Russell does not think arithmetic is made certain by being derived from logic, but that logic is made more certain by arithmetic being derived from it.

As Russell says in *Principia*: "The chief reason in favor of any theory on the principles of mathematics [the justification of the premises that imply mathematics] must always be inductive, i.e. it must lie in the fact that the theory in question enables us to deduce ordinary mathematics" (vol. 1, p. v). What is found by analysis is less certain than what is analyzed. Russell does not seek certainty from the analysis of mathematics, but an understanding of the reasons, however uncertain, for accepting what we normally take for granted.

"In mathematics," Russell further says, "the greatest degree of self-evidence is usually not to be found quite at the beginning, but at some later point . . . . hence, the early deductions [of *Principia*], until they reach this point, give reasons rather for believing the premises because true consequences follow from them, than for believing the consequences because they follow from the premises" (p. v–vi). *Principia* does indeed show that arithmetic follows from logic, which gives us some reason to accept those logical principles as an account of arithmetic's nature.

4 Logical analysis: The theory of descriptions

These concepts of analysis and synthesis may seem vague, but they will get you a long way in understanding Russell's *Introduction to Mathematical Philosophy* and *Principia Mathematica*. At some point, however, to understand Russell's work one must learn his more technical, logical kinds of analysis that are his theory of descriptions and incomplete symbols, his "no-class" theory of classes, his theory of logical types, and his logical constructions.

In the theory of descriptions, Russell analyzes descriptions of objects and classes by translating them into his new logic, where we can see that they do not always mean what they seem to mean in ordinary language. That is, Russell analyzes expressions of ordinary language into more careful logical expressions that are their true meaning. His *Introduction to Mathematical Philosophy* as a whole is the simpler sort of analysis, but within it are several more technical logical analyses using the theory of descriptions.

Russell first published the theory of descriptions in his 1905 article "On Denoting." The theory figures prominently in *Principia Mathematica*, where it is given a fairly clear presentation in the Introduction. Russell's clearest exposition of it is in the 1918 "Philosophy of Logical Atomism," and another is in his 1919 *Introduction to Mathematical Philosophy* (Chapter 16), which is the version most people read in college.

For Russell, the theory of descriptions shows that the grammar of ordinary language is often misleading. Using it, sentences containing singular definite descriptions—descriptions of the form "the so-and-so" such as "the author of *Waverly*" in the sentence "Scott was the author of *Waverly*"—are analyzed so that the description does not occur in the logical analysis of the sentence, but is replaced by a predicate.

For example, "the author of *Waverly*" in "Scott was the author of *Waverly*" is replaced with the predicate "*x* wrote *Waverly*" and the sentence becomes "There is exactly one thing *x* such that *x* is Scott, and *x* wrote *Waverly*," or more briefly, "Scott wrote *Waverly*." The description "the author of *Waverly*" no longer occurs in the logical analysis of the sentence. In particular, the word "the" is gone. That is the whole function of the theory of descriptions.

Why analyze a sentence so that the definite description it contains, and especially the word "the," disappears? Notice that "the author of *Waverly*" seems to function like a name and to denote a particular object. However, the expression that replaces it, "*x* wrote *Waverly*," is a predicate, not a name, and by itself it does not denote any such object. Let us pause here to consider this idea that names denote, but predicates do not. It is an important idea to Russell.

The idea that names refer to, or denote, objects should not be controversial. "Napoleon" refers to the commanding French general at the battle of Waterloo, "Einstein" to the man who created the special and general theories of relativity, and so forth. And as Russell points out, names have these references independently of occurring in propositions. Finally, definite descriptions like "the author of *Waverly*" seem to function like names and refer to particular individuals too, just as "Sir Walter Scott" does.

Predicates, on the other hand, do not name, or refer to, objects. For example, the predicate "*x* is red" does not name or denote any particular individual by itself independently of occurring in a proposition. It does not specify which object or objects it might be used to apply to. So a predicate is definitely not a name. Because definite descriptions are not names but are predicates, Russell calls them *incomplete symbols*. They appear to name objects, but they really don't.

By showing that definite descriptions, which appear to be names of objects, really aren't, we can see how sentences containing descriptions can be meaningful without the sentence asserting the existence of what is described. For example, we can see how sentences like "The present king of France rolled the round square down the golden mountain" can be meaningful without asserting that any of these things exist.

This solves a general problem of logic for Russell—how to logically analyze sentences containing definite descriptions true of no objects. More significantly, Russell uses a variation of this theory, called his "no-class" theory of classes, to remove all references to classes in his logic by treating names of classes and descriptions of classes as predicates. Then, since logic, so interpreted, does not assume that sets exist, the Russell paradox of the set of all sets that are not members of themselves cannot occur—as we will see next.

5 Logical analysis: The "no-class" theory of classes

In addition to analyzing singular definite descriptions so that what appear to be names are seen to actually be predicates that do not name anything, Russell sometimes treats proper names the same way, for example, in *Principia Mathematica* (in *14.21). He suggests there that words like "Homer" that appear to be proper names are actually concealed definite descriptions like "the author of the Homeric poems." They are then treated like definite descriptions and replaced with predicates. By 1918, in "The Philosophy of Logical Atomism," Russell is using this idea aggressively, insisting that *all* proper names like "Socrates" and "Napoleon" are disguised definite descriptions, but in *Principia*, he only suggests it once.

After singular definite descriptions come plural definite descriptions such as "the inhabitants of London." These too are analyzed so that they are replaced by predicates. "The inhabitants of London" in the sentence "The inhabitants of London are cosmopolitan," seems to name a class of objects, the inhabitants of London. But it is replaced by "x lives in London," which, being a predicate, names no object or objects. The sentence then reads "If anyone lives in London, that person is cosmopolitan."

In the slightly different sentence "The class of people who inhabit London is large," the subject is a description that appears to name a single object, the class of people living in London. Again, we replace the description with a predicate. Similarly, when a symbol stands for a set as its name, we treat it like a disguised definite description, just as "Socrates" is treated as the disguised description "the teacher of Plato." For example, when a = the class of even numbers, we translate "$6 \in a$" ("the number 6 is a member of the class a of even numbers") by replacing a with the predicate "x is divisible by two" and get "6 is divisible by 2." We simply replace the class with the predicate that defines it.

Russell uses these techniques to define classes as predicates in *Principia Mathematica*. This replaces apparent references to classes with predicates that do not refer to classes. Thus, *Principia Mathematica* makes no reference to classes. There are then no classes in his logicist thesis, which ensures that paradoxes of set theory cannot arise in it. So Russell eliminates classes from his logic to prevent paradoxes from arising in it or in the logistic theory based on it. This is Russell's no-class theory of classes. (Though in truth it is a little more complex than this, as we will see in Chapter 3.)

Because Russell defines numbers in terms of classes, the elimination of classes from his logic effects his definition of number. In 1903, Russell defines natural numbers as classes of all classes with the same number of members. At that time, classes are objects for Russell. But when Russell replaces classes with predicates in 1910, he effectively replaces numbers with predicates too. They are then no longer classes and so no longer objects.

For Russell, an incomplete symbol is one that is not a name and does not refer, and definite descriptions are "incomplete symbols" because they are actually predicates and predicates are not names. In *Principia*, descriptions, classes, and numbers are all incomplete symbols. They are additionally, Russell says, all *linguistic conveniences* or *logical fictions*. Classes are thus merely symbolic conveniences and not real objects. All this to avoid the paradoxes of set theory which include Russell's own paradox of classes.

For example, in *Principia*, Russell says "The symbols for classes, like those for descriptions, are . . . incomplete symbols . . . merely symbolic or linguistic conveniences, not genuine objects" (p. 75). And in the 1937 Introduction to the second edition of the *Principles of Mathematics*, he says "seeing that cardinal numbers have been defined as classes of classes, they also became 'merely symbolic or linguistic conveniences'" (p. x).

Here is how replacing classes with predicates works for natural numbers. When two classes have the same number of members, the members of those sets correspond to one another in a 1-to-1 relation. Two sets whose members correspond 1-to-1 are called *similar*. A number is thus a class of all the classes that are similar to one another. For example, the number twelve is the class of all classes similar to the class of Apostles.

When classes are replaced with predicates, the class of similar classes is replaced with the relation of similarity itself. And each of those similar classes is replaced by a predicate. So, the relation of similarity is the relation of 1-to-1 correspondence between the objects these predicates apply to. Then, the class of Apostles becomes the predicate "x followed Jesus from the beginning" or some such thing. Other classes with 12 members are likewise replaced with predicates that define them. Finally, the fact that there are 12 Apostles is replaced by the fact that the things these predicates apply to can all be put in 1-to-1 correlation with one another. As you can see, the no-class theory of classes quickly becomes very complicated.

Russell himself does not say that names refer in isolation and predicates do not. Rather, he says that names have meaning in isolation and predicates do not and so are not names and do not refer to objects. But Russell's use of "meaning" here really only means that names refer and predicates do not; there is nothing more he is asserting when he uses "meaning" in this context. Elsewhere, it means other things for him. This special use of "meaning" by Russell is quite similar to the use of "Bedeutung" (German for "meaning") by Gottlob Frege. Frege, an early logicist, used "Bedeutung" in this same special way to mean "reference" while elsewhere using it to mean "meaning" in more standard ways.

6 Logical analysis: The theory of logical types

Though the no-class theory does avoid Russell's paradox of classes, there is a paradox similar to it for predicates that the no-class theory does not eliminate. This of course is because the no-class theory eliminates classes, not predicates. Here is the new paradox: Some predicates are true of themselves, for example, "*x* is a predicate" is itself a predicate. Others are not—for example, "*x* is red" is not red. From this, we can form the predicate "*x* is a predicate that is not true of itself." This predicate is true of some predicates and not of others. But is it true of itself or not? If it is, it isn't, and if it isn't, it is. We thus have a contradiction.

So simply eliminating classes from one's logic and logicism using the no-class theory does not eliminate all self-referential paradoxes from logicism, because similar paradoxes arise in it for predicates. We can try to use something analogous to the no-class theory to eliminate predicates. For example, we might replace predicates with propositions. Unfortunately there are also self-referential paradoxes for propositions. And so on.

Fortunately, Russell has another method for avoiding paradoxes called *the theory of logical types*. Notice that both versions of the Russell paradox result from allowing a set to be a member of itself or a predicate to apply to itself. The many other sorts of self-referential paradoxes similarly arise self-referentially, by allowing sets to be members of themselves, predicates to apply to themselves, propositions to be about themselves, and so forth. The theory of types prevents the paradoxes from arising by banning self-reference.

In the mature "restricted" logicism of *Principia*, then, as well as adopting the no-class theory of classes, Russell adopts the rule that a set cannot be a member of itself and a predicate cannot apply to itself, that is, it cannot take itself as an argument. This rule is the *theory of logical types*. And the theory of logical types is justified by the *vicious circle principle*, which says that any sentence formed by a set taking itself as a member or predicate taking itself as an argument is meaningless. By adopting the rule that is based on this principle, namely, the theory of types, the paradoxes for both sets and predicates do not arise.

The theory of types works like this: If sets cannot meaningfully be members of themselves and predicates cannot meaningfully refer to themselves, we end up with a hierarchy of different types, or levels, of sets or of predicates, their level depending on what type of things *they* can meaningfully take as members or arguments, and on what sets or predicates can meaningfully take *them* as members or arguments.

At the first level in the hierarchy are individuals. This is the zero-order. Then, there are predicates that apply to individuals. These are called *first-order* predicates. Anything we call an object is an individual—cars, people, molecules, mountains, what have you. A first-order predicate is something like "x is brave." It applies to individuals to form propositions like "Nelson Mandela is brave."

Since first-order predicates now cannot apply to themselves, predicates that apply to first-order predicates are called *second-order* predicates. If courage is a first-order property, we must use a second-order property, like "x is an important virtue" to say something about it such as "Courage is an important virtue." First-order predicates also cannot take predicates of a higher-order than themselves as arguments. Then there are predicates that apply to second-order predicates—these are third-order predicates. And so on.

Sets are structured similarly with individuals again at the zero-order. Sets that take individuals as members are first-order sets, sets that take sets that take individuals as members are second-order sets, and so on. And propositions about objects are first-order propositions, those about first-order propositions are second-order propositions, and so on.

This is the basic idea. The actual theory of types is a few steps more complicated than this and will be explained in full in Chapter 3. But as you can see, stratifying sets and the things they can take as members, or predicates and the things they can apply to, prevents them from being self-referential, so the paradoxes of logic and set theory cannot arise.

Notice though that *both* the no-class theory of classes *and* the theory of logical types are used to avoid the paradoxes of class theory and logic. Why both methods? First, the no-class theory gets rid of sets by converting them to predicates. But since paradoxes also arise for predicates, the theory of types is needed to stratify predicates and prevent paradoxes for predicates from arising.

There are also predicates that apply to sets, but since the no-class theory transforms these sets into predicates, there is no need to create a separate hierarchy for them. This keeps the theory of types from getting any more complex than it already is. There are also *philosophical* problems with stratifying predicates that apply to sets. By converting the sets to predicates, the philosophical problems such as the one described below are avoided.

Notice that there is still a hierarchy for sets in type theory. Why? Although it is understood that symbols for sets are "really" predicates in *Principia*, the mathematics in it is done using symbols for sets anyway. They still need stratifying in order to be used, even though we know they are really predicates. And because there are self-referential paradoxes that arise for propositions, the hierarchy of propositions is included in the theory of types as well.

One last point: notice that the paradoxes for set theory only arise from some sets. But the no-class theory eliminates all sets. This is clearly overkill. Why do it? Answer: As well as needing to avoid the set-theoretic paradoxes, Russell has separate philosophical reasons for wanting to eliminate classes from his logic altogether, for example, to avoid the ancient problem of the one and the many.

Sometimes symbols for sets are treated as representing many things (its members), other times they are treated as representing one thing (the set itself). But it cannot be both. Because of this and other such philosophical puzzles, as well as in order to simplify the theory of types, Russell eliminates *all* classes from his logic using the no-class theory and the idea of logical fictions to define them away.

These, then, are the broad outlines of Russell's mathematical philosophy called logicism. We have seen that Russell uses several different kinds of analysis in his mathematical philosophies. He also applies these methods outside of mathematics to answer philosophical questions about the world at large. We have already seen four varieties of analysis: the general kind that seeks the most basic concepts and principles, the theory of descriptions, the no-class theory of classes, and the theory of logical types. A fifth kind is Russell's analysis of entities with logical constructions, which he uses to analyze physical points, space and time, mental phenomena, matter, and even moral and political concepts. These topics will be introduced in the remainder of this chapter, and discussed at greater length in Chapters 4 through 6.

7 Analysis and metaphysics

Russell's ideas about the nature of reality are often responses to problems in logic, mathematics, and analysis. His views on reality in early work (1900–17) are expressed in *Principles of Mathematics* (1903), "On the Relations of Universals and Particulars" (1912), and "Analytic Realism" (1911). In them, a defense of analysis is part of his view of reality.

Philosophical monists, who were common in England in Russell's time, argue that analyzing the whole of reality into parts is impossible. They feel that the nature of objects is determined by the role they play in larger wholes, and that analyzing wholes into parts leaves out these larger connections. And if the nature of an object lies in the role it plays in a whole, and the nature of that whole lies in the role it plays in some larger whole, reality is ultimately one undivided whole—the plurality we experience is an illusion.

To defend analysis, Russell rejects the monists' arguments and concludes that reality is plural and "atomistic," that is, composed of parts that can be understood independently of their role in the whole. Details about reality in Russell's atomism are reached by analysis of logical principles—it is a *logical* atomism. He believes that logic and grammar reveal the nature of reality. This avoids beliefs about reality not warranted by logic. For example, if reality consists of things that can be analyzed into parts, the parts themselves are either complex and further analyzable or not complex and simple. If they are complex, they presuppose the existence of still simpler entities.

Russell's logical atomism is also based on understanding grammar. Monists assume that the logic of sentences always has a subject-predicate form, where a predicate applies a property to a subject—as in "Socrates is wise" where the predicate "x is wise" applies the property of wisdom to Socrates. If all sentences are really subject-predicate sentences, relations expressed by verbs in sentences like "Socrates is wiser than Plato" must also be properties.

Instead of understanding "Socrates is wiser than Plato" as expressing the relation "x is wiser than y" between Socrates and Plato, monists understand it as saying that "x is wiser than Plato" is a property of Socrates. Treating relations this way makes being wiser than Plato seem like an essential property of Socrates. Treating all relations this way—as essential properties of objects—makes everything seem interrelated to every other thing as a part of its essential nature. Thus, they can only be understood as parts of wholes. This view takes relations as "internal" (i.e., essential) properties of objects.

With his logic of relations, Russell can say that verbs are not predicates and relations are not properties of things. Rather, relations are entities in their own right, not part of the things related. Relations between things are thus "external" to the nature of things. They are not facts about the essential nature of the things related. This is the view of "external relations." Complexes of things are thus external relations among simpler things.

Using grammar as a guide, Russell also assumes that entities occur in specific ways in propositions. Some occur only as subjects of propositions. Others occur as relations or properties of propositions but can also occur in other propositions as subjects. Those that can only be subjects he calls "things" or "particulars." Those that can be both subjects and predicates or relations he calls "concepts" or "universals."

Russell also examines logic and grammar to find the basic elements of nature. These include numbers, classes, concepts, properties, propositions, universals, particulars, particles, points, and instants. As analysis develops, the list of elements changes. The theory of descriptions says descriptions are not names, and soon that "Socrates" is a disguised description and not really a name either. Instead, they are properties or relations. Similarly, the no-classes theory replaces classes with properties, so classes need not be assumed to exist. Both theories are metaphysical: they eliminate the need to assume the existence of certain entities, assuming others instead. The theory of types is also metaphysical in distinguishing these elements into different logical types of things.

In Russell's middle period (1918–34) logic and metaphysics continue to be linked in works such as "Philosophy of Logical Atomism" (1918), his introduction to Ludwig Wittgenstein's *Tractatus* (1921), *Analysis of Mind* (1921), and *Analysis of Matter* (1927). He now thinks his earlier ideas are mistaken. In 1911, properties and relations are abstract entities, *universals* that can occur in propositions as predicates or as things and subjects, for example, as "Robert is a man" and "*Man* is a concept." He now thinks relations and properties cannot be subjects and that universals are not among the data of experience. We only experience particulars.

Russell uses logical constructions now to show that "mind" and "consciousness" can be defined in other terms and eliminated from psychology's basic vocabulary. He earlier thought that consciousness was something distinct from the abstract and concrete things to which it is related. Now he defines cognitive acts and entities in terms of constituents that are neither mental nor physical, but something "neutral." This is the view of neutral monism. *Monism* has different meanings. The neutral monism Russell adopts now says there is one *kind* of thing, not just one thing. Thus, he remains a pluralist and atomist.

His neutral monism asserts that the ultimate constituents, which are all particulars, are of the same "neutral" substance, whether they form objects outside the mind or the mind itself. The neutral stuff includes sensations and images, which are the same, but occur in different contexts: images obey psychological laws of association and cannot have effects for anyone else but the one person. Sensations obey both physical and psychological laws and can have effects on more than one person. The difference between the mental and the physical is thus only a matter of the arrangement of elemental neutral stuff.

By 1920, Russell also has a different view of the nature of logic and mathematics. Rather than viewing them as about the most general features of the world, as he had earlier, he now regards them as merely assertions about symbols. He also begins to respond to advances in physics, specifically, to the theory of relativity and the quantum theory of the atom. He remains committed to particulars as the ultimate neutral stuff but begins to speak of them as "events." Logical techniques are then used to define points of space, instants of time, and matter in terms of neutral events.

Russell does not abandon neutral monism in his late period, from 1935 to 1950, but he focuses on other issues. The main works here are *Inquiry into Meaning and Truth* (1940) and *Human Knowledge* (1948). He is an antiempiricist both in his early and late period. In his late period, he analyzes language to show that though we can explain most general words without assuming universals, we cannot eliminate all universals. For example, we can define "red" in "this is red" without assuming the universal *redness* by replacing "red" with "similar to this." Yet we need at least one universal to define "similar." Thus, particular experienced events alone are not enough to account for the meaning of sentences. Universals are not experienced, but to explain meaning we must assume the existence of at least one.

8 Analysis and the theory of knowledge

Russell's theory of knowledge concerns both empirical and *a priori* knowledge. His early views here occur in "The Philosophical Importance of Mathematical Logic" (1911), "Knowledge by Acquaintance and Knowledge by Description" (1911), *Problems of Philosophy* (1912), and *Our Knowledge of the External World* (1914). Logical and mathematical propositions are thought to be general truths that relate universals existing apart from space and time. These propositions are *a priori*—known independently of experience.

Knowledge in general is consciousness of particular or universal entities known by awareness (direct acquaintance). These are not physical objects, which Russell says we construct, but data of sense, memory, introspection, or logical intuition—patches of color, sounds, feelings, or mind-independent universals like *similar*. We also know about things by description, but then our grasp on them comes from our grasp on names of the things of which we are directly aware.

Throughout his career, Russell's epistemology focuses on verifying the propositions of physics to show how physics as a branch of pure mathematics applies to the world. His view is that physical propositions are not completely verified until terms like "matter" and "instant" are defined by sentences about sense data. The definitions are produced in accord with the theory of descriptions, where phrases apparently naming entities are defined with names for sense data.

By defining physical concepts in terms of sense data, Russell seeks to avoid assuming any more than is necessary about the physical world. That is, he seeks to justify the laws of physics by sense data alone, without having to also assume physical objects that cause our experiences but are not directly experienced and so themselves transcend experience.

In his middle period theory of knowledge of *Analysis of Mind* and *Analysis of Matter*, Russell no longer believes logic and mathematics consist of general truths about the world, though he still thinks knowledge of them is *a priori*. But this is because they are now viewed as definitions, which are uninformative. With empirical knowledge, he no longer thinks we are conscious of particulars and universals or know them by acquaintance. The proper method of philosophy is still to make as few metaphysical assumptions as possible, and neutral monism lets him avoid assuming a non-physical relation called "awareness." He now defines mental occurrences using logical words, assuming only the particulars of neutral monism.

The construction of minds and objects occurs by gathering particulars together in different ways. At any moment, for example, a star is a class consisting of various sensation-particulars. Your momentary experience of the star, that is, what occurs in you, is a different class of the same particulars. The whole collection of classes over time defines the star, and the whole collection of your experiences of stars and other things defines you.

After constructing mental phenomena in *Analysis of Mind*, Russell returns to the study of matter. This is due to changes in his views he thinks general relativity and quantum theory require. In *Analysis of Matter* (1927), he argues that all experiences—all data—are subjective and determined by a person's standpoint. He now accepts inductive inferences from our experiences to events in the physical world that cause them. He thus gives an account of induction and of scientific reasoning which assumes events continuous with those we perceive and extrapolates from perceived relations to relations among events in physical space-time.

In the 1930s and 1940s, Russell's late period, these themes dominate his discussion of knowledge, especially that of the *a priori* principles that guide scientific reasoning. The principal texts are *Inquiry into Meaning and Truth* (1940) and *Human Knowledge* (1948). The paper "On Verification" (1938) is also important. The postulates are those actually involved when scientists or ordinary people pursue a line of reasoning. Of all possible inferences that might be drawn from the data, what governs the decision to follow one and ignore the others? On his view, it is the presence of *a priori* expectations about the world.

These have a psychological origin. They are caused by experience but not inferred from it and exist as primitive beliefs or habits. For example, if idly watching the path of a cat crossing an empty room, you would be astonished if it winked in and out of sight, or if it should be here and then suddenly somewhere quite different. This is because we bring expectations about continuity and permanence to experience that are created by experiencing certain qualities and general patterns in the world, not just by our psychology. Our expectations, which, made explicit, are postulates of science, are therefore about the world but known *a priori*, since we bring them to experience. His late period also focuses on "linguistic epistemology," that is, with constructing languages to aid us in discovering what the data are and what we must infer.

9 Analysis and the theory of meaning

In his early period, Russell's theories of meaning are confined to what words and sentences denote. These occur in his early metaphysical works such as the *Principles* (1903). Russell thinks the meaning of a name, verb, or predicate, is the entity it denotes, which may be concrete or abstract, in time and space or outside them. Words that occur as subjects of sentences denote either particulars or universals (things or concepts), while predicates and verbs denote only universals.

Though the things corresponding to words and phrases are their *meanings*, this is not to say that we are aware of them as meanings. Russell explains this with his doctrine of acquaintance with universals. We can be acquainted with a patch of color and not know that it is an instance of the word "yellow." For this, the particular patch is not enough: we need to grasp the universal *yellow*. The understanding of meaning is by way of universals.

The above remarks concern words. Until 1910, the meaning of a sentence is also viewed as a single complex entity—the proposition *aRb* of two objects *a* and *b* with relation *R* to one another. On this view, a sentence has a meaning (the complex entity) even if it is not believed or judged. Eventually, Russell finds this doctrine unacceptable and replaces it with the theory that a sentence has no complete meaning until it is judged or supposed or denied by someone. On this view, *judging* is not a relation between a person and a single entity *aRb*, but a relation between a person and *a*, *R*, and *b*. The proposition is broken into parts and enters into a person's belief, which arranges them in a meaningful way.

There is now no single entity *aRb* that is the meaning of a sentence. There are only sentences, which are incomplete symbols, and the context of belief that gives the sentence a complete meaning. This is another analysis using the theory of descriptions: a sentence "*aRb*" is an incomplete symbol that acquires meaning when judged or believed but is otherwise meaningless. That a person has a belief is a fact, and the entities that constitute the meaning of the sentence are gathered together with the believer in that fact. Just as the theory of descriptions replaces descriptions with predicates, so here it replaces propositions with facts of belief.

This theory requires that a person is acquainted with the things that enter into the belief, for example, with *a*, *R*, and *b*. But acquaintance with this data is not enough to make a judgment. To believe or judge, a person must also be acquainted with the *form* in which things are put together. In this case, he or she must grasp what it means to assert a relation.

In his middle period, Russell's analysis of language and meaning develops well beyond his early views, which hardly constitute a theory of meaning at all. Some texts are "Philosophy of Logical Atomism" (1918), "On Propositions" (1919), *Analysis of Mind* (1921), "Vagueness" (1923), "Logical Atomism" (1924), and "The Meaning of Meaning" (1926). The novelty is the attempt to explain language and meaning in terms of causal relations to the world.

For words, Russell adopts a partly behaviorist account where words are classes of sensations (mouth movements, sounds, etc.) and acquire meaning by association with other sensations of the things meant. For example, a child experiences certain sensations that are collectively a toy and learns to make certain sounds that are collectively the word "toy." Departing from behaviorism, Russell says the sensations of the toy give rise to images associated both with the toy and the word "toy." The meaning of "toy" and the images are products of cause and effect where the word or image can come to have the effects the original sensations had.

Russell had, in his early period, resisted reliance on images in his theories of meaning, but in his middle period he embraces them. Belief is no longer a relation among things (*a*, *R*, *b*, and a person). Instead, the content of belief consists of images and feelings (acceptance, doubt, etc.). And verbs occur in sentences under new constraints. They now do not name anything (denote no universal) but merely create a structure of words that is the sentence. Just as an egg carton is not a kind of egg but a means of holding eggs in a pattern, verbs are now merely means of creating a spatial (if written) or temporal (if spoken) relation among words in sentence.

Russell's late period work on language occurs in *Inquiry into Meaning and Truth* (1940). There he tries to solve philosophical problems by constructing proto-languages and artificial languages. As before, we have feelings toward images or words. He now builds on this by developing a psychological or causal theory of a hierarchy of languages having logical constraints. In the logically fundamental language, we use single-word sentences for immediate experiences. But our utterances also convey feelings like doubt or certainty toward beliefs, as when we wonder "Is it true that this is sugar?" With this idea, Russell explains the psychological meaning of logical words like "true."

We also find a new analysis of indexical words like "I," "this," and "here." At the same time, he tries to identify a minimum vocabulary for sciences like physics and to identify the kinds of sentences that can serve as premises. Since he is interested in physics and psychology, he asks whether the words and sentences that report the observations of a physicist will also serve in the same way for psychology.

Philosophers besides Russell have pursued their own conceptions of analysis. Russell's friend G. E. Moore, who influenced Russell as well as later philosophers, is an important example. But there is no doubt that Russell is most responsible for founding the movement of analytic philosophy. In the following pages, Russell's contribution to that philosophy is described in greater detail. The next chapter describes Russell's logicism, and the chapter following describes the elaborations he added to it to avoid paradoxes it faced. Following that, in Chapters 4 through 6, we return to the broader doctrines about things, knowledge, and language sketched above.

CHAPTER TWO

Naïve logicism

Bertrand Russell's greatest achievement after the invention of modern logic was his use of that logic to analyze mathematics and show that its true nature is logic. The view that mathematics is logic is called *logicism*. To demonstrate his logicist thesis, Russell analyzed mathematics to show that all mathematical concepts, and especially the concept *number*, can be defined in terms of logical concepts and that all mathematical truths can be deduced from logical truths. The attempt to demonstrate that mathematics is just logic is called the *logicist program*. Russell first described his logicist program in his 1903 *Principles of Mathematics*, carried it out in elaborate detail with Alfred North Whitehead in their 1910–13 three-volume *Principia Mathematica*, and presented it informally in his 1919 *Introduction to Mathematical Philosophy*.

Russell was not the only person to argue that mathematics can be derived entirely from logic. Gottlob Frege (1848–1925) had argued for the view informally in 1884 and Richard Dedekind in 1888. Frege then argued for it rigorously in 1893 and 1903, though he did so using a strange and difficult notation.[1] And before this, the philosopher Rudolf Hermann Lotze had asserted though had not argued for the view that mathematics is just logic. But Russell's reduction of mathematics to logic is the one that brought the attention of the world to the subject and that developed the idea in its greatest detail and sophistication.

In May 1901, while writing his 1903 book on logicism, Russell discovered a contradiction in his logic. The contradiction is now called *Russell's paradox*. Similar contradictions were discovered soon after by Russell and others. Russell wrote to Frege of his discovery of the paradox in June 1902, just as volume two of Frege's own work on logicism was going to press.[2] Frege hastily tacked an appendix onto the end of his book meant to fix the problem, but he decided later that neither it nor any other solution could fix it, and he abandoned logicism. Russell similarly tacked a hasty appendix to the end of *his* book that was meant to at least suggest a solution to the paradox: it was a simple version of his later theory of types.

Russell spent the next five years searching for a solution to the paradoxes, eventually settling on a more elaborate version of the type theory of his 1903 appendix, along with his "no-class" theory of classes based on his theory of descriptions. These were first published in 1908 in his article "Mathematical Logic as Based on the Theory of Types" and described in full elaboration in the 1910–13 *Principia Mathematica*. Adding the theory of types and no-class theory to *Principia*, as well as adding his theory of descriptions for other reasons, greatly complicated the simpler version of logicism of his 1903 *Principles of Mathematics*.

This chapter examines Russell's original logicism of his 1903 *Principles*—a version containing none of the complexities later introduced to avoid the paradoxes. We call this simpler logicism without the apparatus for avoiding the paradoxes *naïve logicism*. Frege's logicism is also a naïve logicism. In the next chapter, we show how Russell's paradox arises from naïve logicism, then describe the more complicated logicism of the 1910–13 *Principia* that resulted from the modifications and complexities that were added in order to avoid the paradoxes that we call *restricted logicism*.

1 Historical background to logicism

The nineteenth century was a period of radical innovation and change in mathematics, and Russell, who principally studied mathematics when he was a university student at Cambridge, was both an heir and a contributor to it. Among the new ideas, methods, and subjects created during this period are the rise and development of non-Euclidean geometries from the work of Gauss, Johann Bolyai, Nikolai Lobachevsky, and Georg Riemann, the "arithmetization" of the real number system following from the work of Cauchy, Riemann, Karl Weierstrass, Dedekind, and Giuseppe Peano, and the rise of modern set theory and transfinite arithmetic from the work of Dedekind, Georg Cantor, and Peano. Though Russell embraced Cantor's set theory and incorporated much of it into his logicism, what most concerned him in this movement was the arithmetization of the real numbers.

The ancient Greeks had discovered lengths in geometry that cannot be expressed as ratios of natural numbers. More specifically, they discovered that squares with sides whose lengths are expressed as ratios of natural numbers have diagonals whose lengths cannot be expressed as a ratio of natural numbers. Those lengths expressible as ratios of natural numbers were called *rational* while those that cannot be expressed as ratios of natural numbers were called *irrational*. This discovery led to arithmetic, with its discrete numbers and ratios of discrete numbers, and geometry, with its continuous magnitudes that sometimes cannot be expressed by rational numbers, being treated as separate disciplines within mathematics.

Some 2300 years later, in the seventeenth-century C.E., after a long, slow development of mathematics, particularly of arithmetic and algebra, René Descartes created analytic geometry. Analytic geometry correlates the points on a line with numbers and correlates curves with equations, in a partial bringing together of geometry and arithmetic, a partial expression of geometry's magnitudes in terms of arithmetic's numbers. Since the calculus is concerned with geometric concepts, Descartes' analytic geometry is also the beginning of what is called the "arithmetization of analysis." (Analysis is advanced calculus.) The most important step after Descartes in this development was taken by Richard Dedekind in 1872, who showed how to define the real numbers, especially irrational numbers and their properties, in terms of rational numbers and their properties.

After the real number system and its operations such as addition and multiplication had been defined in terms of rational numbers by Dedekind, the rational numbers were defined in terms of the natural numbers. (This is not hard to do.) With this, the real numbers had been reduced to the natural numbers. In 1889, Giuseppe Peano took the next step by deriving the natural numbers and their operations of addition and multiplication from just three basic undefined concepts and five axioms. Dedekind has shown the same thing, with a little less elegance, in 1888. Hence, these axioms are often called the *Dedekind-Peano* axioms.

Since the real numbers and all their properties and operations can be derived from the natural numbers, and the natural numbers can be derived from Peano's five axioms and three primitive concepts, that means that all classical mathematics can be derived from Peano's five axioms and three concepts. Russell then only needed to show that Peano's three undefined concepts can be defined with logical concepts and his five axioms deduced from logical truths to show that all classical mathematics can be derived from logic, thus showing that mathematics is just logic.

The reason why Russell had to define Peano's primitive concepts in terms of logical concepts before deriving Peano's axioms from logical axioms is this: to deduce a statement from other statements, all of the concepts the first statement contains must be possessed by the other statements, or else definable in terms of concepts they possess, otherwise the first statement cannot be deduced from them. Peano had deduced all the principles of arithmetic from his axioms using just three undefined concepts—*zero, number*, and *successor*, plus logical concepts such as *any, all, the same as, not*—to express his axioms. Russell thus had to define *zero, number*, and *successor* in terms of the logical concepts before he could deduce Peano's axioms from logical propositions.

2 Introducing Peano's axioms

Before looking at how Russell defines Peano's concepts in terms of logical concepts and derives Peano's axioms from logical truths, let us first see how Peano derives the natural numbers and arithmetic from his axioms, and the reasons why Russell thinks Peano's primitive concepts need further defining at all. For now, let *number* mean *natural number*. Peano's axioms are then:

1   0 is a number

2   the successor of any number is a number

3   no two numbers have the same successor

4   0 is not the successor of any number

5 any property belonging to 0 and to the successor of any number which has it belongs to all numbers (mathematical induction)

Using these five axioms expressed in terms of *zero*, *number*, and *successor*, Peano defines the natural numbers as follows: 1 is the successor of 0, 2 is the successor of 1, and so on. This gives us an endless series of continually new numbers, because, by axiom 2, we can go on endlessly defining, and by axiom 3 no new successor is the same as an earlier successor, and by axiom 4, no successor is 0. This insures that the series is not circular but is an endless progression beginning with 0 and such that every successor is a new number.

Finally, axiom 5 guarantees that the series contains *all* the natural numbers, because by the first axiom, 0 is a number, and by axiom 2 if something is a number so is its successor. Axiom 5 says that if 0 has a property and the successor of every number with the property also has it, then all numbers have the property. And since 0 is a number and the successor of any number is a number, axiom 5 lets us assert that every natural number is a number in this series. Put another way, saying that all the natural numbers are in the series of numbers defined by Peano's axioms is the same as saying that all natural numbers are in the set N of numbers generated by these axioms and definitions. And because 0 is in N and the successor of any member of N is in N, axiom 5 guarantees that all natural numbers are in the set N of all the numbers generated by Peano's axioms.

Peano began the series of natural numbers with the number 1: his first axiom is "1 is a number." In Russell's version of Peano's system, the natural numbers begin with 0: Russell's first axiom is "0 is a number." We will use Russell's definition of the Peano axioms. Though we have defined 0 and all the natural numbers with them, there are no positive or negative numbers yet, much less fractions or irrational numbers. These are all defined later in terms of natural numbers.

As well as defining the natural numbers, Peano must define addition and multiplication for them. Here are his definitions: Let Sn mean the successor of n. Then $m + n$ for any numbers m and n is the number such that

6 $m + 0 = m$, and

7 $m + Sn = S(m + n)$

From these two rules, we can calculate $m + n$ for any numbers by applying the rules repeatedly until we arrive at the answer. (It is a *recursive* definition.) For a simple example, we calculate $3 + 2$:

$3 + 2 = 3 + S1$

$3 + S1 = S(3 + 1)$

$S(3 + 1) = S(3 + S0)$

$S(3 + S0) = SS(3 + 0))$

$SS(3 + 0)) = SS3$

$SS3 = S4$

$S4 = 5.$

This definition presupposes that we have already defined each number in terms of its successor and so know that $S0 = 1, S1 = 2$, and so on. Peano's definition of addition essentially defines $m + n$ as being m applications of the successor function, first to n, then to the successor of n, then to the successor of the successor of n, and so on for m applications.

Multiplication is similarly defined: $m \times n$ is the number such that

8 $\quad m \times 0 = 0$, and

9 $\quad m \times Sn = m + (m \times n)$.

For a simple example, we calculate 2×3:

$2 \times 3 = 2 \times S2$

$2 \times S2 = 2 + (2 \times 2)$

$2 + (2 \times 2) = 2 + (2 \times S1)$

$2 + (2 \times S1) = 2 + (2 + (2 \times 1))$

$2 + (2 + (2 \times 1)) = 2 + (2 + (2 \times S0))$

$2 + (2 + (2 \times S0)) = 2 + (2 + (2 + 0))$

$2 + (2 + (2 + 0)) = 2 + (2 + 2) = 2 + 4 = 6.$

In other words, $m \times n$ equals m added to itself n times. And we have already defined addition and so may use it in defining multiplication.

The statement of definitions like "$m + 0 = m$" and "$m + S(n) = S(m + n)$" may appear to be more like axioms than definitions, that is, like extra principles added to the Peano axioms to permit addition and multiplication. And if by "definition" we mean something that adds nothing new to a system, but only introduces new notation for what can already be asserted with other symbols, then because Peano's definitions of addition and multiplication do seem to introduce new principles not stated by Peano's axioms, thus extending the expressive power of Peano's axioms, the definitions themselves seem more like axioms than definitions.

In deriving arithmetic from Peano axioms, we are allowed to use logic (indeed, we must use logic to derive anything from anything else), and for Dedekind, Peano, and Russell, set theory is a part of logic. As Russell shows in *Principles of Mathematics*, addition and multiplication can be defined in terms of set theory using the operation of set union. This makes Peano's definitions of addition and multiplication for arithmetic *theorems* of logic, and since nothing new is introduced by them, they are *definitions* as well. So if set theory is a part of logic, addition and multiplication are both definitions and theorems.

Russell defines addition and multiplication in terms of set theory as follows: The union of two sets is the set whose members belong to either of the original two. Then, $m + n$ is the number of members of a set that is the union of two sets, one having m members and the other n members, where no item belongs to both. Multiplication is similarly defined. Take two classes, one with m members and the other with n members. Let their multiplicative class be the class formed from all possible ordered pairs consisting of one member from each of the two sets. The product $m \times n$ is the number of ordered pairs in the multiplicative class.

Independently of set theory, addition and multiplication can be derived from second-order logic in ways corresponding to these set-theoretical definitions. So second-order logic can also justify Peano's definitions of addition and multiplication as theorems of logic. Addition and multiplication can thus be derived from logic when logic includes either second-order logic or set theory. And from this, Peano's principles of addition and multiplication are both theorems and definitions of the logic.

Following W. V. Quine, many people view set theory as part of mathematics rather than logic. Also following Quine, and to avoid paradoxes of second-order logic, many people limit the logic they use to first-order logic. Then, in a first-order system of logic without set theory, Peano's principles of addition and multiplication cannot be proved from prior logical assumptions but must be explicitly added as axioms to the original five axioms. But when logic includes set theory or second-order logic, and Russell's logic includes both, the Peano definitions of addition and multiplication are both theorems and definitions.

3 The definition of number

We can now define *logicism* in terms of Peano's axioms: logicism is the program of defining Peano's three primitive concepts *zero*, *number*, and *successor* in terms of logical concepts and deriving Peano's five axioms from logical truths. But how, specifically, does Russell do this? Quite simply, he both defines the three concepts and deduces the five axioms from his definition of *number*. Russell's definition of number—commonly called the "Frege-Russell" definition of number because Russell and Frege each proposed it—is this: a number is the set of all sets having the same number of elements in them, 2 being the set of all couples, 3 the set of all triples, and so forth.[3]

At first glance, this definition of a number seems circular. It defines number in terms of itself, and uses specific numbers like 2 to define 2, 3 to define 3, etc. But *number* can be defined without using the concept itself, like this: A number is a class of all classes having the same number of members. Two classes have the same number of members when they are *similar*. A number is thus a set of all sets similar to each another. We then only need to define similarity without the concept of number.

Before doing this, however, we introduce some logical notation: Russell's symbols for relations. We use capital letters *R*, *S*, or *T* to represent relations Then, if *R* is a two-place relation—if it relates one thing to another—we use two variables, *x* and *y*, to represent the two things, and write *xRy*, which says *x* has relation *R* to *y*. For example, if we let *R* represent the relation *greater than*, *xRy* says that *x* is greater than *y*. Some people write this as *R(x, y)* instead of *xRy*. But again, if *R* is the relation *greater than*, *R(x, y)* says *x* is greater than *y*. In this guide, we write two-place relations as *xRy*. Now let's return to the definition of similarity.

According to Russell, two sets are *similar* when their members can be correlated by a 1-to-1 relation (when every member of the first set corresponds to a member of the second, and vice versa). This seems to use the number 1 in "1-to-1 relation," but the following definition does not: a 1-to-1 relation is a relation R such that if x has relation R to y and x also has relation R to y', then $y = y'$, and if x has relation R to y and x' has relation R to y, then $x = x'$.

The concept *number* is not used to define a 1-to-1 relation here, nor is any particular number. We define the concept *number* with the concept of similarity and the concept of similarity with the concept of a 1-to-1 relation. Then, the concept *number* is not used to define itself—the definition is not circular. Saying that a number is the set of all sets with the same number of members is just a manner of speaking that sounds circular but really is not, as the same thing can be said without using the concept of number.

4 Peano's axioms without definitions

We now know Russell's definition of *number* and can define it without circularity. But before considering how Russell defined Peano's primitive concepts and derived the five basic axioms, let's consider what is involved in defining *number* and Russell's reasons for believing his own definition is the true meaning of *number*, and that in defining *zero* and *successor* with his definition of number, he defined their true meaning as well.

Although Peano's three primitive concepts are undefined in his system, there is one intended interpretation of them that we intuitively suppose them to mean. This intended interpretation is what we ordinarily mean by

(a) 0, 1, 2, 3, 4, 5, . . .

where we have 1 nose and 2 eyes, and there were 3 Stooges, 4 Beatles, and 12 Apostles. But there are really an infinite number of ways we can define Peano's concepts so that the axioms are true and each definition is different from our standard interpretation of them.

Each of the infinite alternative definitions specifies a progression other than the progression that is the natural number series we ordinarily use, yet Peano's axioms are as true for these other progressions as for the standard one. But it makes a difference which interpretation we choose if we want to apply arithmetic to the world so that we have 1 nose and 2 eyes. For this, we must specify the intended standard interpretation of the three concepts.

Here is an example of a nonstandard interpretation that makes Peano's axioms true. Let *zero* have its usual meaning, let *number* mean *even number*, and let *the successor of n* mean $n + 2$ in our sense of 2; thus $n' = n + 2$ for our sense of 2. Then, the progression of numbers 0, 1, 2, 3, 4, 5, ... for this interpretation will mean what we normally mean by:

(b) 0, 2, 4, 6, 8, 10, . . .

In interpretation (b), what we normally mean by 2 is now expressed by the numeral 1, what we mean by 4 is expressed by 2, and so on. But the Peano axioms are just as true for this interpretation as for the standard one: 0 is still a number, the successor of any number is still a number, it is still true that no two numbers have the same successor, and so forth. Even addition works just as well in (b). For example, $2 + 3 = 5$ is just as true for the new interpretation as it is for the standard one, for $2 + 3 = 5$ will mean what the standard interpretation means by $4 + 6 = 10$. Both are true for our meaning of " $+$."

However, multiplication does not work exactly the same in both interpretations: " $\times$ " does not mean the same thing in each. But this is not a problem, since the new interpretation reinterprets what we mean by $m \times n$ and Peano's definition of multiplication is as true of the new interpretation as of the standard one. For example, in the new interpretation, $1 \times m = m$ is no longer true *according to our ordinary understanding of multiplication*. To see this, consider $1 \times 3 = 3$, which is true for the standard interpretation. In the new interpretation, this means $2 \times 6 = 6$, which isn't true according to our meaning of " $\times$." And by interpretation (b), $2 \times 4 = 8$ means what we mean by $4 \times 8 = 16$. Clearly, multiplication now means something different.

In fact, $m \times n$ now means what we normally mean by one half the product of $2m$ and $2n$, that is, by $m \times n \times 2$. (Try it with a few examples and see.) The new interpretation of *zero*, *number*, and *successor* redefines $m \times n$ so that it is true in the new interpretation.

Peano's definitions of addition and multiplication are thus also true for the new interpretation. The Peano axioms, including addition and multiplication, are as true for interpretation (b), 0, 2, 4, 6, 8, 10, . . . , as they are for 0, 1, 2, 3, 4, 5, ...

In the same way, other interpretations make Peano's axioms true. For another example, let the numerals, 0, 1, 2, 3, 4, 5 . . . , mean what we usually mean by:

(c) 100, 101, 102, 103, 104, 105 . . .

Here 0 means what we usually mean by 100, but *number* and *successor* stay the same. Addition and multiplication get redefined so that $m + n$ now means what we ordinarily mean by $m + n + 100$, and $m \times n$ means what we ordinarily mean by $m \times n + 100$.

Here is another oddity: how do we say what we ordinarily mean by 0 and 1 with interpretation (c)? If negative numbers are developed, we can then use "–100" to mean what we usually mean by "0." This seems to go beyond the Peano axioms. We have a similar problem with interpretation (b). With it, we can only count couples of things, say, pairs of socks. But we cannot count odd numbers of socks. We must first extend the system beyond the Peano axioms, in this case, by developing fractions. Then 1/2, 3/2, 5/2 can mean what we usually mean by 1, 3, 5.

Differing interpretations that each satisfy a set of axioms are *isomorphic* to one another. Specifically, if each makes the axioms true and there is a 1-1 correspondence between the objects of the interpretations, they are isomorphic. For Peano's axioms, each will be a progression of objects with one object, 0, having no successor. More new words: an interpretation making a set of axioms true is a *model* of those axioms and is said to *satisfy* the axioms. There are an infinite number of interpretations of Peano's axioms that satisfy them. Which interpretation should we use to interpret the axioms and the numerals?

5 The true meaning of "number"

Mathematicians commonly say that for the purposes of pure mathematics, it doesn't matter what the symbols for numbers mean—they can even be left uninterpreted and pure mathematics will get along just fine without them. In fact, alternative geometries have been worked out without clarifying what they mean by *point*, *line*, or *plane*. As long as the axioms are consistent (i.e., don't lead to a contradiction), it is acceptable mathematics. Still, mathematicians also often claim that an intuitive sense of the symbols guides their work. Moreover, logicians and set theoreticians who analyze mathematics into fundamental concepts want to understand what it is all about whether their work matters to mathematics or not. So again, which interpretation should we use?

Russell argued that our numbers cannot be just any of an infinite number of progressions that satisfy the Peano axioms, because we want them to "apply in the right way to common objects. We want to have ten fingers and two eyes and one nose. A system in which 0 means 100, 1 means 101, and so on, might be all right for pure mathematics, but would not suit daily live."[4] Russell's definition of number picks out this standard interpretation. Still, Russell understands that we can use an interpretation in our everyday lives where 0 means what we now mean by 100. The model we choose to interpret our numerals is wholly a matter of convention, and Russell understands that. So what is he saying?

Even though the model we use for arithmetic is a purely conventional choice, there is just one interpretation that almost all members of the human race have chosen, and that is the interpretation that says people have one nose and two eyes. This is the interpretation Russell's definition of number gives us. It is wholly a matter of convention that humans have chosen this model, but it *is* the convention we have chosen. Thus, picking Russell's definition of number to interpret Peano's axioms may entirely be a matter of convention, but being the established human convention, it is still the true meaning of "number" as we use the word.

By saying that his definition of number is the right one, Russell also means that by his definition, numbers apply to classes. By his definition—that a number is a set of similar sets—to say that there are 12 Apostles means that the *class* of Apostles has the property of being 12. And this is just how we use numbers. It cannot be the case, for example, that the number 12 is a property of each Apostle, so that Peter is 12, Paul is 12, and so on. Being the property of a class is how natural numbers actually work. Not all definitions of number make this clear. Only by viewing numbers as properties of sets will numbers apply properly to the world.

Russell's definition of number is thus again the one needed for applied mathematics. This does not mean that his interpretation of Peano's axioms is itself applied mathematics. A system of applied mathematics, Russell says, must contain nonlogical constants, and Russell's definition of number and interpretation of the Peano axioms is purely logical. Logicism is pure mathematics, not applied mathematics. But pure mathematics cannot be used for applied mathematics unless numbers are something like sets of similar sets.

(Note: First we say that for Russell a number is a set of all sets similar to one another, then we say that for Russell a number is the property of a set. But these are just two ways of saying the same thing. Take the set of all the dogs in the world. To say that something belongs to the set of all dogs is to say that it has the property of being a dog. Similarly, to say that the number 12 is the set of all sets having 12 members is to say that each set in it has the property of having 12 members.)

According to one standard theory, the meaning of a word is either its extension, its intension, or both. A word's intension is a definition picking out every object the word applies to. Its extension is the set of things the intension picks out. By Russell's definition, the number 3 is the set of all sets with 3 things. Thus, Russell defines numbers as the extension of a numeral, so for those who believe the meaning of a word is its extension, Russell's definition of *number* gives the true meaning of the word.

For those who think the true meaning of a word is its intension, that is, a definition that picks out all and only those things in its extension, Russell's definition of number—*the set of all sets similar to one another*—is what defines the set of things numerals pick out. And for those who think the meaning of a word is both its intension and its extension, they can have both the definition and the set it defines.

Philosophers sometimes say that Russell's logicism substitutes classes for numbers, and that the use of his definition of number is justified *as a substitute* only because the classes do everything numbers do in mathematics. But this is a misunderstanding. If the meaning of a word is its extension and/or intension, then Russell's definition of number is exactly what we mean by a number, it is not just a substitute for it.

Peano was aware that an infinite number of interpretations satisfied his axioms, but he intended that we use his system with an intuitive understanding of its three fundamental concepts. He also thought that we could define those concepts by "abstraction," where we abstract from the different interpretations what is common to all of them. But what is common to all of them is just that they satisfy Peano's axioms, that is, the axioms themselves are the only things that are common to all the different interpretations. Peano's idea for defining *number* thus does not pick out any particular interpretation. And without a particular interpretation, and especially one that applies numbers to classes in the way that humans actually do, we will not be able to apply mathematics to the world properly, or really, at all. With Russell's definition, we can.

6 The concepts defined and axioms derived

We now show how, with Russell's definition of number, one can define Peano's primitive concepts and deduce his axioms from logic. Russell's most accessible account of this is in his *Introduction to Mathematical Philosophy*. But there are places in it where people sometimes get stuck. We thus take special care in what follows to explain what we feel are the difficult spots of the *Introduction*. In particular, we find that people first encounter difficulty reading it with the definitions of posterity (N-posterity, R-posterity, P-posterity). These are really not hard to understand, but pay attention when we get there. We will make them clear to you. But first we will go through Russell's simpler 1903 version of logicism.

From Peano's five axioms and three undefined concepts, the natural numbers and their properties can be derived along with addition and multiplication. And once we have the natural numbers, we can define negative and positive numbers (when $a = b + x$, x is negative when $a < b$ and positive when $a > b$) and fractions (as ratios of natural numbers in the form m/n). And with the rational numbers, we can define the irrational numbers with what is called a *Dedekind cut*, explained in detail below.

To derive all this from logic, Russell will logically define Peano's three undefined concepts and deduce Peano's five axioms from logic using those definitions and logic. In 1903, in Chapter 14 of his *Principles of Mathematics*, Russell does this in a simple and straightforward way. First he introduces his logical (i.e. set-theoretic) definition of *number* as a set of sets all having the same number of members, that is, that are *similar* to one another. Then he defines the individual natural numbers, beginning with 0 and 1, using his general definition of number. With addition and the number 1, he defines *successor of*. And with these concepts logically defined, he derives the rest of the natural numbers, proving that Peano's axioms are logical truths. Now let's go over this in detail.

First, in the 1903 *Principles*, Russell defines the natural numbers with his general definition of number like this:

(a) 0 is the class of all classes whose only member is the null set

(b) a number is a class of all classes similar to any one of themselves

(c) 1 is the class of all classes not null and such that if x and y belong to them, $x = y$

(d) $n + 1$, the successor of any number n, is the number of the union of a class a of n members and a class of one member x, when n is a number and $x \notin a$

(e) the natural numbers are the members of every class s that 0 belongs to, and that $n + 1$ belongs to if n belongs to it

(Russell sometimes defines 0 as the class of all classes whose only member is the null set, but often says more simply that it is the class whose only member is the null set. These definitions are the same. In set theory, two sets are identical when they have exactly the same members—not the same *number* of members, but exactly the same members. All classes containing only the null set have exactly the same member, the null set, and so are identical, that is, they are all the same set. There can only be one set whose only member is the null set.)

Russell's definitions above define *zero, number, successor,* and each natural number. And given these definitions one can prove that the five Peano axioms are logical truths, expressed wholly in logical terms and true for all possible cases. (A logical truth, after all, is true for all possible cases of it.) Specifically, from these definitions the following Peano axioms are obviously true:

1 0 is a number

2 if n is a number, $n + 1$ is a number, where $n + 1$ means the successor of n

3 if $n + 1 = m + 1$, then $n = m$

4 if n is a number, then $n + 1 \neq 0$

5 For any class s, if 0 belongs to s, and $n + 1$ belongs to s if n belongs to it, then every natural number belongs to s.

Definition (b) defines *number* as a class of classes similar to one another, and definition (a) defines 0 as the class of all classes similar to a class containing only the null set. Being a class of similar classes, 0 is thus a number, which justifies axiom 1. Definition (d) says $n + 1$, the successor of n, is a number if n is a number. Axiom 2 follows immediately from that. Definition (d) assumes axiom 3: if a number n has a particular successor $n + 1$, then if another successor equals $n + 1$, it must be the successor of the same number $n + 1$ is the successor of. Axiom 4 follows from definition (d), of *successor*: the successor of a number must contain at least one member, but a set with 0 items contains no members. Axiom 5 is justified because it is already assumed in definition (e) that a natural number is whatever is true of mathematical induction.

This shows that the natural numbers, as defined by Russell, have all the properties a series of objects must have to satisfy the axioms, that is, to make them true. And the fact that Russell's interpretation of the Peano axioms makes them true shows that they are logical truths. Normally, if just one interpretation satisfied the axioms that would not prove that they are logical truths; logical truths must be true for *all* interpretations of them. But Russell has in effect adopted his definition of number as an axiom of Peano's system by asserting it is the one true definition of *number*. There is then only one interpretation that satisfies the Peano-Russell definition and Peano's axioms. And since there is now only one interpretation of Peano's axioms that satisfies them, that means that all interpretations satisfy them.

Russell uses mathematical induction to define the natural numbers, then he justifies mathematical induction (axiom 5), by deducing it from that very definition! How Russell uses mathematical induction to define the natural numbers, and then uses them to justify mathematical induction can be seen more clearly in his derivation of Peano's axioms in his *Introduction to Mathematical Philosophy*. These same arguments appear in *Principia* itself and roughly follow Frege's arguments for logicism. So by looking at Russell's argument in his 1919 *Introduction*, we will come to more clearly learn the argument of *Principia Mathematica*, and as well, of Frege's logicism. It will also make clear how Russell uses mathematical induction to define *finite* and *infinite* both there and in *Principia*.

7 A more careful definition and derivation of the axioms

In *Introduction to Mathematical Philosophy*, Russell derives Peano's axioms from logic by first defining one of Peano's basic concepts in terms of the other two—specifically, he defines *natural number* in terms of *zero* and *successor*. He does this using mathematical induction, which he defines with the following concepts: hereditary property, hereditary class, inductive property, inductive class, and a class called the "posterity" of some number *n*. Posterity is just a precise formulation of mathematical induction and is defined in terms of the concepts that precede it in the list above. These concepts are defined immediately below. (Note: $p =df q$ means that q is the definition of p and is read *p equals q by definition*.)

1 a hereditary property $=df$ a property such that if *n* has the property, then *n'* has it, for any natural number *n*.

2 a hereditary class $=df$ a class such that if *n* is a member of it, then so is *n'*.

3 an inductive property $=df$ a hereditary property that belongs to 0.

4 an inductive class $=df$ a hereditary class that has 0 as a member.

It may seem that *natural number* can be defined just using these concepts, for the objects that belong to inductive classes, that is, to classes containing zero and the successor of any member of that set, seem to be the natural numbers. But an inductive class cannot define the natural numbers completely. We define an inductive set using just one inductive property. But natural numbers don't just have one inductive property; they must have *every* inductive property. So to define numbers, we need to define objects that belong to *every* inductive class. And for that, we need the concept of *posterity*.

5   the posterity of *n* =df the class containing all the members of *every* hereditary class that *n* belongs to (where heredity is defined in terms of *successor of*).

And from this we can easily define the posterity of 0.

6   the posterity of 0 =df the class of objects that belong to every hereditary class 0 belongs to (where heredity is defined in terms of *successor of*).

The posterity of 0 is thus the set of numbers that belong to *every* hereditary class 0 belongs to. This is just a precise definition of mathematical induction (axiom 5), that every property that belongs to 0, and to the successor of every number with that property, belongs to all numbers. In other words, natural numbers have *all* the hereditary properties 0 has. We can now define the natural numbers in terms of posterity.

7   the natural numbers =df the posterity of 0

This defines *natural number* in terms of *zero* and *successor* by defining *posterity* in terms of *zero* and *successor* and defining *natural number* in terms of *posterity*.

Two of Peano's axioms can be inferred from the definition of *natural number* in terms of *posterity* alone. The definition of natural number implies Peano axiom 1, that 0 is a number, because the natural numbers are defined as the posterity of 0, and the posterity of a number includes the number itself, so 0 is a natural number. The definition of natural number also implies Peano axiom 5, the principle of mathematical induction, because the posterity of 0 just is the definition of mathematical induction. In other words, since the natural numbers are defined with mathematical induction (posterity), they must imply mathematical induction in return (axiom 5). The definition of natural number also allows one to weaken Peano axiom 2, which says the successor of a natural number is a natural number. We can drop the last part, because we have just defined natural numbers in terms of successors, so the successor of a natural number is already a natural number by definition.

We now define 0 and *successor* with the Frege-Russell definition of number, and derive the other three Peano axioms from them. 0 is the set whose only member is the null set, and the successor of a number *n* is the number of a class with *n* items to which an item *x* is added where *x* does not belong to the original class. Note: the concept *number of a class* in this definition is already defined by the Frege-Russell definition of number.

We then prove Peano axiom 4, that 0 is not the successor of any number: by the definition of successor, the successor of a number is the number of a class with at least one member, but this is not true of 0, so 0 does not succeed any number. The weakened version of axiom 2—every number has a successor—follows from the definition of successor: since any class can have a member added to it, its number of members is then the successor of its earlier number of members. It only remains to define axiom 3, that no two numbers have the same successor.

If the universe contains an infinite number of things, then for each natural number there will be other natural numbers greater than it, specifically, for any number *m*, there will always be the number $m + 1$. Then we can say that $m + 1 = n + 1$ only if $m = n$. But if the universe is finite, this is not the case. If there are, say, 10 things in the universe, the successor of 10 is null, because there is no class of 11 things, and the successor of 11 is likewise null. Then $10 + 1 = 11 + 1$. Peano axiom 3 holds only for an infinite universe.

In 1903, Russell thought he could logically prove that the universe contains an infinite number of things, if only abstract objects like propositions, numbers, or classes. By 1910, he realizes this cannot be proved logically. He therefore has to accept as an *assumption* that the universe consists of an infinite number of things. This assumption is called the "axiom of infinity." By assuming an infinite universe, Peano's third axiom is valid. In his early logicism, however, Russell did not realize that he needed this assumption.

If the universe is infinite, Russell can define Peano's three basic concepts in terms of logical concepts, and derive Peano's five axioms from them. Granting him this one assumption, his logicist thesis seems vindicated. Also, by defining the basic concepts this way, one can say what it means for something to be finite. Each natural numbers is finite. With the natural numbers, one can define this important property.

8 Ordering the natural numbers

Because *natural number* is defined with *posterity*, and *posterity* is defined with *successor*, natural numbers are finite. Proof: finite natural numbers can be reached from 0 by successive additions of 1. Thus, finite natural numbers obey mathematical induction starting from 0. Thus, finite natural numbers possess every property possessed by 0 and by the successor of every number possessing the property. Thus, finite numbers are the posterity of 0 as defined by the successor relation.[5] And by definition, these are all the natural numbers.

Any natural number can therefore be reached from 0 by a finite number of steps from n to $n + 1$. Or really, any natural number can be reached from any other natural number by a finite number of steps from n to $n + 1$, or from $n + 1$ to n if moving toward 0. So every natural number is finite. This defines *finite number* in terms of mathematical induction.

There are only a finite number of numbers between any two natural numbers, because defining natural numbers with mathematical induction makes them so. The only progressions that make mathematical induction true have a finite number of steps between any two of their members. After all, if there were an infinite number of steps between them, you would never reach one from the other, and could not define the unreachable one with mathematical induction.

For example, moving step-by-step from −1 in the series −1, −1/2, −1/4, −1/8 . . . 1/8, 1/4, 1/2, 1, you will never reach 1, for there are an infinite number of steps between the two—the steps from −1 to 1 go on forever. But a series of numbers defined as those reached by repeatedly adding or subtracting 1 starting from any other member of the series makes every number in it finite, with the number of successor or predecessor steps between any two of them also finite.

Finally (before discussing order), though each natural number is finite and the number of steps with the successor or predecessor function between any two is finite, the class of finite natural numbers itself is infinite. There are an infinite number of finite integers: the successions go on forever, but each element in the progression, being a finite number of steps from any other, is itself finite. The number of natural numbers thus cannot be a natural number, but must be a higher "infinite" number. In fact, it is $\aleph_0$ (aleph null), the smallest infinite number.

In addition to defining the natural numbers and their finitude, mathematical induction (posterity) also defines their order. In fact, it defines the order of magnitude, 0, 1, 2, 3, . . . that we are so familiar with. Simply defining the natural numbers with the Frege-Russell definition of number, as a set of similar sets, does not define their order. What organizes objects into a series is some relation among them. But the natural numbers do not have just one order. As Russell says in *IMP* (p. 29), they have all the orders of which they are capable, and the natural numbers are capable of an infinity of orders. For example, you might start with 0, list all the odd numbers, then all the evens, like this: 0, 1, 3, 5, . . . , 2, 4, 6, and so on. Or you might start with 1, then take all the evens, then all the odd multiples of 3, then the odd multiples of 5 but not 2 or 3, and so on. Each order is defined by a different relation among them. Their most important order is their order of magnitude.

To order any set of objects, an ordering relation R must have three properties. It must be:

1 asymmetrical—if a has relation R to b, b does not have relation R to a.

2 transitive—if a has relation R to b, and b has R to c, then a has R to c.

3 closed for the series—for any two objects x and y being ordered, either x has relation R to y or y has relation R to x.

The successor relation might at first seem capable of ordering the natural numbers according to magnitude by itself, for 1 is succeeded by 2, 2 by 3, 3 by 4, and so on, in what seems like a series. But the successor relation is not transitive: though 1 is succeeded by 2, and 2 is succeeded by 3, 1 is not succeeded by 3. Nor is the successor function closed: it cannot tell us whether 3 comes before 7 or vice versa, and that is what an ordering relation must do. We can, however, use the successor relation to define a transitive relation, namely, the relation of a number n to its posterity.

Remember, a property is hereditary if, whenever a natural number n has it, its successor n' has it; a class is hereditary if, whenever n is a member of it, so is n'; the posterity of n is the class of numbers with every hereditary property n has; and the posterity of 0 is the class of numbers with every hereditary property 0 has. Now 0 has every hereditary property that 0 has, so 0 belongs to its own posterity, and so does every other natural number, because the natural numbers are *defined* as the posterity of 0. Clearly, then, posterity is the relation "less than or equal to" ($\leq$).

Posterity ($\leq$) is a transitive relation: for any natural number x, y, z, if $x \leq y$ and $y \leq z$, then $x \leq z$. However, it is not asymmetrical: when $x \leq y$, we don't know if $x < y$ or if $x = y$. The relation *less than* ($<$), however, *is* asymmetrical. When $x < y$, y cannot be less than x. To define an ordering relation with the successor relation, we want *less than* ($<$), which Russell calls *proper posterity*, not *less than or equal to* (*posterity*). Here is the definition: a number n is in the *proper posterity* of m if n possesses every hereditary property possessed by m'. This is transitive, asymmetrical, and also closed—for any two numbers m and n, either $m < n$ or $n < m$. With this, we can define the natural numbers in their familiar order of magnitude.

Both posterity and proper posterity are defined with the *successor* relation $n' = n + 1$, because they are defined with heredity and heredity is defined with *successor*. A relation defined with this sense of successor will clearly order the natural numbers: moving from n to $n + 1$ is the very essence of the natural numbers. But not all objects can be ordered using this sense of *successor*, for example, consider the series of kings of England. Here, we move from one member of the series to a successor, but here "successor" means "eldest legitimate son," not $n + 1$.

Or consider fractions. The relation *less than*, being asymmetrical, transitive, and closed, will order any two fractions m/n and p/q, determining whether one precedes the other or the other precedes the one. But fractions do not have successors the way natural numbers do. Fractions are *dense*. For any two fractions there is always a third between them in order. The notion of *less than*, when defined as proper posterity with a notion of *hereditary* which itself is defined with *successor*, will not do. A different sense of *less than* is needed, one specifically defined for fractions. More generally, different *successor* relations are needed to define different ordering relations for different kinds of objects.

In *Introduction to Mathematical Philosophy*, Russell first defines a *general* concept of posterity and proper posterity using a *variable* R that stands for *any* relation rather than any specific successor relation. Then, to produce a specific concept of posterity or proper posterity to order a specific set of objects, one replaces the variable R with the specific successor relation that is needed. Russell calls the generalized concepts of posterity and proper posterity *R-posterity* and *proper R-posterity*. The concepts of posterity and proper posterity defined with the successor relation $n + 1$ he now calls *N-posterity* and *proper N-posterity*, N indicating the successor relation for the natural numbers.

R-posterity is defined in terms of *hereditary property*, and *hereditary property* is defined in terms of *successor*, just as we would expect. But instead of using the arithmetical *successor* $n + 1$, we replace the successor function with a *variable* relation R and define a hereditary property with this variable, calling it *R-hereditary*. Then, to use these definitions to order a *particular* set of objects, we replace the variable R with the particular successor relation that will order those objects. In detail, then, we have: P is an R-hereditary property when, if x has property P and x has relation R to y, y has P; a is an R-hereditary class when, if $x \in a$ (i.e. if x is a member of a) and x has relation R to y, $y \in a$. The R-posterity of x is then every y that has every R-hereditary property x has. And the proper R-posterity of x is every y that belongs to the R-posterity of some x' that x has relation R to.

Here is a little more. Every relation R has a converse relation R^* where if xRy then yR^*x. For example, when n' is the successor of n, n is the predecessor of n'. It is often more convenient or intuitive to use a relation's converse than the relation itself, and where you can use a relation, you can use its converse. For example, for greater than ($>$) and its converse less than ($<$), if you can use $x > y$, you can use $y < x$. Similarly, the converse of *posterity* is *ancestor*. In detail, *R-ancestor* is defined like this: x is the R-ancestor of y when y has every R-hereditary property x has, and x is a proper R-ancestor of y when y belongs to the proper R-posterity of x.

9 Positive integers, negative integers, and fractions

We have seen how Russell defined and derived the natural numbers from logic by justifying the Peano axioms with logical concepts and principles. We will now see how Russell defines the rest of mathematics—negative numbers, positive numbers, fractions, and irrational numbers—with the natural numbers. The definitions in this section, of positive and negative integers and fractions, are clear enough in the *Introduction to Mathematical Philosophy*, though parts of our exposition may be clearer. The derivation of real numbers, in the following sections, is more interesting.

Russell does not develop numbers as we do—by starting with natural numbers, defining negative numbers, adding them to the natural numbers to have positive and negative integers, adding fractions to them to have rational numbers, and adding irrational numbers to them to have all the real numbers. For Russell, each kind of number is in a separate number system. Thus, the natural number 1 and positive integer + 1 are different numbers, the fraction 1/1 is different from 1 and + 1 because it is in yet another number system, and likewise for the real numbers, so that 1, + 1, + 1/1, and $\sqrt{1}$ are all distinct. They can be correlated with one another, but they are not the same number.

Why is this? Why are they all different numbers? Answer: because each kind of number is *defined* differently. Natural numbers are classes of classes, positive and negative integers are relations between natural numbers, fractions are different relations between natural numbers, and real numbers are classes of fractions. This will all be explained, but one can see right away that a fraction, say, 3/4, is a relation between the natural numbers 3 and 4 rather than a class of classes. A similar situation holds for negative and positive integers and real numbers.

Defining positive and negative integers is easy. They are the *successor* and *predecessor* relations of the natural numbers. *Predecessor* is the converse relation of *successor*: When b is the successor of a, a is the predecessor of b. When S is the successor relation, bSa means $b = a + 1$, that is, that S is the relation of $n + 1$ to n, which defines + 1. Similarly, when S^* is the predecessor relation, aS^*b means $a = b - 1$, that is, that S is the relation of n to $n + 1$, which defines − 1.

We then generalize this to define all positive and negative integers, not just $+1$ and -1. When c is the successor of b and b the successor of a, the relation between c and a is 2 applications of the successor function. Denote this as S^2. Then, cS^2a means c is the successor of the successor of a, that is, $c = a + 2$ and that means that S^2 defines $+2$. Now let S^x mean x applications of the successor function where x is any natural number. Then $+x$ will be S^x, that is, the successor function applied x times. Similarly for negative numbers, $-x$ will be S^{*x}, the predecessor function applied x times. Addition and multiplication for positive and negative integers are defined like those for natural numbers.

Fractions (ratios) are as easy to define. The fraction m/n is the relation between two natural numbers x and y when $xn = ym$. For example, $2/4 = x/y$ when $2y = 4x$, which is true when $x = 1$ and $y = 2$, or $x = 2$ and $y = 4$ or $x = 3$ and $y = 6$, and so on. This thus defines fractions in terms of multiplication of natural numbers, and $1/2 = 2/4 = 3/6 = 4/8$, and so on. We then define addition for them in terms of addition and multiplication of natural numbers: $m/p + n/p = (m + n)/p$ and $m/n + p/q = [(m \times q) + (n \times p)]/(n \times q)$, just as in ordinary arithmetic. Multiplication for ratios is similarly straightforward, namely, $m/n \times p/q = (m \times p)/(n \times q)$.

Fractions are relations between natural numbers, and so different from natural numbers. Natural numbers are classes of classes; fractions are relations between natural numbers, and so relations between classes of classes—not the same at all. (When Russell introduces his theory of types—described in the next chapter—natural numbers and fractions become different logical types and even more different from one another.) Positive and negative integers are also relations between natural numbers, but not the same relations, so fractions are also different from positive or negative integers.

The fractions $0/m$ and $m/0$ are zero and infinity for any natural number m. The zero of the fractions is not the zero of the natural numbers, as explained above. And the infinity of the fractions, symbolized as ∞, is not the Cantorian infinite $\aleph_0$. It is a potential infinite; Cantor's is an actual infinite. It is like the series 1, 2, 3, 4, . . . getting progressively larger and larger, rather than like the set of *all* natural numbers {1, 2, 3, 4, . . . } taken at once, as with Cantor's infinity. Cantor's infinity assumes the axiom of infinity—that there are an infinite number of things. The infinity of the fractions does not.

To order the fractions in a series, Russell defines *greater than* and *less than* for fractions. From here on, let m, n, p, and q be nonzero natural numbers. Then, for two ratios m/n and p/q, m/n is less than p/q if and only if $mq < pn$. Similarly, m/n is greater than p/q if and only if $mq > pn$. In the series of ratios, 0 and ∞ are the smallest and largest numbers. If they are omitted, there is no smallest or largest fraction. For any fraction, $m/2n$ is smaller than it and $2m/n$ is larger, and between any two fractions m/n and p/q when $m/n < p/q$, $(m + p)/(n + q)$ is always greater than m/n and less than p/q.

There are thus always an infinite number of fractions between any two other fractions, unlike the natural numbers and integers. This property is called "compactness" by Russell and density by contemporary mathematicians. Also, there is no fraction p/q that immediately follows another fraction m/n in the series of fractions: no two fractions are consecutive. These are properties of Cantorian infinity, not the infinity of fractions: they cannot be proved without the axiom of infinity.

Our fractions are so far signless. Russell defines positive and negative fractions as he did for the integers: $+p/q$ is the relation $m/n + p/q$ to m/n, where m/n is any fraction at all. This relation means "greater than by p/q," that some number is greater than another by p/q. And $-p/q$ is defined as the converse relation, m/n to $m/n + p/q$, which means "less than by p/q." Positive and negative fractions are clearly different from positive and negative integers: positive and negative integers are relations of classes of classes; positive and negative fractions are relations of relations of classes of classes.

Though the definitions of positive and negative integers and rational numbers are straightforward, it is interesting that both ratios and signed integers are relations of classes of classes but not the same relation, and so not the same, and that signed ratios are relations of relations of classes of classes. Only natural numbers are classes of classes. The difference between the potential infinity of fractions and the actual Cantorian infinite is also of interest.

10 Background to defining real numbers

Other than its answer to the question "What is a natural number?" what is most interesting in logicism is its answer to the question

"What is a real number?" What are new in real numbers are irrational numbers, for example, $\sqrt{2}$ and π. Irrational numbers, or really, irrational lengths or magnitudes, were discovered by the ancient Greeks when they discovered that squares with sides 1 unit by 1 unit long will have diagonals whose lengths cannot be expressed by any fraction or any other numbers known to them, and then discovered many more such magnitudes.

Because irrational lengths cannot be expressed as fractions, and lengths are the subject matter of geometry rather than arithmetic, not all objects of geometry can be expressed in terms of arithmetic. Arithmetic and geometry thus had relatively separate developments from the Greeks on. With the development of algebra, irrational numbers were encountered again, this time as possible solutions to equations. But these made even less sense to mathematicians than irrational lengths in geometry: at least lengths are real. The divide between geometry and arithmetic, and later algebra, thus persisted into the nineteenth century.

Whitehead and Russell define irrational numbers as lengths in *Principia Mathematica* (*PM*), specifically, as the lengths of number lines in analytic geometry, where numbers are correlated with points on a line. They define irrationals as line segments of a number line—as a series of numbers—rather than as single points on it. Russell defines irrational numbers similarly in *Introduction to Mathematical Philosophy* (*IMP*).

Fractions are similarly defined in *Principia* as relations between line segments This differs from *IMP*, where fractions are relations of natural numbers as we defined them in the last section. In *PM*, however, fractions are relations of line segments. For example, 2/3 is the relation between two lines A and B, where A is two-thirds as long as B, and this is defined as being the case when 3 lengths of A equal 2 lengths of B. In *Principles of Mathematics* (*POM*), Russell distinguishes between ratios and fractions (*PM* and *IMP* do not), ratios being relations of natural numbers, as in IMP, and fractions being ratios of lengths as in PM. But Russell's POM definition of fractions as ratios of lengths was unclear, and so is replaced in *PM* with a better one by Whitehead, namely, the one described above.

Three volumes of *PM* were published. A 4th volume—on geometry—was planned but never written. However, one will find places in *POM*, *PM*, and *IMP* where Russell, and Whitehead in *PM*, discuss various geometric subjects as a part of logicism, giving ghost-like hints of what a logicist treatment of geometry might have been like. The definitions of fractions and real numbers in *PM* and of real numbers in *IMP* are examples of this.

The definition of real numbers in *Principia Mathematica* did not originate with Russell and Whitehead, but with Dedekind as a part of the arithmetization of analysis. Dedekind defined certain sets of rational numbers, known as Dedekind cuts, that correspond to points on the number line and represent both rational and irrational real numbers. Russell added the definition of mathematical concepts in terms of logical concepts and the derivation of mathematics from logic.

Mathematicians often conceive of real numbers differently than Russell, as points on a number line. Sometimes that point is described more carefully as the limit of a particular series of fractions that progresses toward it. But for Russell, real numbers are the whole series of ratios approaching that limit, not just the limit itself. In this way, Whitehead and Russell treat them as segments—something geometrical. These make it easier to apply mathematics to the physical world.

11 Real and complex numbers defined

Russell defines both rational and irrational real numbers with what is called a *Dedekind cut*, in honor of Richard Dedekind who first used them to define real numbers. A Dedekind cut divides all the members of a number series into two sets, where every member of the series is in one of the two sets and every number in one set is less than every number in the other. Each set is called a *section*. The section with the lower numbers is the *lower section*, the other is the *upper section*.

There are several different kinds of cuts, depending on how the "point of section"—the point where the two sections are divided —is defined. For a cut in the series of fractions, where a is the lower section, β the upper section, and c a fraction in the series, we might define a as every fraction less than c and β as c and every fraction greater than c. Then, the upper section β has a *minimum* value, namely, c, but the lower section a does not have a maximum value.

The fraction c is thus the minimum value of β; no member of β is less than c. The lower section a has no maximum value, it contains every fraction less than c, but not c itself. As the values of its members increase in size they come closer and closer to c but never reach it; for every one of them, there are always others that are closer to c, and for these too there are still others that are closer. There is no greatest number in a that is greater than all the others.

This lower section a does however have an *upper limit*: it is the number in the series that the members of a approach but never reach as they increase in value, namely, c. Though a has no maximum, it has c for an upper limit. If we reverse the matter and make a cut in the series of fractions where every member of the lower section a is less than or equal to c and every member of the upper section β is greater than c, then a will have a maximum value, namely c, but β will have no minimum. It will, however, have c as a *lower limit*.

Two sets of fractions where one contains every fraction lower than c and the other contains every fraction greater than c would not be a cut. A cut must place *every* member of a series in either the lower or upper section. The two sets just described do not contain every fraction—they leave out c itself. And two sets where one contains every fraction less than or equal to c and the other contains every fraction greater than or equal to c are also not a cut, because the same fraction cannot belong to both sets.

For some cuts, the lower section has a maximum value and the upper section has a minimum value, for example, a cut in the positive integers. Then, if the lower section is every integer less than or equal to 7 and the upper section is every integer greater than 7, the lower section has 7 as its maximum value and the upper section has 8 as its minimum value. Finally, there are cuts with neither a maximum nor upper limit for the lower section and neither minimum nor lower limit for the upper section. These are used to define irrational numbers.

Can we make a cut in the fractions at $\sqrt{2}$? Not exactly. $\sqrt{2}$ is not a fraction at all, so we cannot define a cut in the fractions by letting $c = \sqrt{2}$, $a = $ the fractions less than c, and β the fractions greater than c. But we *can* let $c = 2$ and define a as the set of fractions whose square is less than 2 and β those whose square is greater than 2. Then, a has neither a maximum nor upper limit, and β has neither a minimum nor lower limit, yet between them they contain all the fractions.

An *upper boundary* is either a maximum or upper limit. A *lower boundary* is either a minimum or lower limit. In the case above, neither a nor β have a boundary. The values of a increase steadily toward β, and the values of β decrease steadily toward a. While we do have to include every fraction in one or the other of the two sections for it to be a cut, we do not include $\sqrt{2}$ in either. because it is not a fraction at all, as the ancient Greeks proved long ago. So in this case, there is nothing between the two sections, since all the fractions are accounted for and are in one section or the other. There is then said to be a *gap* between them and they are called *irrational sections*. Cuts with gaps correspond to irrational numbers. In fact, they represent irrational numbers. But this must be carefully defined.

Let a *segment* be is a lower section with no maximum: it either has an upper limit or no boundary at all. The segments of the series of fractions represent real numbers. Those with upper limits represent *rational* real numbers; those without upper limits represent *irrational* ones. The series of fractions thus define a series of segments that are the real numbers. A rational real number is itself a segment and at the same time a series of segments that approach an upper limit. This is the same as saying it is a segment of the series of fractions that approach an upper limit.

An irrational number seems to be a series of fractions with no upper limit, but only a "gap" between it and its upper section. But we cannot say the fractions approach an irrational number as a limit, because irrational numbers do not belong to the series of fractions at all. But rational numbers do belong to the real numbers. And since the series of fractions defines a series of segments and thus a series of real numbers, we can say that an irrational number is the upper limit of a series of segments that approach it and have no rational upper limit while at the same time, the series of segments makes up one segment that contains them all, namely, the segment that is the real number the series defines.

A segment is a geometrical conception of a real number—it corresponds to a segment of the number line and not just a point on it. A segment thus contains every segment less than it, just as any length does. These segments that make up a single segment that is the real number they define can be ordered using the relation of whole to part: one segment is greater than another when it is not a part of the other, but the other is a part of it. And since real numbers are segments, a real number contains every real less than it. In the end, though, to say a real number is a series of segments is the same as saying it is a series of fractions, since each segment is defined in terms of fractions.

Both Richard Dedekind and Giuseppe Peano following him made a Dedekind cut with a point of section having no boundaries and then *postulated* the existence of a real number that the ratios approach as a limit, rather than *defining* real numbers in terms of fractions as Russell does. This can now be seen to be wrong from Russell's perspective because real numbers are not fractions at all, so that with an irrational cut in the series of fractions, there is no real number in the series for the fractions to approach. In introducing an axiom that postulate s a real number as the limit of the series of fractions, one has created an arithmetic object that cannot then be reduced to logic, or even to fractions. To reduce the real numbers to logic, Russell must define them with fractions that can themselves then be defined with natural numbers that can be defined logically.

To define addition and multiplication for real numbers, let the sum of two reals u and v, which are sets of fractions, be the set of sums of one member of u and one member of v for each possible combination of members of u and v. The set of all such sums are fractions making up the segment that is the sum of u and v. The product of u and v is the set of products of every combination of one member of u and one member of v. The set of all such products is the set of fractions making up the segment that is the product of u and v. Though impractical as a method of calculating sums and products, it is a satisfactory theoretical definition.

Complex numbers are more straightforward, and presented clearly by Russell, so need not be covered here, except to describe Russell's treatment of them in outline. A complex number is of the form "$x + y\sqrt{-1}$" for real numbers x and y. We let $i = \sqrt{-1}$ and write the complex number as "$x + yi$." We then represent it with an ordered pair of real numbers $<m,n>$ that are the values of x and y in $x + y\sqrt{-1}$ and define addition and multiplication for them so that the sum or product is the same as what the addition or multiplication of actual complex numbers would result in.

This is the basic outline of Russell's naïve logicism. In addition to this, Russell shows how to define infinite numbers and their arithmetic following Cantor. But what we have covered here is the core of logicism, and enough to discuss the modifications Russell made to logicism in *Principia Mathematica* to prevent paradoxes from arising in it. These modifications amount to what we call Russell's *restricted logicism*, described in the next chapter. Russell's logical definition of infinity and its arithmetic, and the problems that arise for it, are discussed in Chapter 7, on "The Infinite."

CHAPTER THREE

Restricted logicism

Russell conceived of logicism—the thesis that mathematics is nothing more than logic—in January 1901 and described it in detail in his 1903 *Principles of Mathematics*. But even before finishing the book, he discovered a contradiction in its logic. Unless he could find a way of expressing his logic so that it did not imply the contradiction, the logicism of the 1903 book, which presupposed this logic, would be unacceptable, for any theory that implies a contradiction contains at least one false premise.

By the time the book was ready to print, Russell still had not found a way to modify his logic so that it would avoid the contradictions. (By this time there were several.) He thus left the book in its original form, contradictions and all, appending a proposed solution to them at the end of the book. The solution, however, was inadequate: only when he presented the mature version of logicism in the 1910–13 *Principia Mathematica*, which contained many complexities in its logic the earlier version did not, was he able to avoid the contradictions and save his logicism.

The original 1903 version of logicism, presented without any of the complexities introduced later, we call *naïve logicism*. This simpler form of logicism was described in the last chapter. In this chapter, we describe Russell's mature logicism of 1910–13. In particular, we describe the complexities added to the theory in order to avoid the contradictions. Essentially, these complexities restrict the use of logic so that the contradictions cannot be stated. We thus call this mature logicism *restricted logicism*.

What are these restrictions? The most important, and the principal difference between naïve and restricted logicism, is Russell's theory of types. But the theory of types makes Russell's logicism *so* complex that the axiom of reducibility must then be introduced to simplify it. This axiom, however, is itself quite complex: Russell has simplified his logicism by adding more complexity to it! Finally, for good measure, Russell defines classes, or really, explains them away, with a "no-class" theory of classes based on his theory of descriptions. He also uses the theory of descriptions to define, or again, explain away, mathematical functions (things like "$f(x) = x^2 + 1$"). These too add a lot of complexity to logicism.

The version of type theory described here is that of *Principia Mathematica*, as Russell's discussion of it in his 1919 *Introduction to Mathematical Philosophy* is inadequate. In this chapter, then, we take the reader straight to the heart of *Principia Mathematica* itself. Similarly, our descriptions of Russell's axiom of reducibility, theory of descriptions, and no-class theory are described as they occur in *Principia*. It is time for the reader to begin understanding that book directly.

1 Background to discovering the Russell paradox

Russell did not begin writing the *Principles of Mathematics* with logicism in mind, much less with any idea of the paradoxes to come. He had written a final draft of it between October and December 1900. Only after that, in January 1901, did he conceive of logicism. In May 1901, he wrote Part One of the book, describing his logic, and began writing Part Two, on logicism, the same month. Then disaster struck: while writing the part on logicism, he discovered a contradiction in the logic of Part One. The contradiction threatened to be fatal to his logic, and so to the theory of logicism based on it.

A contradiction is a statement or set of statements making two claims that cannot both be true. For example, in "It is both raining out and not raining out at the same time and place" at least one claim must be false, and we would have to look out the window or go outside to decide which we should throw out. Similarly, because

Russell's logic implied a contradiction, at least part of it was false and had to be thrown out. But logicism was based on this logic, so if part of the logic was thrown out, the logicism might not work anymore. Russell had to both reject part of the logic and replace that part with something that did not imply any contradictions and yet did all the work of constructing mathematics from logic that the discarded part had done.

At first Russell did not appreciate the difficulty that eliminating the contradiction would present. Though aware of it while writing the section on logicism for his book during June 1901, he did not revise his logic or modify his approach to logicism at that time to avoid the paradox. Similarly, when he rewrote the section on logic in May 1902 again, nothing was modified to avoid the contradiction. In fact, he turned the manuscript into his publisher in its unmodified form, thinking he would find a solution to the contradiction quickly later on, write a brief account of how to avoid it, and get this to his printer and into the book before it went to press.

A solution to the paradoxes, however, was not readily forthcoming, so in November 1902 Russell added a hasty appendix to his book suggesting a tentative solution, while also mentioning the difficulties the proposed solution faced. The solution tentatively proposed was a simpler version of the more complex theory of types he would eventually adopt and publish seven years later in *Principia Mathematica*. Before accepting the theory of types, in *Principia*, Russell would spend five years searching for a less drastic solution. But he could find nothing else that would both eliminate the paradoxes and save logicism.

2 The set of all sets that are not members of themselves

The paradox in the form in which it was first discovered—as the set of all sets that are not members of themselves—arises in Russell's set theory, and also in Frege's, Cantor's, Dedekind's, and Peano's set theories, because, like the others, he assumed what is called the "axiom of comprehension," that for every predicate that can be formulated in the language of logic or set theory, there is a set consisting of all and only those objects the predicate is true of.

In most cases, this assumption is perfectly acceptable; for example, the predicate "*x* is divisible by 2" defines the class of even numbers. No problem arises here. But some predicates can be defined in set theory that *do* produce contradictions such as Russell's paradox. The axiom of comprehension must thus be restricted somehow so these paradoxes do not arise. The paradox as stated above assumes sets and so is a problem for set theory. Another version of it arises directly from logic itself using predicates, and another still from logic using relations. These are thus problems for logic itself and not just set theory. Similar paradoxes arise within mathematics.

Here is Russell's paradox for set theory in full: Some sets, such as the set of mathematical objects, are members of themselves, because sets are themselves mathematical objects. Most are not, for example, the set of prime numbers is not itself a prime number. There being sets that are not members of themselves, there is a set *a* of all sets that are not members of themselves, which can easily be defined: *a* =df the set of all things *x* such that *x* is not an element of *x*. Is *a* a member of itself or not? If it is, then it isn't, and if it isn't, then it is. So *a* both is and isn't a member of itself, which is a contradiction.

Here is the same idea expressed a little more formally in the next four paragraphs, with symbolism for those with logic. (Symbols used are "$x \in a$" for "x is a member of *a*," "$x \notin a$" for "*x* is not a member of *a*," "p$\rightarrow$q" for "if p is true then q is true," "p$\leftrightarrow$q" for "p is true if and only if q is true," "$\forall$" for "all," "$\exists$" for "some.") Let *a* be the set of all sets that are not members of themselves: or symbolically, $a = \{x: x \notin x\}$. Then, for all sets *x*, *x* is a member of *a* if and only if *x* is not a member of *x*: or symbolically, $(\forall x)[(x \in a) \leftrightarrow (x \notin x)]$. Since, this applies to *any x*, it must apply when *x* is *a*. But then *a* is a member of *a* if and only if *a* is not a member of *a*: or symbolically, $(a \in a) \leftrightarrow (a \notin a)$. This means that if *a* is a member of *a* then *a* is not a member of *a*, and if *a* is not a member of *a* then *a* is a member of *a*: or symbolically, $[(a \in a) \rightarrow (a \notin a)$ and $(a \notin a) \rightarrow (a \in a)]$. And this is a contradiction.

Using a few more symbols ("$\sim p$" for "it is false that *p*" or simply "not-*p*"; "*p* v *q*" for "either *p* or *q* is true"), here is why this is a contradiction: Logic translates $p \rightarrow q$ (if *p* then *q*) as $\sim p$ v q (not-*p* or *q*). Thus, we translate "$p \rightarrow \sim p$" as "$\sim p$ v $\sim p$." And $\sim p$ v $\sim p$ is simply $\sim p$. And we translate $\sim p \rightarrow p$ as *p* v *p*, which is simply *p*. Applying this to $[(a \in a) \rightarrow (a \notin a)$ and $(a \notin a) \rightarrow (a \in a)]$, $(a \in a) \rightarrow (a \notin a)$ becomes $(a \notin a)$ v $(a \notin a)$, which is $(a \notin a)$, and $(a \notin a) \rightarrow (a \in a)$

becomes $(a \in a) \vee (a \in a)$, which is $(a \in a)$. Thus, the whole expression, $[(a \in a) \rightarrow (a \notin a)$ and $(a \notin a) \rightarrow (a \in a)]$, just means $[(a \notin a)$ and $(a \in a)]$, which is clearly a contradiction.

Using the same symbols (plus one: let predicates like "x is human" be symbolized as "Hx," "x is brown" as "Bx," and likewise for other predicates), we can show that this contradiction follows directly from the axiom of comprehension, which Russell and others assumed. Here is the axiom of comprehension: for any property P and any object x, there exists a set a such that x is a member of a if and only if x has property P. In other words, for every property there corresponds a class, and for every class there corresponds a property, or symbolically, $(\forall P)(\forall x)(\exists a)(x \in a \leftrightarrow Px)$.

Since P can be any property, that is, the axiom is true for *any* P, let P be the property: $(x \notin x)$. We thus replace P in the comprehension axiom with $(x \notin x)$ and drop the first quantifier. The axiom now reads: x is a member of the set a if and only if x is not a member of x, or symbolically, $(\forall x)(\exists a)(x \in a \leftrightarrow x \notin x)$. And since the axiom is supposed to hold for *any* x, let us take the case where x is the set a. We thus replace x with a in the last expression and get: there exists a set a such that a is a member of a if and only if a is not a member of a, or symbolically, $(\exists a)(a \in a \leftrightarrow a \notin a)$. But that is just the Russell paradox.

We can thus see that Russell's paradox follows directly from an assumption of his logic. Similarly, the Russell paradox will follow from any naïve set theory or logic, that is, from any set theory or logic that assumes the axiom of comprehension and so assumes that any predicate or set that can be defined in the language of logic or set theory exists for that logic and set theory.

3 Other paradoxes soon discovered

Russell also found a version of his paradox for predicates; thus it is a paradox of logic that is independent of set theory. Consider the fact that some predicates are true of themselves and some are not, for example, "x is a linguistic entity" is itself a linguistic entity while "x is human" is not itself a human. We then formulate the predicate "x is a predicate that is not true of itself." Is it true of itself? If it is, it isn't, and if it isn't, it is. We have derived a contradiction from any logic that allows us to formulate such a predicate, which includes Russell's logic.

This is a version of the paradox that is independent of mathematics or set theory and arises independently of the axiom of comprehension. Thus, we need a solution that not only prevents the axiom of comprehension from allowing sets that lead to contradictions, but also one that does not allow predicates to occur that lead to the contradiction for predicates. There is also a version of the paradox for relations, as follows: Define the relation T as the relation that holds between any two relations R and S whenever R does not have relation R to S. Then, since this is true for any relations R and S, it is also true when R and S are both T. But then we have the claim that T does not have relation T to T if and only if T has relation T to T. We will need a solution that prevents such relations from occurring in our logic or mathematics.

Along with these three contradictions, Russell found many others that are similar. The oldest and simplest include the barber who shaves all those in the village who do not shave themselves, and the statements "I am lying" and "This statement is false." Others concern Cantor's transfinite ordinals, such as the Burali-Forti contradiction, which goes like this: Every well-ordered series has an ordinal number, and the series of ordinals up to some ordinal number n is $n + 1$. The series of all ordinal numbers is likewise well-ordered and so has an ordinal number—call it Ω. But the series of all ordinals up to and including Ω has the ordinal number $\Omega + 1$. Thus, the ordinal of the series of all ordinals is not Ω. There are many other such contradictions.

4 The vicious circle principle

Since Russell's paradoxes follow directly from his logic, the logic must be changed to eliminate the paradoxes, and the paradoxes must be eliminated to save logicism. The paradoxes seem to arise when sets can be members of themselves, predicates predicated of themselves, relations related to themselves, or sentences about themselves. If we could find a property that all such sentences have, we could stipulate that sentences, sets, predicates, or relations with that property are inadmissible in logic or set theory. This would eliminate all situations in which paradoxes can arise. Russell did find such a property, namely, self-reference, and stipulated a restriction with it on what sentences can and cannot be used in logic and set theory. The stipulation is his *theory of logical types*.

In addition to this, if we could explain what is wrong with sentences, predicates, relations, or sets that possess this property, we would have a *rationale* for stipulating some rule that made them inadmissible in logic and set theory. This would *justify* adopting the rule restricting their use. Along with his theory of types, which makes such entities inadmissible in logic, Russell provides just such a rationale saying what is wrong with them: it is that they violate the *vicious circle principle*.

The paradoxes all seem to arise from self-reference. The Russell paradox, for example, arises because it is possible for the set of all sets not members of themselves to be a member of itself. And this is because in the definition of the set, "all sets" includes the set itself: the set is part of its own definition. The case is the same for the other paradoxes. For example, the sentence "This sentence is false," makes an assertion about itself. In particular, the sentence is defined in terms of its own truth or falsity. That is, it is self-referential, and this circularity means that the proposition is defined in terms of itself. Similarly, when predicates or relations apply to themselves, this likewise means that they are defined in terms of themselves.

The vicious circle principle claims that linguistic things defined circularly—such as a predicate that may be true of itself, a set that may be a member of itself, a relation that may relate itself to something, or a sentence that may be true of itself—are all meaningless. This is because the circularity of definition caused by self-reference makes it impossible to determine whether or not a proposition about itself is true or false of itself, or a predicate that may apply to itself actually does or doesn't, and so forth. Given this, we have the perfect justification for adopting a theory of types that bars such entities from logic and set theory.

This claim also applies to those things whose truth is defined circularly yet are *not* contradictory. For example, in *Principia* (p. 39), Russell argues that the law of excluded middle, that "All propositions are either true or false" seems to apply to itself in making a claim about *all* propositions, and is therefore meaningless. To see this, assume that the law of excluded middle is true of all other sentences. But you can still ask: Is it true of itself? This, however, cannot be determined. If it is, it is. If it isn't, it isn't. That's all we can know. Russell assumes that to be meaningful, a generalization must be well-defined for *every* case it applies to. The law of excluded middle, understood as applying to itself when it says "all propositions," is therefore meaningless.

Similarly, the class of all classes that *are* members of themselves is a member of itself if it is, and it is not a member of itself if it isn't. We can never determine if it is a member of itself or not. So, it is meaningless (not well-defined). Why call it meaningless if it is indeterminate for just one case? After all, it works for all the others. But the definition of a class should tell us of any object whether or not it is a member of the class. Definitions of predicates and relations must be similarly determinate.

Russell concludes that logical principles like the law of excluded middle, which purport to apply universally, cannot meaningfully apply to themselves. A logical proposition about "all" propositions is not about itself but is of a different "logical type" than the propositions it is about. And propositions about these logical propositions are of a different logical type yet, but again are not about themselves. We say that each such proposition is of a higher type than the type it is about.

More specifically, propositions making claims about the world are all of the same logical type and are called "first-order" propositions. Propositions about first-order propositions are of another logical type and are called "second-order" propositions. All propositions about second-order propositions are third-order propositions, and so on. No proposition can be about any proposition of its own order or about any proposition of a higher order than it. There are similar hierarchies of type for predicates, relations, and classes. These will be discussed later.

We can see that if we want to say that absolutely all propositions are either true or false, we have to go on forever up this hierarchy, claiming that propositions of ever-higher order are either true or false of the propositions below them in order. The problem here is one of special concern to Russell, for logical propositions like the law of excluded middle *are* about all propositions absolutely. If such propositions are inadmissible, it seems to be impossible to assert any logical truths and thus to even state the principles of a system of logic. Russell must find a way to specify the principles in his system of logic so that they *do* apply to all sentences whatsoever.

To fix this problem, Russell first points out that logical propositions such as the law of excluded middle are *typically ambiguous*—they do not state what logical type or order of proposition they are meant to apply to: they are ambiguous with respect to type. More than this, Russell claims that such propositions "ambiguously" refer to *all* levels or types *at once*, the assertion being valid for each level. Problem solved! But how is this done? By a method called *ambiguous assertion*, which we will explain after we have gone through the ramified theory of types and axiom of reducibility, where the subject comes up again. First, let us look at the theory of types in detail and see exactly what we mean by the level or type or order of a proposition, propositional function, or class.

5 Some logic for the theory of types

Logic starts with *individuals*—people, atoms, perceptions, what have you—and predicates such as "*x* is tall" or "*x* is taller than *y*." Russell calls such predicates *propositional functions*. They are formed by replacing one or more subjects of a proposition with a variable. The *argument* of a propositional function is whatever can replace its variables to create a meaningful sentence. Some propositional functions, like the two just given, take individuals as arguments: "*x* is tall" becomes the true and meaningful sentence "Yao Ming is tall" when it takes "Yao Ming" as an argument; it becomes the false but meaningful sentence "Tom Cruise is tall" when it takes "Tom Cruise" as an argument.

A propositional function that takes individuals as arguments is called a *first-order* propositional function. The proposition formed when a first-order function takes an individual as an argument is called a *first-order proposition*. The function "*x* is tall" is a one-place propositional function; "*x* is taller than *y*" is a two-place propositional function, that is, a relation. But both are first-order propositional functions because both take individuals as arguments. There are also three-place propositional functions (three-place relations) like "*x* is between *y* and *z*," four-place functions, and so on. Arguments of propositional functions are also called "values of the function's variable." Similarly, a proposition that a propositional function becomes when its variables are replaced by arguments is called a *value of the propositional function.*

Functions can also be used to form propositions called *generalizations,* such as "someone is tall" or "someone is taller than everyone." Generalizations are formed when quantifiers like "all" and "some" (words that say how many) are applied to variables of functions. Assume for the sake of simplicity that the variables x and y only take people as values. In the first case, we have "some x's are tall" which is formed from "some" and "x is tall"; the second example, "some x's are taller than all y's" is formed from quantifiers "some" and "all" and the function "x is taller than y." Generalizations formed from first-order functions are also first-order propositions.

Some propositional functions take other propositional functions as arguments. These form propositions that are about properties and relations rather than about individuals. The function "The natural numbers are ϕ" takes properties as arguments. When ϕ is replaced by the property of being discrete, we get "The natural numbers are discrete" and so forth. But "x is a natural number" is a first-order function—it becomes meaningful by taking individuals as arguments. Let us assume for now that numbers are individuals. Then, for example, by taking "seven" as an argument it becomes "Seven is a natural number."

Propositional functions that take individuals for arguments are *first-order* propositional functions, those taking first-order propositional functions as arguments are *second-order* functions. Propositions formed by replacing the variables of first-order functions with individuals are first-order propositions. Those formed by replacing variables of second-order functions with first-order functions are second-order propositions. Generalizations formed from first-order propositional functions are still just first-order propositions. Those formed from second-order propositional functions are second-order propositions, and so on into infinity.

6 The theory of logical types

The theory of logical types states that functions can only take lower-order functions or individuals as arguments. First-order functions can thus only take individuals as arguments, but not other functions. This means that first-order functions cannot take themselves as arguments, which prevents self-referential paradoxes from arising. And since propositions that refer to themselves are meaningless, this rule also prevents meaningless propositions from being formed.

Second-order functions or individuals take first-order functions or individuals as arguments, but not functions of their own order or higher. This bars them from taking themselves as arguments and creating paradoxes. It also prevents meaningless propositions from being formed. Third-order functions or lower take second-order functions or lower as arguments but not third-order functions or higher, and so on to infinity. This is the basis of the theory of types.

But why prevent a function from taking *every* function of the same order or higher as an argument? Why not just bar a function from taking itself as an argument? Isn't that what causes the paradoxes? Answer: no. Paradoxes can also be formed when functions take other functions of the same or higher order as arguments. For example, if function F can take function G of the same order as an argument, and G can in turn take F as an argument, then F has in effect taken itself as an argument, which can result in a paradox. Similarly, a 3-function circle of functions of the same order, F, G, and H, can result in a paradox when F takes G, G takes H, and H takes F as an argument. And if F takes a higher-order function as an argument, it too can take F as an argument, and again we have a circle.

This basic structure of type theory thus creates a hierarchy of functions, with functions at each level only taking lower-level functions or individuals as arguments. We similarly have hierarchies of propositions and sets. The order of a proposition is the same as the order of the function that forms it, and propositions cannot be about functions or propositions of the same order or higher. But since the order of the proposition is determined by its function, we only need to define a hierarchy of functions (something we have not completely done yet) in order to have defined a hierarchy of propositions. Similarly, since sets can be formed from propositional functions, a hierarchy of functions defines them as well. We need not define these hierarchies separately.

Russell's actual theory of types is three steps more complicated than what we have seen so far. In the next section, we will learn the last three steps of the strange dance of hierarchies Russell has created for us. The complete, more complex theory of types is called the *ramified* theory of types. It is the theory of types used in *Principia Mathematica*. The basic theory of types described so far is the *simple* theory of types. It describes the hierarchy used for sets, which are first-order when they have individuals as members, second-order when they have sets of individuals as members, and so on.

7 The ramified theory of logical types

The basic theory of types above needs to be made more complex to *completely* prevent contradictions like Russell's paradox from arising, for there are more complex cases that must also be considered—those where a function contains another function within it. With the simple theory of types, paradoxes can still arise from these more complex kinds of functions. A more complex hierarchy must be created to keep these complex functions from allowing paradoxes to arise. This new, more complex hierarchy is the ramified theory of types.

Here is the basic rule of the new hierarchy: for functions that contain other functions within them, if the inner function has a higher order than the main function that contains it, the order of the main function is the same as the order of the inner function. As before, the main function cannot take arguments of the same order as it or higher. However, while the order of a function changes when it contains a higher order function within it, the order of the main function's variable does not change. It will still take the same order thing as a replacement for the variable as it did before. This definition of the order of a complex function containing another function completely prevents paradoxes from arising.

Here is an example of this more complex case. The sentence "Napoleon had all the qualities of a great general" has "x had all the properties of a great general" as its main function, which is a first-order function because it takes individuals like "Napoleon" as arguments. But it contains the expression "all the properties of a great general" within it, which is formed from the propositional function "ϕ is the property of a great general" with the quantifier "all" attached to it. And *this* function is a second-order one, because its variable, ϕ, takes first-order functions as values, namely, properties like courage and tenacity that great generals have. (Inner functions in these more complex cases always have quantifiers attached to them, otherwise their variables would just be variables of the main function and they would not be complex cases.)

Here is how paradoxes can arise from functions containing inner functions of a higher order than them: In the example, the inner function, "ϕ is the property of a great general," is a second-order function, and the main function, "x has all the properties of a great general," is first-order. Because the inner function takes first-order functions as arguments, it can take the entire main function that contains it as an argument. Then the main function contains itself as a part of its own meaning. This is a circular definition. And from these, paradoxes can arise.

The specific rule for the ramified theory of types is this: the order of a function is one higher than the highest order of its own variables or of the variables of any function it contains. In the example above, the main function is now second-order, so the inner function cannot take it as an argument and paradoxes cannot arise from it. But the ramified theory also assigns a second order to the function: one for the function's variable. For "Napoleon had all the qualities of a great general," the main function is a second-order function, because it contains a second-order inner function, but its variable is still an individual variable ("zero-order"), that is, a variable that takes individuals like "Napoleon" as values.

A function having an individual variable could now be a first-order function, a second-order function (because it has an inner second-order function), a third-order function (because it has an inner third-order function), and so on. Similarly, a function having a first-order variable could now be a second-order function, a third-order function, a fourth-order function, and so on. We now have a whole series of functions of different orders for each order of variable a function might have.

Why specify the order of both a function and its variables? The order of the main function, now determined by the order of any higher-order inner function it might contain, determines which *other* functions can take *it* as an argument. This especially prevents any inner function it contains from taking the main function as an argument. And the order of the main function's variable determines what order object the function can take for *its* arguments, which is now no longer obvious from the order of the function itself, just as the order of the main function is no longer obvious from the order of its variable. Note that a function might also have an inner function of a *lower* order than the main function. Then, the order of the main function is determined by the order of its own variable, not that of the inner function. The highest order of any variable within a function, whether its own or that of an inner function, is what determines the function's order, which is one order higher than that of the variable. Here, the variable of the main function determines its order even though it contains an inner function.

8 Observations about ramified type theory

We now have a fully defined hierarchy of propositional functions, and, as mentioned earlier, a hierarchy of propositions and a hierarchy of sets, both defined by the hierarchy of propositional functions. But there are still more hierarchies. In *Introduction to Mathematical Philosophy*, Russell says: "individuals, classes of individuals, relations between individuals, relations between classes, relations of classes to individuals, and so on, are different types" (p. 53). One-place functions of individuals and relations between two individuals are not the same type and not in the same hierarchy, but in separate hierarchies. And a two-place relation is of a different type than a three-place relation, so each type of relation will form its own hierarchy as well, and so forth.

The relation of set membership (as in "One is a member of the set of natural numbers.") is a relation between things of different types, for example, between individuals and classes. Russell calls this a *heterogeneous* relation. Relations between objects of the same type are *homogeneous* relations. Predication, which relates a property to the object it applies to, also relates things of different types and is also heterogeneous. And heterogeneous relations are of a different type than homogeneous relations, and thus form hierarchies distinct from those of homogeneous relations.

Some argue that Russell's type theory assigns yet another number to functions as a third kind of order, namely, the number of variables a function has. This is just the distinction between one-place predicates, two-place relations, three-place relations, and so on, mentioned above. These *are* different logical types, and Russell says that they are several times. (At times, Russell says there is a distinction between different logical types based on the number of *apparent* variables, i.e. variables attached to quantifiers, that a function has, but he means to make the same distinction—that between one-place predicates, two-place relations, etc.) Also, in practice in *Principia*, Russell does distinguish functions into further logical types depending on the number of variables they have. That is why, in *10 and *11, and again in *20 and *21 of *Principia*, Russell defines some theory (formal implication in the first case, incomplete symbols in the second) for classes, and then does it all over again in the following section for relations.

However, whenever Russell explicitly describes the hierarchy of logical types, he never states it in a way that requires a function to have more than two kinds of orders. This is because the third distinction, between one-place predicates and two-place relations, is already clearly made in the basic formation rules of his logical language of *Principia* (or in what pass as formation rules there) and does not need repeating in the theory of types. Formation rules tell us how we are allowed to use the symbols of a symbolic language to form propositions. And on the very first page of *PM* (p. 4), Russell tells us that we would never replace a variable that takes propositional functions as values with a relation if it was meant to be replaced with a one-place predicate, because we could tell that using a relation would make it meaningless. The theory of types is meant to identify meaningless statements that most people may not immediately recognize as such. It does not identify the most basic ones that are already obvious.

9 The axiom of reducibility

Russell's ramified theory of types eliminates the paradoxes of self-reference from logic and mathematics. But another problem then arises—many of the statements of logic and mathematics simply cannot be made in a language constrained by the ramified theory. Specifically, for some object a of any order in ramified type theory, we can only make statements about some, but not all of the functions that can take a as an argument. But in logic and mathematics, we must often make statements about all of the functions of some object. Russell's type theory needs fixing.

Take Russell's favorite example of ramified types again—Napoleon. We can say that Napoleon was brave and that Napoleon had all the qualities of a great general, but the ramified type theory does not let us refer to both of these qualities with the same expression. They are properties of two different orders (as we have seen earlier), and so cannot be referred to by a single function or by a single statement.

The problem also occurs in mathematics, where we often need to speak of all the different order properties of entities of a single order. This occurs, for example, in mathematical induction, which we need in order to define the natural numbers. The principle of mathematical induction is defined using the concept of *posterity*: a number x belongs to the posterity of another number n if x has every hereditary property that n has (a *hereditary property* is a property possessed by the successor of a number if it is possessed by the number itself).

To define the posterity of n, we thus need to be able to say of any member x of its posterity that it possesses *all* the hereditary properties that n possesses. But this cannot be done. A statement about all the hereditary properties of n will be of a higher order than statements that some particular property is a hereditary property of n, which themselves will be of a higher order than n itself. In fact, the statement that a number possesses all the hereditary properties of n will itself be a higher order *hereditary* property of n.

Thus, this new higher-order hereditary property also needs to be asserted of n, since it was excluded from being asserted of n in the first assertion about n's hereditary properties by the ramified theory of types. In like manner, any attempt to say something about a "totality" (i.e. about *all* things of a certain kind) will be incomplete, because it will generate a function of a higher order that cannot be included in that totality due to the ramified theory of types. But again, we need a way to make statements about totalities in order to express many standard propositions of logic and mathematics.

To fix this problem, Russell introduces the axiom of reducibility. It asserts that all the functions of different orders that are about one object, or about a set of objects of a single order, are each equivalent to a function about the same object or objects that is just one order higher than the order of the objects. This makes all the different order functions about the objects equivalent to same order functions about the objects. Since one can say something about all the functions of a single type, one can thus make assertions about all these equivalent functions, and in so doing, make assertions about *all* of the functions of different orders to which they are equivalent. Here is how it works. We can replace the quantifiers (words "all" or "some") in generalizations (propositions containing quantifiers) with strings of propositions each about a single argument the variable can take. For example, if I say (falsely) "everyone can speak English" and $(a, b, c, \ldots, a_1, b_1, \ldots a_2, b_2, \ldots)$ are the names of all the people in the world, I can replace the generalization with the conjunction "*a* can speak English and *b* can speak English and *c* can speak English and . . . ."

Taking this idea, we can apply it to a statement like "Napoleon had all the qualities of a great general" and replace it with a conjunction that attributes to Napoleon each property of a great general, one at a time. We then get something like "Napoleon was brave and Napoleon was smart and Napoleon was tenacious and Napoleon could go without sleep for three days and . . . " which is a conjunction of first-order propositions constructed from first-order functions. We no longer have a proposition with a second-order function in it. It has been reduced to a first-order one.

Similarly, we can now express the concept of posterity, and so define mathematical induction. Again, a number x is in the posterity of a number n when x has every hereditary property n has. Assume numbers are individuals, and so zero-order. We then use the method described above by first replacing each hereditary property of n with an equivalent one expressed as a first-order function. Then, using the same method, we replace "all the hereditary properties n has" with a first-order conjunction of all the now first-order hereditary properties of n. With both the hereditary properties of n and the function that refers to all of them at once now both equivalent to first-order functions, we can effectively refer to all of them with one function.

Notice that we began with a simple theory of types, where there are zero-order individuals, then first-order functions that take individuals as arguments, then second-order functions that take first-order functions as arguments, on to infinity. This theory became more complex as the ramified theory, where we identified a whole hierarchy of different order functions that take individuals as arguments, a whole hierarchy of different order functions that take first-order functions as arguments, a whole hierarchy of different order functions that take second-order functions as arguments, and so on.

In effect, we began with an infinite hierarchy of functions in simple type theory and split each level of this infinite hierarchy (one for each order of argument a function could take) into an infinite hierarchy of different order functions in the ramified theory of types. So in the ramified theory, we get an infinite number of levels of functions where each level itself gets split up into an infinite number of sublevel functions.

Now what the axiom of reducibility does *not* do is reduce all these infinite sublevels of an infinite number of levels to one single order. Rather, it reduces each of the infinite sublevel hierarchies of functions, where the different order functions in a sub-hierarchy take arguments of a single type but contain different order inner functions, to a set of equivalent functions that are all of the same order. So we start with a hierarchy with an infinite number of levels, ramify it so that there are an infinite number of sublevels for each of the original infinite levels, and then use the axiom of reducibility to "shrink" this back to just an infinite number of levels again, replacing each of the infinite sublevels of functions with a single level, or order, of functions. With just the infinity of levels we end with, we can then refer to all the functions that take a certain object as their argument, or all of the functions that take objects all of the same order as their argument.

10 Reference to an infinite number of propositions

Though we can now refer to all the functions of a particular level in our infinite hierarchy of levels, how on earth can we refer to all the functions on all of the levels at one time. Yet propositions such as logical and mathematical truths must be able to make assertions about *all* propositions or *all* propositional functions of *any* type. But we have already seen above how Russell thinks we can do this—we do it with *ambiguous assertion*. But we did not explain then how it works. Here is the explanation now.

Principles of logic that seem to refer to *all* propositions or functions are, according to Russell, really an infinite number of assertions made all at once, with each assertion applying to a single order of propositions or propositional functions one order below it.

This is because a proposition that refers to all propositions cannot refer to itself or any of its own type or of a higher type. Still, Russell says, some assertions are ambiguous and are meant to refer to all levels at once. This is *ambiguous assertion*. (Russell believes that ambiguous assertions are properly made using the quantifier *any* while an assertion about all of a single type and lower is made with *all*, though logicians today generally take the two terms to mean the same thing in such cases.)

With ambiguous assertion, we can assert something about every proposition in some infinite hierarchy of propositions, for example, that they are all true. And for logical or mathematical truths that are asserted ambiguously, Russell claims that they are actually true all the way up—not just asserted for every level, but true at every level—and that we can know this.

To see how ambiguous assertion works in this way for truths of logic and mathematics, let us take the example of the law of excluded middle again, that all propositions are either true or false. Let us also adopt the theory of types, so that no proposition can meaningfully apply to itself. The law of excluded middle is then understood to apply to all propositions and thus be of a higher order than them, but at the same time, not apply to itself. And with ambiguous assertion, we do not take it to apply to itself, but to all other propositions of a lower order. Then, to say that it is true, there must be a higher-level statement that applies to it, and another that applies to that one, and so on.

Let us assume that the logical principle of excluded middle does in fact seem to be true of all other propositions (for example, if we know of no exceptions to it). Then, since we understand it to only be about all other propositions of a lower order and we take them to be true of the principle (i.e. they are all either true or false), we can see that the logical principle of excluded middle is itself true, and so either true or false. Now, our statement here, that it is true of itself as well, is a new proposition one level above the logical principle because it is *about* it. But because we can see that the logical principle is true, we know that our statement that it is true is true too, as is this new statement that *that* statement is true, and so on, all the way up.

Here is the same story viewed a little more carefully. If the principle of excluded middle is true of all propositions of a lower level—let us call that the n-level so that the principle itself is of the $n + 1$ level—then, our $n + 2$ level statement that the principle itself is true will not only be an assertion about that one principle, but also that excluded middle holds of all propositions of a lower order, including those at the $n + 1$ level that the original logical principle did not apply to. But since we have decided that the principle seems to be true of all other propositions other than the principle itself (because we know of no exceptions), this will include other $n + 1$ level propositions other than the principle, so we know the $n + 2$ level statement that the principle holds of *all* propositions of the $n + 1$ level and lower is true too, and again, so on up the hierarchy. Russell's assertion that valid logical propositions can be known to hold for each level thus makes good sense, whether or not you think this is actually how language works.

The axiom of reducibility is sometimes thought to completely undo everything achieved by ramified type theory. By this view, Russell begins with a simple theory of types, where a function's order depends on its argument's order. Then, with his ramified theory, he sorts the functions of a particular argument into their own hierarchy of orders, doing this for each of the original orders. Finally, he introduces the axiom of reducibility so that the functions of *different* orders that take the same argument are equivalent to functions of the *same* order that all take the same argument. It is with this "reduced" hierarchy that is used to make ambiguous assertions about all functions.

But what really happens is a little different. Applying the axiom of reducibility to a ramified hierarchy of functions does not produce the same simple hierarchy one had before ramification. Applying type theory to functions removes the functions that refer to themselves. Simple type theory removes some; ramified type theory removes the rest. When one then simplifies the ramified theory with the axiom of reducibility, there will be no functions that can refer to themselves. Problem solved.

Some claim that the axiom of reducibility is not a logical principle at all. In the 1910–13 edition of *Principia*, Russell defended the axiom against this charge, but in his 1919 *Introduction to Mathematical Philosophy*, he thought it was an empirical principle rather than a logical one. Russell seems to have been right the first time. While the axiom is not self-evident, self-evidence by itself is not a good reason for accepting logical principles. A better reason for accepting a principle is that it is true for all known instances of it and false for none. This is inductive evidence, but as Russell rightly points out in the preface to *Principia*, this is the only good reason for accepting *any* logical principle. This looks like a good argument to us. The axiom seems to work. That is the most you can say for a logical principle.

11 Introduction to the no-class theory

In the naïve logicism of Russell's *Principles*, set theory is a part of logic and Russell uses it to do much of the work of explaining mathematics logically. In the restricted logicism of *Principia*, Russell likewise uses set theory to do much of the work of explaining mathematics, but this time without the sets! He manages this by defining symbols for sets in terms of propositional functions, then letting these definitions, or "constructions" do all the work the sets did. More or less.

Actually, Russell defines symbols for sets in terms of propositional functions in *Principia* and says that the definition is what symbols for sets *really* mean. Then he uses symbols for sets to explain mathematics anyway. He and Whitehead then claim that no sets are used in *Principia* because the symbols for sets they use really mean some arrangement of propositional functions. This definition of sets in terms of propositional functions in *Principia Mathematica* along with the claim that no sets have been used in it is called the "no-class" theory of *Principia*.

While symbols for sets seem to name objects, namely, sets themselves, when they are defined in terms of propositional functions, they no longer seem to refer to any set at all. Names refer to objects, but propositional functions are not names and so do not refer to objects and so do not refer to sets. So if symbols for sets are really propositional functions, they too are not names and do not refer to objects, and so do not refer to sets.

Let's go over this more carefully. Russell says that names have meaning "in isolation." They have meaning by themselves, independently of occurring in propositions. This just means that names refer to objects and we know what they refer to whether they are part of a proposition or not. Propositional functions, on the other hand, are not names and they do not independently refer to or name any object. For example, the propositional function "x wrote Waverly" by itself does not name any object.

Russell shows by analysis that symbols for sets are really propositional functions, which means that they are not names and do not refer. Russell calls symbols that do not refer independently of their occurrence in propositions "incomplete symbols." Propositional functions themselves do not refer independently of propositions and are thus incomplete symbols. They are only meaningful in propositions—that is, only then is there a reference to objects. And even then, it is not the predicate that refers to these objects, though the predicate can contribute to reference by the proposition. So it is because symbols for sets are really predicates (as is shown by analysis) that they are nonreferring incomplete symbols.

More than this, because symbols for sets do not really refer to objects and sets are a kind of object, symbols for sets do not really refer to sets. As Russell describes the situation in 1914 (in *Our Knowledge of the External World*), because symbols for sets, though they appear to refer to specific sets, are really incomplete symbols and so do not actually refer to sets, they are "logical fictions" instead. This is the main point of the no-class theory of classes, for on the basis of it, Russell can claim that *Principia Mathematica*, along with the logic it presupposes, does not assume the existence of sets but only propositional functions, even though it uses symbols for sets throughout.

As the reader may notice, Russell's no-class theory of classes of *Principia* is very much like his theory of descriptions. In the theory of descriptions, Russell replaces singular definite descriptions with propositional functions. In the no-class theory, he replaces symbols for sets with propositional functions. In each case, he replaces what appears to be a denoting expression with a definition of it in terms of functions that do not denote anything. The singular definite description and the symbol for the set are both incomplete symbols, and so logical fictions. They appear to refer to objects but really do not.

By claiming that sets are incomplete symbols and so do not name any object, Russell is not claiming that there are no sets. He only means that he is agnostic about the existence of sets and that *Principia* does not assume that any sets exist. His theory does not need them. And because his notion of a set does not occur at all in his logic, it will not be confronted by the Russell paradox of sets.

But why eliminate *all* classes, you might ask? After all, only some of them lead to paradox. And besides, Russell has just gone to great trouble to protect himself from the paradoxes with the theory of types—he even has a hierarchy of classes that prevents classes from being members of other classes of the same or higher order. Isn't that enough to prevent paradoxes of sets from arising? The answer, however, is *no*.

Even with ramified type theory, Russell has not entirely accounted for the use of sets in logic. He has a hierarchy of functions and a hierarchy of sets, but he does not have one for functions that take sets as arguments. In this last case, *all* sets seem to be individual objects. But letting any set be an individual leads to paradoxes, for as we know, we must distinguish between sets of individuals, sets of sets of individuals, and so forth. But adding a hierarchy for functions that take sets as arguments would add even more complexity to type theory. So the no-class theory keeps type theory simpler than it would otherwise be.

And all sets *do* seem like individual objects. So functions taking *any* set as an argument do seem to be first-order functions to Russell, not functions that are *truly* different logical types. This is a philosophical problem, but a real one to Russell, who thinks different logical types are true differences in reality. Stratifying functions that take different kinds of sets as arguments would thus create artificial, not real, distinctions of logical types. However, taking sets as propositional functions stratifies them with the hierarchy of functions into truly different logical types, and functions that take them as arguments are now also stratified into truly different logical types.

Another philosophical problem solved by taking sets to be functions is that there appears to be more classes than individuals, so sets could not be individuals. The reason why there are more sets than individuals is because any set of things can be subdivided into more subsets than the number of members in the set. Specifically, a set with n members had 2^n subsets. Thus, the set of *all* individuals has more subsets than it has members, so there are more sets than individuals in the universe, so sets cannot be individuals. Russell had always been uncomfortable with the idea of a set. What is it? Is it a single thing—an object, an individual? Or is a set many things, namely, its members? Or is it something that is both one and many? And isn't the idea that it is both one and many things a contradiction? Replacing sets with functions solves these philosophical problems.

12 The theory of descriptions in *Principia Mathematica*

Russell's no-class theory of classes in *Principia Mathematica* is based on his theory of descriptions. To see how the no-class theory works in detail, it is useful to examine the theory of descriptions more carefully. Another reason for examining it is that in *Principia* the theory of descriptions is used to eliminate mathematical functions from mathematics, just as the no-class theory is used to eliminate sets. Mathematics uses mathematical functions extensively. These are expressions like $2 + 2$ or 4^3 or $x^2 + 7$ or $\log x$ or $\sin x$, etc. But a mathematical function is a definite description, and the theory of descriptions would have us replace descriptions with predicates.

Russell's theory of descriptions analyzes singular definite descriptions of the form "the so-and-so" such as "the author of *Waverly*" as they occur in propositions such as "The author of *Waverly* was a poet" or "Scott was the author of *Waverly*." "The author of *Waverly*" seems to function as a name in these cases. But Russell analyzes the sentence so that the description "the author of *Waverly*" no longer occurs in it. This new proposition is claimed to be the true meaning of the proposition containing the description.

For example, "The author of *Waverly* was a poet" is analyzed to mean "There exists exactly one thing that wrote *Waverly*, and that thing was a poet." A little more technically, it is "There exists at least one thing that wrote *Waverly* and there exists at most one thing that wrote *Waverly* and that thing is a poet." Notice that in rephrasing "The author of *Waverly* was a poet," the word "the" disappears and the description itself has been replaced by "x wrote *Waverly*." And "x wrote *Waverly*" is not a name, it is a predicate.

To symbolize this example, let "the" be symbolized by the Greek symbol ι (iota). Then, using Wx for "x wrote *Waverly*" we can write "the author of *Waverly*" as $(\iota x)(Wx)$, which technically is "the x such that x wrote *Waverly*." Then, using Px to mean "x was a poet" we substitute the definite description for the variable in Px, and "The author of *Waverly* was a poet" becomes $P(\iota x)(Wx)$. Note that this symbolizes the first example, which contains a definite description.

Now we symbolize the sentence without the definite description that replaces the example containing the description to see the difference. Wx still means "x wrote *Waverly*" and Px still means "x was a poet." The upside-down A ($\forall$) means *all* and the backwards E ($\exists$) means *some* (at least one). $\&$ means *and*. To keep things simple, assume that variables take people as values. Then, "At least one person wrote *Waverly* and at most one person wrote *Waverly*, and whoever wrote *Waverly* was a poet" is symbolized as $(\exists x)(\forall y)\{[Wx$ $\&\ (Wy \to (x = y))]\ \&\ Px\}$.

The two parts, $(\exists x)(Wx)$ and $[(\forall y)(Wy \to (x = y))]$, say that at least one person x wrote *Waverly* and that if y wrote *Waverly*, then $x = y$, that is, that at most one person wrote *Waverly*, Together they say that exactly one person wrote *Waverly*. The third part says that this one person who wrote *Waverly* was a poet. This formula can be rewritten as $(\exists x)(\forall y)[(Wy \equiv (x = y))\ \&\ Px]$, which means exactly the same as $(\exists x)(\forall y)([Wx\ \&\ (Wy \to (x = y))]\ \&\ Px)$. In either case, we can see that *the* (iota) has disappeared and the description $(\iota x)(Wx)$ has been replaced by the predicate Wx.

A brief excursus for logic students. These two statements, $(\exists x)$ $(\forall y)\{[Wx\ \&\ (Wy \to (x = y))\ \&\ Px)$ and $(\exists x)(\forall y)[(Wy \equiv (x = y))\ \&\ Px]$ do not appear identical. The first makes the existence claim $(\exists x)$ (Wx), that at least one person wrote Waverly. The second makes some indirect claim about there being an x such that for any y, y wrote *Waverly* if and only if $x = y$, but it does not seem to directly say $(\exists x)(Wx)$. But those with logic can prove that from the second statement one can infer $(\exists x)(Wx)$, so that it does indeed imply that there exists at least one person who wrote *Waverly*. '(Try it.)

It might also seem that the two statements are not the same because the second asserts that for some x and every y, Wy is true if and only if $x = y$ is true. The first however only asserts that if Wy then $x = y$, but not the other way around. But it can be easily proved from the first version that one can infer that if $x = y$, then Wx. (Try proving this one, too.) This, plus the proof that the second version does in fact imply $(\exists x)(Wx)$ shows that the two statements are equivalent.

Similarly we restate "Scott is the author of *Waverly*" as "There is exactly one person such that that person wrote *Waverly*, and that person is Scott." Following the idea and symbolism of the previous example and letting $c = Scott$, we can then symbolize it as $(\exists x)(\forall y)$ $[(Wy \equiv (x = y))\ \&\ (x = c)]$, or more simply, $(\forall y)[Wy \equiv (y = c)]$. Again, the word *the* (iota) is gone and the description, $(\iota x)(Wx)$, is replaced by the predicate Wx.

Here is how Russell justifies the view that definite descriptions are really predicates and not names: First, note that the descriptions "the round square" and "the present King of France" are meaningful yet clearly denote nothing. Thus, they are not names. So it is *possible* for descriptions to be meaningful yet denote nothing, so it is possible for descriptions like "the author of *Waverly*" that appear to name objects that *do* exist to be meaningful yet not name the object.

Second, Russell argues that it is *necessary* that descriptions not be names to be meaningful—even descriptions like "the author of *Waverly*," that describe existing objects. Russell assumes that if two terms denote the same object, they have the same meaning. So we should be able to substitute one for the other in a sentence without changing its truth value. If Tony Curtis was a famous Hollywood movie star, and Tony Curtis was Bernie Schwartz (and he was), then Bernie Schwartz was a famous Hollywood movie star.[1]

But consider "George IV believed that Scott was the author of *Waverly*." We cannot substitute "Scott" for "the author of *Waverly*" and equally assert that George IV believed that Scott was Scott, for this is not what George IV was concerned about. More simply, if "the author of *Waverly*" was a name for "Scott," then "Scott is the author of *Waverly*" would have to be true whenever "Scott is Scott" was, yet this is not the case. "Scott is Scott" cannot be false, but "Scott is the author of *Waverly*" could be. "The author of *Waverly*" and "Scott" clearly have different meanings, so "the author of *Waverly*" cannot simply be a name of Scott.[2] Generalizing from these arguments, it follows that definite descriptions are not names. Instead, they are predicates as described above, which do not themselves name.

In addition to modeling his no-class theory of classes on this theory of descriptions, Russell uses it in *Principia* to analyze and eliminate mathematical functions, for mathematical functions also seem to be names—in particular, they seem to be names of numbers. But if numbers are classes and classes are predicates that are not names, then numbers are predicates that are not names. Since they are definite descriptions, Russell's theory of descriptions can explain what they really are.

Mathematical functions such as $x + 2$ or $\log x$ seem to be names of numbers. Russell calls them "descriptive functions" because they are definite descriptions. We treat the operations they perform on x as predicates and view the functions as on a par with "the author of Waverly." We thus use the symbolism "$(\iota x)(\phi x)$," described above and read as "the x such that ϕx," to describe the mathematical function, where ϕ is a predicate that describes the operation the mathematical function performs on values of x.

More specifically, mathematical functions are relations, just like "the author of *Waverly*," which we replace with "x wrote *Waverly*," which relates x and the book *Waverly* using the relation "x wrote y." Similarly, a mathematical function like x^2 means "the number that is x times itself." We thus treat $y = x^2$ as the relation yRx, or "y is x times itself." In the simpler cases of ordinary language descriptions, it seems as though we replace them with one-place predicates. But a more careful analysis will show that, like mathematical functions, we actually replace them with two-place relations.

13 Russell's no-class theory of *Principia Mathematica*

Russell's no-class theory of *Principia Mathematica* replaces sets with propositional functions that "simulate" sets—they do all the work that sets do without themselves being sets. He replaces a sentence containing a symbol for a set with another not containing the symbol, but containing a predicate instead. Russell can then assert that no sets are used in *Principia*. By eliminating sets, he need not complicate his type theory further by stratifying functions that take sets for arguments. And since *Principia* no longer contains sets, the set-theoretic paradoxes and other philosophical problems with sets cannot arise in it.

Russell's analysis of sets as propositional functions is similar to his analysis of definite descriptions. Sets are incomplete symbols or "merely linguistic conveniences," he would say They are not names but predicates. Being incomplete symbols, they do not name objects, nor does the predicate that replaces the set name any object. They do, however, contribute to reference within the sentences they occur in. One thus shows their function in referring by defining the statements they occur in, which is done by replacing the sentence containing the set symbol with one that does not.

Another reason why the meanings of descriptions and sets can only be defined within propositions is that they both make assumptions only expressible as propositions. For example, we replace the definite description "the author of *Waverly*" with the predicate "*x* wrote *Waverly*." But part of the meaning of the definite description is that there is only one such *x*, which requires us to say "There exists exactly one *x* such that *x* wrote *Waverly*" to completely express it. Sets are similar.

Russell has a strong argument for his view that propositions containing definite descriptions can only be meaningful if the descriptions are actually disguised predicates. But he has no similar argument to justify his analysis of classes. Still, something can be said in its favor. One is that the analysis avoids the paradox of sets and another is that it simplifies the theory of types. Also, it solves certain philosophical problems (discussed above).

In effect, the no-class theory is this: We say there were 12 Apostles and commonly understand this to mean that the set of Apostles has the property of being 12. But we might also take this to mean that the function "*x* was an Apostle" has the property of being satisfied by 12 arguments. It is this second way of understanding it that Russell claims we really mean when we speak of sets.

Specifically, sets occur in propositions as arguments of some function. Let $f(\phi)$ be a propositional function that takes a as an argument, describing it in some way (ϕ is just f's variable). Let a be the set of Apostles and f the function "ϕ has the property of being twelve." Then, $f(a)$ means "There were twelve Apostles," that is, "The set of Apostles has the property of being twelve." Every meaningful function defines a set, and every set is definable by a meaningful function. The set of Apostles is defined by the function "*x* is an Apostle." Let Ax be the function "*x* is an Apostle." Then we can replace a with the function Ax in $f(a)$ to get $f(A)$, which, like $f(a)$, says roughly "There were twelve Apostles," that is, "The property of being an Apostle is satisfied by twelve things." The predicate that replaces the set is the same one that defines the set. As might be expected, however, the situation is actually a little more complex in *Principia Mathematica* than described above. The complete theory is described below.

14 Defining sets

Mathematical functions are extensional and Russell wants to use logic in *Principia* to explain mathematics, so his definition of sets as functions holds only for sets occurring as arguments of extensional functions, but not intensional ones. This saves Russell the trouble of describing cases where they occur as arguments of intensional functions.

To say that a function f is extensional means that if f can take both the functions Gx and Hx as arguments and Gx and Hx are formally equivalent, then $f(G)$ will be true whenever $f(H)$ is true and vice versa. And Gx and Hx are formally equivalent when they are both true for all the same values of x. For example, "x is a creature with a kidney" and "x is a creature with a heart" are equivalent functions: when one is true the other is too, because all and only creatures with kidneys have hearts. Then, the function "x crawled across my backyard today" is extensional, because "A creature with a kidney crawled across my backyard today" is true whenever "A creature with a heart crawled across my backyard today" is true, and vice versa.

Russell's symbol for a set is $\hat{x}(\psi x)$, which means "the set of all things x such that x has property ψ." (The hat over the first x means that the whole symbol denotes the set, not the set's members.) As with descriptions, Russell defines sets contextually, that is, he defines the proposition in which the set occurs, not the set itself. In particular, he defines sets by defining propositions where the set $\hat{x}(\psi x)$ is an argument for a propositional function f, that is, he defines the proposition $f(\hat{x}(\psi x))$. And he defines $f(\hat{x}(\psi x))$ more or less (but not exactly) as follows:

$$f(\hat{x}(\psi x)) =\mathrm{df}\ (\exists \phi)(\forall x)[(\phi x \equiv \psi x)\ \&\ f(\phi x)].$$

Technically this says: when a set $\hat{x}(\psi x)$ of all things having property ψ is the argument for the function f, thus forming the proposition $f(\hat{x}(\psi x))$, (which says "the set $\hat{x}(\psi x)$ has the property f"), there is a function ϕx equivalent to ψx such that $f(\phi x)$ is also true. Roughly, the function defining the set will replace it. But not quite. We actually replace the set with a function *equivalent* to the one that defines it. This makes the equation that replaces $f(\hat{x}(\psi x))$ extensional.

There is still one more step to the definition: Russell requires that the function ϕ that is formally equivalent to ψ must also be what he calls a *predicative* function. A predicative function is a function that contains no inner quantifiers and so is just one order higher than the order of its arguments. If ϕx is a function, Russell uses an exclamation mark to indicate when it is a predicative function, like this: $\phi!x$. The *actual* definition of a set is thus:

$$f(\hat{x}(\psi x)) = \mathrm{df} \ (\exists\phi)(\forall x)[(\phi!x \equiv \psi x) \ \& \ f(\phi!x)]$$

This says we can always replace a set with a predicative function equivalent to the function that defines the set. Since the function ϕ that replaces ψ is predicative, and since the mathematics in *Principia Mathematica* is done with sets, this means that the mathematics of *Principia* is really done with predicative functions.

Let's review what it means to be predicative. Some functions take individuals as arguments. They are normally first-order functions, one order higher than their arguments. *Except* when the function contains an inner function of a higher order, as in the case of "x had all of the properties of a great general." Then, though the function takes individuals as arguments, the function itself is second-order because it contains a second-order inner function. Functions without inner functions, those just one order higher than their arguments, are predicative. Functions more than one order higher than the order of their arguments are nonpredicative.

Now let's go back to Russell's axiom of reducibility. It says that for a function of any order, including nonpredicative ones that are at least several orders higher than the order of their variables, there is always an equivalent predicative function, that is, an equivalent function that is just one order higher than the order of its variable. How can Russell be sure this is true? For one reason, there are no known exceptions. So it is at least inductively true. And that is the most that can be said for any logical principle.

Now let's go back to Russell's definition of a set. It says that for any set there is a predicative function equivalent to the function that defines the set. This guarantees that sets are replaced with predicative functions. And how do we know there will always be a predicative function equivalent to one of any order? The axiom of reducibility guarantees that. And because this means mathematical functions are all predicative, mathematics then only requires a simple theory of types, not the ramified theory, to avoid the paradoxes. And this allows us to make assertions about *all* propositions of mathematics using ambiguous assertion. In effect, the definition of a set asserts the axiom of reducibility for sets, and so for mathematics.

In set theory, all sets are just one order higher than the order of their members, and so equivalent to a function just one order higher than its arguments. By requiring that a function that replaces a set be predicative, we ensure that it is the same order as the set it replaces, thus ensuring that propositions about the set that obey type theory will continue to obey it when we replace the set with a function. This ensures both that paradoxes will be avoided and meaningful mathematical propositions about sets will continue to be meaningful when we replace the sets with predicates.

As Russell points out (*Principia*, *12), using classes in language guarantees that because every function has an extension, every function corresponds to a set a of all its arguments. This in turn means the function is equivalent to the expression "x belongs to the set a" which is a predicative function just one order higher than the order of its objects. Classes thus guarantee that for functions of any order there is an equivalent predicative function. If we assume set theory, we can actually prove the axiom of reducibility.

Russell removes classes from mathematics, but introduces the axiom of reducibility in their place, which, he says, does everything that we need classes for, but without assuming classes themselves. In other words, it asserts that every function is equivalent to a predicative function. The no-class theory takes something out of mathematics (sets), and the axiom of reducibility, which does everything we want sets to do, puts something back in without assuming that there are sets themselves.

CHAPTER FOUR

Metaphysics

What is number? That is a question about existence, about what there is. In preceding chapters, queries about what exists and other philosophical questions have remained in the background so that Russell's definitions of number and related proofs could be presented in detail, along with his theory of descriptions and other analytic techniques. But larger philosophical questions about mathematical objects and objects in general are very much in the forefront of Russell's thought. This chapter and the two after it consider the philosophical doctrines about reality, knowledge, language, and meaning that surround Russell's logic and his logical analyses of mathematics. We begin with metaphysics.

Metaphysics is the branch of philosophy that studies being. This may be understood as the study of the first principles or the study of God or the study of the ultimate constituents of reality. It is inquiry into the ultimate constituents of reality—their nature, kinds, modes of existence, and relations—that characterizes Russell's metaphysics. Besides investigating the basic constituents of reality, Russell at times examines and invokes principles that transcend any possible experience. Though such principles are often considered a dimension of metaphysics, Russell regards them as belonging to epistemology and, following his lead, they are discussed in the chapter on knowledge.

In turning to Russell's metaphysics, a word of explanation is necessary. Metaphysics is often associated with purely speculative flights of fancy, regarded as an exercise in unrestrained imagination without serious bearing on anything. Russell shares this attitude and is dismissive, even contemptuous, of speculative metaphysics, which he often refers to simply as metaphysics. Russell does not think that his investigation into the ultimate constituents of reality is a form of speculative inquiry. On the contrary, he sees himself as engaged in logical ontology: the study of the kinds of beings that logical analysis shows must exist. Because this inquiry is supported by logic, it has an objective basis that makes it independent of the whims of a philosopher. It is this sort of analytic inquiry into the ultimate nature of things that he believes ought to replace the musings of traditional metaphysicians. Russell is therefore never a speculative metaphysician, or not willingly. Having pointed this out, we can nevertheless proceed to refer to Russell's inquiries as metaphysical. We acknowledge that there is room for debate as to what metaphysics is and whether his doctrines are metaphysical. But by calling them this we place Russell's work in a context of historical debates about ultimate reality and the ultimate constituents of things.

A final observation concerns what is novel in Russell's approach to metaphysics. There is nothing unique in the fact that he sometimes argues that we need to assume a certain kind of entity and at other times argues that an entity is needlessly assumed. What metaphysics does, in part, is to establish an inventory of entities. What is more noteworthy is his use of mathematical logic to dissolve longstanding philosophical problems, and it is largely due to his efforts that this approach has become commonplace. Thus, this practice is also not entirely unique to him. Modern logic was not available to Russell as it is to us, as a more or less established body of knowledge; for him, logic is both a means of solving philosophical problems and itself a philosophical problem. *That* is perhaps the most distinctive feature of his philosophy.

I The Early Russell

1 Platonism, dualism, pluralism

In his early work, Russell is decidedly Platonist. *Platonism* refers to the belief that there are entities and relations of entities that do not exist in space and time but have being and are a part of reality. A number or a class is such an entity. In *Principles of Mathematics*

(1903), anything that can be thought or mentioned is said to have being, and anything that has being is called a *term*. Thus, the category of *being* includes any quality we can think of and any absence of a quality; it includes what is simple and what is complex, what exists and what does not, what is concrete and what is abstract, what is particular and what is universal. In short, "a man, a moment, a number, a class, a relation, a chimera, or anything else that can be mentioned, is sure to be a term" (p. 43).

Russell is also a *dualist*: some parts of reality are characterized by consciousness and others are not. Since he accepts a Platonic world of nonmaterial and nonmental entities, his dualism is not limited to mind and matter. Rather, the mental realm is distinguished from both the material world in space and time and the Platonic domain. Consciousness is not a means of knowing an object but *is* the knowing of the object, and his dualism therefore involves the belief that when we are conscious of something we apprehend it directly and not through a medium of ideas. This apprehension of entities by a nonphysical act of "seeing" might be called "insight."

Moreover, his early philosophy is a species of *pluralism*. Russell's pluralism results from believing that the relations between things are "external" to them. This means that relations do not belong to the things they relate or alter them in any way. In contrast, the doctrine of internal relations holds that relations are properties of the terms they relate in the same way that *redness* seems to belong to a red apple. For example, if *a* is left of *b*, then *being to the left of b* is a property belonging to *a*. But if *being to the left of b* is a property belonging to *a*, then it begins to seem that *b* is part of a property of *a*. Likewise, if *being to the left of a* is a property of *b*, then *a* begins to seem to be a part of *b*. In short, on the doctrine of internal relations, the distinctions between things begin to collapse, lending support to the monistic assertion that the divisions between things are illusion and that the universe is one. Russell's doctrine of external relations rejects monism and supports the plurality of the universe by ensuring that items related do not belong to each other as properties do to a subject. It supports a view of the world as "composed of an infinite number of mutually independent entities, with relations which are ultimate, and not reducible to adjectives of their terms or of the whole which these compose" (1903a, p. xviii).

Among the groups of entities in external relations to each other, some are of the kind he calls *propositions*. For example,

Caesar himself, the abstract entity *death*, and their relation are a "proposition." The sentence "Caesar died" means this proposition. As a logician, Russell has no interest in a sentence as a string of words or in the mental images or feelings it might call up. A logician, he thinks, has to look *through* sentences and phrases to their meanings, which are objects. Since this is the only sense of meaning that he thinks is relevant to logic, he calls the complex object that corresponds to a sentence a *proposition*.

Summing up, Russell is Platonist, dualist, and pluralist, and he believes there are complex entities called "propositions." His reasons for these views have to do with his conception of the nature of propositions in logic and mathematics, which must consist of timeless relations that are independent of the mind and always true. Thus we read that "pluralism," and "the non-existential nature of propositions . . . and their independence of any knowing mind" are "indispensable to any even tolerably satisfactory philosophy of mathematics" (1903a, p. xviii).

2 Types of entities

Russell wishes to focus on propositions, properties, and other entities relevant to logic, and yet early on he confesses that he has been unable to apprehend any entity corresponding to the word "class" and that the discovery of a paradox of classes (Russell's paradox) shows that something is wrong (1903a, pp. xv–xvi). This is problematic given that he has defined *number* in terms of classes. There are additional difficulties. What he has discovered, it seems, is an entity that cannot occur. For example, when he attempted to form the class of all the classes that are not members of their classes, the result was that the class of these classes is and is not a member of itself. Given his Platonist conception of classes, this is a contradictory entity and it seems that such an entity is not even thinkable—as he said, he could not apprehend it. Beside classes, there also seem to be paradoxical concepts. If we accept that paradoxical entities cannot actually occur, as Russell seems to think, then the solution to the issue is not a matter of preventing them but of exposing the principle in the nature of things that precludes their formation and has hitherto escaped notice. In resolving on how to manage the paradoxes, Russell therefore assumes that the nature of reality determines what combinations of entities can occur. Since he wants to show what prevents contradictory complexes from occurring, "solving" them is not simply a matter of specifying formation rules from which the paradoxes cannot arise. The rules must capture some general fact of reality (which, articulated, is a principle of logic) that excludes impossibilities. He finally decides that it is the vicious circle principle that does so.

The vicious circle principle asserts that a propositional function (a concept) cannot take itself as an argument. That is, a propositional function that applies to individuals cannot apply to itself. What can apply to it is a propositional function that applies to propositional functions of individuals. This also cannot apply to itself, though what can apply to it is a function that applies to functions that apply to functions of individuals—and so on, without limit. This principle has implications for the kinds of entities there are and their relation to each other. In the *Principles*, Russell distinguished terms into *things* and *concepts*. The distinction between things and concepts needs revising once there are distinct types of concepts. A concept can still occur as a subject, as he had thought in *Principles*, but the concept applying to it must be the right type. The theory of types resulting from the vicious circle principle thus limits both what complexes can occur and what can meaningfully be said. It is metaphysical theory of things and a technical rule defining what sentences in a system of logic are well formed.

The need for yet more distinctions emerges as Russell turns to paradoxes not accounted for by the hierarchy of types of entities, such as the Liar paradox ("this sentence is false"). He explains these as due to ignoring the vicious circle principle and then uses the principle to justify drawing distinctions among propositional functions that take the same arguments. Propositional functions of one type (e.g. individuals) are thus subdivided into elementary functions of individuals, first-order functions of individuals, second-order functions of individuals, and so on. This solves the liar paradox but it makes it impossible to refer to all propositions or all functions as such: we can only talk about all properties of some order. Since mathematics needs to refer to such totalities, this doctrine is prohibitive. To preserve the forms of mathematical reasoning that his theory prohibits, Russell introduces the axiom of reducibility. This is problematic because it seems not to be a logical axiom. Despite these weaknesses, the fully elaborated theory of types eliminates the paradoxes, and for many years Russell remains committed to it.

3 Concepts, classes, and propositions

A different kind of help with paradoxical entities emerges early on when Russell discovers how to eliminate descriptive phrases like "a man" and "the last man" from his logical vocabulary. This is his theory of descriptions. The background to it is a problem about meaning and denoting. He had thought that a word like "man" means the concept *man* and that the concept *man* denotes individual humans (1903b, pp. 306–7). Thus, we apprehend the concept directly but only know about its denotation. The trouble is that it seems we cannot talk about the concept itself. If we try, we find ourselves talking about another concept, for example, "the meaning of 'man'." To avoid this and other problems, in "On Denoting" (1905) Russell shows that descriptive phrases can be eliminated from sentences that contain them without any loss of meaning. The phrase has to be replaced by other symbols and those have to mean entities (properties), but we do not need to assume the existence of the putative entity hitherto presumed to be the meaning of the original phrase. *That* entity is a fiction of logic, and since the original phrase has meaning only by being translated by other words, it is an incomplete symbol (1905a, pp. 415 ff.). This technique helps with the paradoxical notion of a *class*. Sentences containing class expressions do not have to be interpreted as being about classes if these sentences can be shown to have meaning without that ontological assumption. Defining classes in terms of propositional functions achieves this. Hereafter, propositional functions are to do the work of classes, since something must do that work if logicism is to define mathematics.

Besides its application to classes, the theory of descriptions can be used to show that the meaning of sentences can be explained without assuming that there are propositions, that is, entities like *Caesar died*. In *Principles*, a proposition is a complex entity. Because a proposition like *Caesar died* consists solely of entities in external relation, it is in a sense the same entity as *the death of Caesar*. The difference between these cases is that the first is true or false and the second is neither true nor false. Thus Russell's view requires him to say that an entity—the proposition—is true or false. We do not usually say that entities are true or false; this use of these words is unusual. Moreover, on his view entities may either exist in space and time or subsist in a Platonic domain. This applies to propositions also. *Beijing is in Ireland* is not in space and time but it subsists. It is a false, subsisting proposition. The desire to eliminate false, subsisting entities is one reason Russell begins to look for a way to revise his theory of propositions.

In papers like "On the Nature of Truth and Falsehood" (1910) and "Knowledge by Acquaintance and Knowledge by Description" (1911), and in *Principia* Russell argues that a proposition is a logical fiction. On this analysis, when a person believes that Caesar died, a certain object (Caesar) is asserted or judged to have a certain property (*death*). When a person doubts that Caesar (i.e. a collection of sense data) died, the entities are the same but the psychological attitude differs. Russell thinks of these kinds of occurrences as involving a relation of belief (doubt, etc.) holding between a believer and the various terms whose relation is believed in. Because belief holds of several entities, it is called the "multiple relation theory of belief." A person's belief that Caesar died consists of the same entities or meanings as those that were supposed to be provided by the proposition *Caesar died*. Since we can account for the meaning of the sentence "Caesar died" by reference to such beliefs and their constituents, it follows that the meaning of the sentence need not be a single entity and that there are no propositions after all.

Like a descriptive phrase, a sentence is now an incomplete symbol, not a symbol that corresponds to some entity. More precisely, a sentence is an incomplete symbol when considered apart from a person's state of belief, and it is that belief state that gives it a complete meaning. Since it is a psychological occurrence that provides them with complete meaning, as Russell remarks in *Principia* (p. 44), there need be no verbal difference between a sentence occurring as an incomplete symbol and as a symbol that has a complete meaning. The psychological context that distinguishes a sentence as a complete symbol from the incomplete symbol is brought into view by mentioning the believer, the relation of believing, and the objects of the belief. To be rendered in words, this belief fact requires a sentence of the form "A believes *p*."

While the meaning of the sentence "Caesar died" is provided by the fact of someone's belief in Caesar's death, its truth or falsehood is not. Since there are no propositions, subsisting or existing, truth and falsehood is explained in terms of the correspondence of a belief to a fact. If a belief is true, the entities that are judged to be related or to have a property will occur in that relation or with that property. They will not if the belief is false. The theory brings facts into prominence while propositions as single entities vanish from Russell's metaphysics. Because there are no propositions as entities, there are now no false and subsisting entities, though certain subsisting entities, like universals, remain.

4 Universals and particulars

By 1911, Russell no longer thinks that there are propositions, and the distinction between things and concepts has given way to a doctrine of particulars and universals. In "Analytic Realism" (1911), he describes this new view as a realist philosophy that defends analysis and is pluralistic: he calls it *logical atomism*. Here, "logic" does not mean the axioms and inference rules of mathematical logic but philosophical logic, the inquiry into the ultimate constituents of reality, its complexes, and their parts. This philosophy is called *logical* atomism because it describes only what is logically necessary to reality and avoids any additional metaphysics. Complexes are necessary and so are simples, since reason tells us there must be complexes and that their existence must be logically dependent on what they contain, which Russell calls simples. Just as a bowl of cherries presupposes cherries, a complex aRb is "logically dependent" on its constituents, a, R, and b. Complexes depend logically on simples, and simples depend logically on nothing. Since the existence of everything else depends on them, simples are called *logical atoms*.

They are also called logical atoms because they occur in complexes in a way analogous to the way that words occur in sentences. Russell continues to think that entities occur in distinct roles, though now they occur in complexes rather than propositions. He uses the terminology of *particulars* and *universals* to highlight the different roles simples play in a complex. Particulars can only occur as subjects. Universals—properties or relations—can occur either as predicates and verbs do in sentences or as subjects do (1911b, p. 135). Russell further describes particulars as having all the logical properties of substances, but not their traditional metaphysical properties. Thus, contrary to traditional metaphysics, particulars (substances) do not need to persist; they can be fleeting, as a patch of color is. Though particulars are logically independent entities, their existence may be causally dependent on other objects. For example, some particulars are data of sense, such as a patch of color, and these exist only when we perceive them. Despite this causal dependence on perception, a sense datum is not a mental entity existing in the mind. The data of sense are physical events or qualities. They will not exist if physical conditions are not of the right kind, for example, if there is no brain in a body, or no light source, but they exist in the extramental world and have physical causes (material particles, light, and so on).

Russell still speaks as if sense data are signs of something other than themselves, namely, their unseen causes, pieces of matter, but he is beginning to question that notion, which belongs to commonsense, traditional metaphysics, and physics. On the commonsense view, a desk can appear different colors to different people at the same time or different colors to one person from different angles because there is a thing, the desk, that changes color. It is assumed that the real desk exists independently of the existence of anything else and continues to exist when we close our eyes, leave the room, and so on. The underlying thing is also supposed to be unchanging; even if the desk is destroyed, the real stuff the desk is made from continues to exist. Because physics builds on commonsense, this is how physical atoms have been viewed. They exist, making up larger objects, and they persist indefinitely: you can destroy the larger things they compose, but not the atoms. Russell is denying that particulars persist and that they are mental entities. The notion that there is something that undergoes change and the belief that sense data are mental are ideas that contribute to the metaphysical hypothesis of a *ding an sich*, a thing beyond the appearances, and this is a hypothesis he soon argues ought to be avoided if possible.

5 Essence and existence

The doctrines above lead into Russell's account of the propositions of mathematical logic and their relation to propositions of applied sciences, such as physics. He works on this issue in the spring of

1911 in "Analytic Realism" and "The Philosophical Importance of Mathematical Logic." To begin with, any valid argument is valid because of its form, not its subject matter, and so, if all of the terms are replaced by variables, what results is a valid argument form. If the valid form is then expressed in a conditional form, it is a logical truth. Thus, logical truths arise from particular valid arguments and generalize them (1911c, p. 35). In replacing particular terms with variables to arrive at a logical truth, some will be found that cannot be replaced (1911c, p. 35). What cannot be eliminated in this manner is a constant of logic, that is, a formal concept like *is-a*, *all* and *if, then*. Thus, logic is "composed of propositions which contain only variables and logical constants, that is to say, purely formal propositions—for the logical constants are those which constitute form" (p. 38).

As noted above, the propositions of mathematical logic are conditional or hypothetical; they assert of any indeterminate subject that a hypothesis implies a certain thesis but they do not assert either the hypothesis or the thesis. Because their hypotheses are made of no particular thing, such propositions do not involve knowledge of the "actual world" (p. 37). It is by giving specific values to the variables that we arrive at the propositions of applied mathematics. Though these are also hypothetical, they concern particular terms and it is therefore possible to verify the hypothesis in question, that is, to determine whether the objects satisfy the hypotheses. Having done so, "this permits us to assert, not merely that the hypothesis implies the thesis, but that, since the hypothesis is true, the thesis is true also" (p. 36). The possibility of verification is not relevant to the truth of the propositions of pure mathematics and logic, but these propositions gain importance to us when their variables are given a definite meaning, enabling them to by applied and verified.

In a formal system of propositions the primitive undefined concepts are open to multiple interpretations; in effect they occur as variables. For example, in pure geometry, *space* occurs as a variable: it can take as its meaning anything that satisfies the axioms of geometry. A similar point can be made about *matter* in pure physics. In applied physics, this variable is interpreted in terms of physical objects and particles of matter. But this does not yet make a sentence of applied physics verifiable, since physical objects and matter are not observable. The astronomer talks about the moon as cold and distant, but we do not experience the moon; we experience qualities that we infer to be of the moon and these are neither cold nor distant. In general, the statements of applied physics are not about things we experience, which are colors, shapes, and so on. Thus, the sentences of applied physics transcend experience.

In order to verify sentences of applied physics, we must relate them to sentences about what we sense. Since we do not see or feel *things*, but only various sensory qualities from which we infer to things, to verify statements of applied physics we must relate them to sentences about pure sensations, in other words, to sentences whose variables are interpreted with sense data. The last step is the transition from "the world of essence" to "the world of existence" (1911b, p. 138).

This step is problematic. Physics infers that what we sense is the result of causal processes involving physical objects. Physical objects are a hypothesis and many other hypotheses might account for our experience: what we experience might remain the same even if there were no external world at all.

6 Data and the external world

The problem of our knowledge of matter and the external world belongs to epistemology but metaphysics enters into it in several ways. In "On Matter" we read that physics assumes the existence of particles of matter and "hypothetical coordinates," such as distance, occurring in an inferred physical space (1912c, p. 90). Since sense data cannot justify the belief in physical particles or physical space, these assumptions are metaphysical. Moreover, physics says that these objects are the causes of sense data, but physical causes are hypothetical and there is no greater probability that sense data are caused by physical objects than that they are caused by Mind or by nothing, since any of these hypotheses are compatible with all available evidence.

Thus, Russell concludes that we ought to abstain from any of these hypotheses. Instead, he proposes to construct matter and pieces of matter in terms of sense data. Since objects will be built up out of qualities, that is, out of what we experience, the statements of physics about physical objects will no longer concern something unobserved and will be verifiable by our experience. In this way, the laws of physics can be justified by sense data without assuming that unobserved physical objects exist.

This constructive approach to objects is an attempt to avoid metaphysical entities and hypotheses, but it is impossible to entirely avoid metaphysics in forming a construction. To try to avoid any metaphysics in the procedure, Russell would have to define objects by means of his sense data and his alone, since the existence of other people is a hypothesis on a par with the external world. But if collections of sense data (qualities) are to substitute for a hypothetical object, the collections have to be complete, and yet no person ever experiences *all* of the sense data that we say "belong to an object." Thus to justify physics, the collection of sense data that is to replace the hypothetical object must consist of data that is sensed as well as all the unsensed sense data. Given an actual sense datum, say, some round shape (a coin) in a person's visual field, we can imagine an infinite series of round shapes diminishing or increasing in size on a continuum with it. These are hypothetical data and it is these that are required by the logical construction. Having used these to construct an object, Russell then can construct physical space from an infinite number of hypothetical perspectives, occurring where there is no known perceiver, and locate constructed physical objects in the constructed physical space.

What is the ontological status of the possible data and possible perspectives? Russell has two choices: he can use them as "place holders" and abstain from saying that they exist or he can argue that such data exist and adopt a form of realism. In either case, they are hypotheses, but in the latter case an effort is made to show that we can infer their existence. Russell adopts both tactics. In the context of verifying physics, he does not think it necessary to make a metaphysical claim. There, the goal is to show that a logical construction has all the properties necessary to verify propositions of applied physics, and unsensed data and unoccupied perspectives can be treated as simplifying assumptions. However, Russell also wants to give reasons why such ideal data might exist. He therefore adopts the principle that sense data (fleeting qualities) exist even if they are not sensed (1912c, p. 86), a position he earlier denied. Russell calls the assumption that sense data can exist even when not sensed the essential axiom of naïve realism. This realist hypothesis is preferable to the metaphysics of physical objects. It is superior because unseen qualities are presumed to be like those we experience, whereas physical objects are assumed to be very different (e.g. relatively permanent), and therefore the inference in the first case is more secure than in the second. Similarly, an inductive inference from seen qualities to unseen qualities is less dubious than an inference from seen qualities to entities that are in principle beyond any possible observation. Metaphysics enters into his constructions, therefore, but in a constrained and limited way.

II The Middle Russell

7 The problem of types

Russell's early work ends with certain aspects of his thought in tension. On the one hand, there is a collective difficulty concerning the logical types, and on the other hand, a problem concerning the kinds of facts necessary to a description of the world. This section and the next two address these general issues, beginning with the problem of types. Both emerge from the reflections on logic prompted by a student, Ludwig Wittgenstein. Russell had thought that logical constants like *is-a*, *all* and *if*, *then* were entities and that logical forms were made up of them. He believed that logical propositions were about these logical objects and forms and that philosophical logic studied them. Wittgenstein has since made him aware that logical constants are not objects and cannot occur as the subjects of propositions. Words like "relation" and "or" are syntactical words, and if a language can say all that it needs to say without them, it is a mistake to suppose that they denote any things that are their meanings. They are on a par with words like "class." This suggests to Russell that language misleads us by its vocabulary, including its logical vocabulary, as well as by its syntax.

He decides that if language is to be a guide to what exists, it needs to have the right syntax and vocabulary. The notion of an ideal language emerges as a result. In lectures given in the fall of 1917 and published as *Introduction to Mathematical Philosophy* (1919), Russell describes an ideal language as one that prevents nonsense from occurring by containing words that refer unambiguously and by having a structure that mirrors the structure of facts (1919b, p. 198). What is true of one structure is true of one that mirrors it. Thus, an ideal language will not suggest that the world contains relations if it does not: it will exhibit relations among things by relations among words, that is, by syntactical structure. It will "show at a glance the logical structure of the facts asserted or denied" (p. 176).

The deeper reason for adopting an ideal language emerges in "The Philosophy of Logical Atomism", the text of a lecture series given in the spring of 1918. In these lectures, Russell says that if you try to refer to relations, properties, facts, and so on, you make a type error. As noted earlier, the young Russell built a theory of types of entities into his logical system in response to the threat of various paradoxes. The gist of that theory is that a symbol cannot be substituted for any symbol we like: a symbol that is meaningful in one role in a sentence will result in nonsense if used in another role in a sentence. He now realizes that if we take the theory of types seriously, we ought not say things like "yellow is a property," since in doing so we treat it as a different type of entity.

Since an error in type is an error in making sense, talk about concepts, facts, relations, or any logical primitive or type is nonsense. As Russell observes: "the statement concerning any particular that it is not a universal is quite strictly nonsense—not false, but strictly and exactly nonsense" (1918a, p. 225). Thus, "you can always only get at the thing you are aiming at by the proper sort of symbol, which approaches it in the appropriate way" (p. 233). For example, we cannot say "yellow is a property" but we can say "this is yellow." But if we cannot talk about this or that property, or this or that relation, how can we enunciate a theory of types? Moreover, how can we talk about kinds of entities as we do in metaphysics? We can, Russell says, by referring to the different types of symbols rather than to the different types of things. We may not say "yellow is a property" but we may say "'yellow' is a predicate."

Some sort of metaphysical conclusion might seem to follow from the above problem, and it does. Many of the cases that Russell now regards as nonsensical had previously supported a theory of universals. If it is nonsense to say "yellow is a property," then it is hard to accept that we apprehend a universal, *yellow*. By the early 1920s, he ceases to include universals among the data of experience. This does not mean that there are no universals, but if there are any, they are inferred and not experienced. (And if there are any, they will be universal relations like *similar* but not nominatives like *similarity*, since that would violate type theory.) What is meant by the predicate "is yellow" is something in experience, a recurring sensation, and not a single, nonphysical entity, the universal *yellow*. Though Russell begins to call classes of recurring stimuli "universals," they are not universals in his old sense and are not part of his metaphysics.

8 Forms of facts

Despite the difficulties of expression noted above, Russell's logical atomism unfolds in many respects as it did before. He describes reality as consisting of a great many ultimate constituents or "atoms" and lays out what he thinks these entities must be. The accent is on the constituents of facts rather than of complexes and on the different forms of facts. What is ultimate are facts and their constituents since most of what we regard as entities (tables and chairs and people) are logical fictions, that is, constructions of sense data.

The starting point of his analysis is the conviction or primitive belief that there are facts. A fact is what makes a sentence true or false, and while it is likely that different kinds of facts exist, it is not obvious what kinds of facts are needed to account for the truth of the various kinds of sentences. In logic, sentences are classified as atomic, molecular, general, or logical. Atomic sentences are of various forms (with monadic relations, dual relations, triadic relations, and so on), and they correspond, if true, to atomic facts containing the same complexity. Thus, to explain the truth of an atomic sentence, such as "this patch is darker than that one," we have to assume the existence of a relational atomic fact. But no such new form of fact has to be introduced to account for the truth or falsehood of a molecular sentence like "this is blue or green" since the facts that verify or falsify its component sentences suffice. Such a sentence, if true, corresponds to a disjunction of atomic facts and not to a disjunctive fact. Thus, Russell denies the existence of molecular facts and of any entity that is the disjunctive form.

Russell had regarded the form as an abstract entity. One reason for holding this view is that something must enter into our understanding of a disjunctive sentence like "this is blue or green" to distinguish it from one with an entirely different meaning, such as "this is blue and green." His present difficulty is to explain where the meaning comes from if not from the fact and not from its form. The problem remained unresolved for some time. Though Russell decides there are no molecular facts, he makes an exception for negative facts, such as "This sauce is not sweet." He thinks that attempts to try to explain negative sentences without assuming negative facts (e.g. by reference to incompatibility) ultimately assume negative facts anyway.

Generalizations like "All humans are mortal" and "Some humans are mortal" raise related problems. What forms of facts correspond to them? For example, if, as Russell now says, propositional functions are mere symbols and denote nothing, and if there are no forms, what are we to say about what verifies or falsifies "for all x, if x is a man, then x is mortal"? Russell believes that there must be facts corresponding to such sentences, but he does not know how to analyze their form. The issue, which is not resolved in the lectures, is analogous to the problem posed by logical propositions. Logical propositions are completely general and are always true. But because they contain variables and are about nothing particular, if there are no logical forms for them to be about, it seems that nothing is distinctive to them, nothing is their content. To put it another way, we arrive at logical truths by abstracting from the subject matter of empirical generalizations, but logical propositions cannot be distinct from empirical generalizations merely by an absence of content. In 1918, this issue is unresolved. A few years later, Russell decides that logical propositions are not about anything other than language: they express relations between symbols that mean the same thing.

9 Sensations and images

By 1918, Russell begins to be aware of weaknesses in his earlier arguments against neutral monism, a philosophy defended in different ways by John Dewey, William James, and Ernst Mach. Neutral monism argues that reality is more fundamental than the categories of mind and matter, and that "mental" and "physical" are labels given to different arrangements of a single and more fundamental kind of stuff. On this philosophy, the consciousness of a red patch and the red patch are explained as different classes or series containing the same neutral material. Since neutral monism analyzes mental life in terms of the same stuff it uses to analyze the physical world, Russell had resisted it, believing that there is a uniquely mental character to all mental life and a mental domain distinct from the physical. This idea rests on the notion that what is sensed (a sense datum) is distinct from our sensation of it, where *sensation* means a nonphysical form of awareness or "acquaintance." On this view, a noise that we hear is distinct from our consciousness of it.

One reason the above doctrine of acquaintance had been attractive to Russell is that it seemed necessary to explain the perspective of consciousness. Insensible objects are in the world but are not aware of the world. Anything that is conscious is aware of the world that it occupies and of the vantage point from which it is aware—we are at a center and things are here or there relative to that center. If nothing were conscious, the world could be described neutrally, in a list of objects, but so long as there is consciousness, the perspective characterizing experience requires an account. Though Russell had admired the scientific tenor of the work of the neutral monists and conceded that their view is superior to his own with respect to employing the fewest metaphysical assumptions, so long as it could not account for subjectivity, it was unacceptable to him. Since he has come to think he can explain these phenomena with a neutral monist philosophy, he is now willing to abandon dualism.

These are largely epistemological issues, but they bear on his metaphysics. Thus, having rejected his dualist theory of acquaintance, in *The Analysis of Mind* (1921) Russell ventures to construct mental phenomena (such as belief) and mental entities (such as a mind or person) from the same elements that go into a construction of a piece of matter. To do so, he employs as the neutral stuff what he calls "sensations" and images. Both are particulars. A sensation may be a member of the class that constitutes an object or of the class that is a person's perception of the object. Thus, sensations fall under physical as well as psychological laws. Images might appear unsuited to neutral monism if we think of images as mental entities, but this is not his view. They do not differ intrinsically from sensations though they occur in different classes or causal series. Thus an image falls under psychological laws only, for example, under laws of association. For metaphysics, the result of the turn to neutral monism is the elimination of mental entities and acts (mind, person, consciousness, etc.), and the adoption of an ontology that consists of sensations and images. The emphasis is on particulars and universals are no longer treated as among the data. Russell's metaphysical position remains pluralistic. Adopting neutral monism does not mean abandoning logical atomism, and the two are merged into a new philosophy.

10 Structure and realism

Besides the changes in metaphysics that come from alterations in Russell's logical theory, there are shifts that arise due to developments in physics. Physics assumes an indirect realism of chains of events leading from some external cause, say, the sun, to our eyes and our experience of light. This is nothing new to physics, and Russell had earlier assumed there are causal chains leading from external events to the brain and ending in sense data. In his earlier work, however, physics seemed committed to entities, particles, whose persistence made them quite unlike the fleeting colors and sounds we experience. Inference to the existence of such entities was hard to justify, and he chose, instead, to construct objects from sensed and unsensed sense data. This made it possible to interpret the variables of the propositions of physics with objects that are built out of what we experience.

The 1919 confirmation of Einstein's general relativity theory changes his assessment of the issue. Among other things, *matter* has ceased to be a central physical concept; physics speaks instead of fleeting *events*. This draws physics closer to Russell's philosophical doctrine, where fleeting sensations are ultimate constituents. But it is still a leap to connect what occurs in the external world assumed by the physicist, such as light waves, with the colors and shapes of experience. What is needed is a philosophical account that shows how these elements are continuous with sensations, which he now prefers to call *percepts*.

Russell works this out in detail in *The Analysis of Matter* (1927). To connect the world of physics to the world of sense requires several things: a philosophical account of entities based on neutral monism, a theory of perception, and the use of constructions and inference. Concerning inference, Russell is neither hunting for principles that justify inference to unobserved events nor attempting to explain them. He assumes there are such principles and has some in mind.

For example, he assumes that the principle "difference in effects, difference in causes" justifies inferring from groups of *percepts* to unobserved *events* occurring in related patterns. Like the pattern of ripples on a pond, when we cannot see, structures among percepts imply corresponding structures among events that continue the pattern. But to use such principles, he must show how percepts *can* be connected causally with unobserved events: this is the purpose of *Analysis of Matter*.

Russell has not abandoned constructions. Events believed to be continuous with percepts are part of a construction, just as were the hypothetical entities he used to assume. We infer from percepts to the existence of these events using the inductive principle that warrants inferring from something observed to unobserved things of the same kind. Percepts are a kind of event, so inferring to physical events is inferring to something of the same kind. Yet percepts tell us nothing about intrinsic properties of the events causing them and we cannot assume that unobserved events would be similar to percepts if we could but observe them. This is related to Russell's emerging *structural realism*. On that doctrine, inferences from structural properties of groups of percepts to structural properties of events in the external world are justified but we can know nothing about the intrinsic nature of events in the physical world.

11 Substance and analysis

In his early period, Russell sometimes treated the unobserved data used in his constructions as if they were simplifying devices useful in expressing a theory. For the purpose of addressing the verification of physics it did not matter whether they existed or not and the question could be set aside. This did not prevent him from raising the question in other contexts, however. And he also defended a realist view of unsensed data, suggesting that inference from sense data to unsensed data is more justifiable than inference to entities wholly unlike sense data. His position has now changed on both points. He no longer abstains from assuming the existence of unobserved events in the course of his constructions, but he now does abstain from asserting that unsensed data are similar to what we would sense were we to occupy the right perspective. We can in fact infer the existence of events continuous with what we experience, as when we infer that the paint on a wall continues under the pictures on the wall, yet we can know nothing about the intrinsic nature of physical events. Moreover, we cannot infer from percepts to an underlying substance having qualities. The only object we can legitimately infer from perception is the constructed object consisting of percepts and inferred events. Nothing is meant by "physical object" other than this group of events, and it can be called an "inferred entity" because much of it *is* inferred.

The metaphysical importance of this position is that it explicitly rejects the concept of a substance existing in different states, for example, the concept of matter in motion. There is no basis in experience for this idea: as far as we know, objects are groups of events that we flesh out by assuming unobserved events. The point can be applied to the entities assumed by physics. It is clear that physics does not require "permanent entities with changing states or relations" (1927a, p. 238). We can retain the truth of physics by interpreting matter, such as electrons, as strings of successive events. Physics and his neutral monist philosophy are thus in accord in rejecting the notion of substance.

What is the impact of eliminating substance on Russell's conception of particulars? To cast doubt on the notion of substance as an unknown and unknowable substrate underlying changing qualities or states is not to cast doubt on whether there is something in our experience that can be considered particular and given a name. The emphatic rejection of substance or substrate is merely a deepening of a view he has held for a long time. Neither in his early work nor earlier in this middle period has a particular been a permanent substrate. Since there are particulars, either percepts or constructions of them, there is no disruption in grammar and no impediment to finding something to be the subject of a proposition.

Russell argues that as physical structures, noise-events, or spatial series, sentences are similar in structure to other nonlinguistic structures and reveal facts about them. He also looks at the grammar of sentences to draw metaphysical conclusions, as he did in 1918. These ideas later become a theory of two forms of analysis of the world, grammatical and perceptual. Even though he is aware of the great danger of error involved in using grammar as a guide to reality he still thinks that "certain linguistic distinctions . . . may have metaphysical importance" (1927a, p. 242). The distinctions he has in mind are those between proper names, adjectives, and verbs.

12 Events and percepts

It was noted above that part of Russell's task in *Analysis of Matter* is to explain perception and show how percepts *can* be continuous with events we do not see, namely, the events causing the seeing. It is hard to explain how physical events can cause mental events if they are different in kind, as they are assumed to be by most philosophical theories. Neutral monism does not make that assumption and therefore it helps us to understand why the continuity in question is not impossible.

In *Analysis of Matter*, the basic entities are *events*; these are "the ultimate existents in terms of which physics is true" (1927a, p. 293). Percepts are not distinct from events except in their effects. The word "percept" refers merely to those events that, by occurring where there is a brain and at the end of a causal series in that brain, have certain psychological effects, such as habit or perception. If we also bear in mind that events are not in themselves mental or physical, mind or matter, it will not seem strange to say that percepts and events can be grouped spatially together, or to say that percepts can be members of group of events that form a piece of matter. For example, percepts may belong to groups constituting the electrons in the brain. Conversely, matter (in our brains or eyes) may consist of percepts and mental states (p. 322).

The important relations between events are *compresence* and *co-punctuality*. Compresent events are those that overlap in space; co-punctual events are those that overlap in time. Groups of spatially overlapping events form a point, and since these events may include some that are percepts (if the point occurs in a brain), a percept may be a member of a group that is among the groups forming a point. Groups of points construct an electron. Pieces of matter, such as electrons or protons, are collections of groups of events, each of which is arranged about a center. They are constructed out of groups of events as a "causal line." What define these lines are the earlier and later groups of related events in a sequence (p. 318).

Perception, on Russell's account, occurs when a causal line (pieces of matter or light waves), in a portion of space-time containing a brain, terminates in a percept. Percepts are thus at the end of a causal series beginning with light waves external to the brain and leading inward from the eye, optic nerve, and so on. Percepts occur at the end of a physical causal chain but stand at the head of a psychological chain. They are events whose effects we call habit, images, and perception.

III The Late Russell

13 Language and fact

In the 1930s and 40s, Russell focuses on the relation between language and nonlinguistic fact in order to identify the sorts of words necessary for expressing what we perceive and the level of language at which meanings of words are defined by ostension. Viewed in a certain light, these tasks might easily seem to be metaphysical or even mystical. For example, the point of connection between words and things might seem to be something that evades words and is therefore inexpressible. This kind of claim is familiar to Russell. In his *Tractatus Logico-Philosophicus* (1921), Wittgenstein contended that there are things that can only be shown and not said, including the nature of language. Russell rejected this idea and the mystical view Wittgenstein attached to it, arguing in the introduction to that text that we might talk about language by using a higher language. Aside from this point, Russell does not see his subject, language, as an inexpressible one. There are difficulties in talking about what occurs where experiences give rise to language but it is not impossible. His is an inquiry into language as a physical phenomenon and how it is caused by extralinguistic experience. For example, repeated canine percepts in association with the sounds "d-o-g" may cause a child to say "dog" when the stimulus is present and, eventually, even when it is absent. When a word acquires meaning for a person in this way, the meaning of the words is something to which the person must point. This is not because the meaning is mystically inexpressible but because the physical process has to begin somewhere.

Russell's inquiry into language might be seen as metaphysical for other reasons having little to do with its supposed inexpressibility.

Some of Russell's contemporaries might contest the idea that there is a correct or ideal language, or that we ought to be looking for one. From the perspective of some logical positivists of the period, a language (such as a logical language) is not to be judged by some external standard—as if we could stand apart from language and assess how well it reflects the world—but by the purposes for which it was constructed. Questions that appear to be about the world, they would say, are really questions about which language we choose to use. Is the universe infinite? This seems to be a factual question but is really a matter of which logical language we use and the names it contains. Seen in this light, Russell's attempt to identify the "right" language is as metaphysical as his belief that there are factual philosophical questions other than those that belong entirely to logic.

Russell is familiar with this objection too. He has long since come to think that many philosophical problems are really linguistic problems in disguise, but he does not reduce all non-logical philosophical questions to questions about language. That view, he thinks, forgets that the purpose of language is to be about the world. For Russell, language is about the world and part of the world and therefore a key to the nature of the world, if we identify a logically correct language free of the misleading features of ordinary language.

14 Prelude to metaphysics

Besides thinking that it is legitimate to talk about how words acquire meanings, Russell also thinks that avoiding this topic allows spurious metaphysics to creep into philosophy. Some logical positivists prefer to talk about the premises to knowledge without determining how the words in the premises acquire meaning or asking what kinds of words are acceptable in premises expressed in a language suited to science. Russell regards this as a mistake. The kinds of premises we accept determine what we think we can infer and whether we think we can infer anything transcending experience. Those who avoid talking about these issues inevitably smuggle metaphysical assumptions into the very language they employ to state or describe premises. They think they have shown that knowledge cannot transcend experience and so they despise the metaphysics they have unwittingly exploited. Better to ask whether a scientific language ought to include this or that kind of word or sentence, and to determine how the meaning is supplied by experience. If we are careful in these stages, we will be able to see where inference is required, what kind of inference is necessary and on what principles, and we will be able to use language as a guide to what there is.

In *An Inquiry into Meaning and Truth* (1940), Russell asks, "how far, if at all, do the logical categories of language correspond to elements in the non-linguistic world that language deals with? Or, in other words, does logic afford a basis for any metaphysical doctrines?" (p. 21). He wants to use language as a guide to what there is in part so that he can address the question, long put aside, of whether we need to infer the existence of universals. The procedure is more complex than is at first obvious. He has to establish a language with the right grammar and a minimum vocabulary suited to science in order to see if there is anything left unexplained requiring inference to universals. In establishing his language, Russell must first be sure that knowledge from perception is accurately and completely captured. We cannot take for granted what we perceive since it is often overlaid with assumptions. Hence before any inquiry into metaphysics begins, we must identify the perceptual data.

The attempt to determine the perceptual data might be mistaken for a part of Russell's metaphysical inquiry but it is in fact a prelude to that inquiry. It involves asking what we need to perceive to account for our grasp on words and sentences of certain kinds. (At the same time, Russell asks what kinds of words and sentences we need, that is, what kinds of words suffice for formulating sentences of about what we perceive.) For example, Russell analyzes what we perceive when we hear "x precedes y" and decides that we must perceive a relation or we could not tell from the sounds involved whether we heard "y precedes x" or "x precedes y." The conclusions concern perceptual data, not metaphysical entities. In this context Russell uses the word "universal" to refer to what we perceive, that is, to repeatable events that have recurring effects on us and that result in a word, which is also a recurring event. In these contexts he is not talking about universals as inferred single entities. Responding to similar instances of canine shapes does not imply the existence of a universal *dog*, and responding by using similar sounds or marks "d-o-g" does not mean there is a single universal that is the word.

The possibility of stimulus and response leading to habit implies that there are similarities but not that there is a single universal, *similarity*. Russell says, "when we use language, it is not necessary to *perceive* similarity. One black patch causes one verbal utterance "black," and another causes another; the patches are similar, and their verbal effects are similar, and the effects of the two verbal utterances are similar" (1940, p. 58).

None of this constitutes a metaphysical doctrine, though the metaphysical issue of whether we need to infer to universals is not far off. Before turning to it, however, other question require discussion that are not metaphysical, but that ought to be noted because falling within related territory.

15 Egocentric words

Russell considers whether egocentric words like "this" and "I" are needed by a minimal vocabulary adequate for completely describing the world. He concludes that they are not, but his reasons go beyond the fact that physics does not require such words and describes the world neutrally without tense or reference to an observer. All words would be absent from a purely physical world, but the world does contain language users and so the question is whether we require egocentric words for a description of that aspect of the world, an aspect he thinks would remain even if humans were replaced by talking machines (1940, p. 111).

The sentence "this is hot" contains the egocentric word "this," the meaning of which seems tied to a particular individual and moment. Since many sentences contain similar elements of egocentricity, it might appear hopeless to attain knowledge not limited to a particular person's subjective experience. Against this, Russell argues that it is not what is known in perception that gives egocentric words their subjectivity but what causes the words to be uttered. For example, a person or machine utters "this is red" rather than "this was red" because of a different causal chain between the percept and the word user. The egocentricity derives from the causation of the words, which is unique and is not part of its meaning. This does not get rid of egocentricity but it explains it differently. In the 1910s, Russell thought that egocentric words involve reference to the experience of a subject and that this experience of perspective was how they got their meaning. He now sees that words like "this" and "here" are merely "an expression of the causal relation between what is stated and the stating of it (1940, p. 115)." A word like "this" is not a necessary part of a language capable of describing the nonverbal world. The word "this," for example, can be replaced with a name, "W," denoting the bundle of qualities {hotness, etc.} in a person's present experience.

Finally, the word "this" in sentences like "this is red" might appear to be the name of a substance, a thing, distinct from its quality of redness. In other words, we might be encouraged to think of a thing as an unknowable and indescribable subject of its qualities. But if "this" is shorthand for a bundle of qualities called W, then we can interpret the sentence "this is red" as asserting that some quality, redness, belongs to some bundle of qualities: in short, that hotness belongs to W. The advantage of the new interpretation is that it helps with the elimination of substance as an unknown substrate of qualities.

16 Bundles of qualities

In *Analysis of Matter* (1927), Russell dismissed the notion of a substrate and took events as his ultimate particulars. His present work goes further and eliminates the need to assume particulars by analyzing events into bundles of compresent qualities. On this view, a particular is merely the collection of its qualities. We normally think particulars do not occur in more than one place at a time. Bundles of qualities satisfy this requirement since they are unlikely to reoccur. Consider a person's total experience at one moment. It consists of a long list, say, color patches of blue and white, a flapping sound, a sensation of wind, and so on. It is improbable that all of the qualities that make up a person's present experience will ever recur together at another time, though it is not logically impossible. Russell regards as an advantage that the recurrence of a bundle is not logically impossible. It means that sentences like "if A precedes B, B does not precede A," said of bundles of qualities, are empirical generalizations, true in some cases and not in others, rather than *a priori* truths.

Since a total momentary experience is unlikely to occur twice or in two places at once and serves as a particular, it can be used as a point-instant. As such, it is the basis of two series. A total momentary experience—at a point and an instant—is the basis on which a perceiver, assuming laws of perspective, infers the position of what occurs in physical space-time as near or far, left or right, and so on. It is also the way we may assign the perceiver a position relative to other point-instants in physical space-time. The probable uniqueness of total experiences as bundles of qualities also lets us sort a person's experience into a temporal series, assuming that some but not all the qualities overlap from one momentary bundle to the next. We determine a temporal series by noting which bundles of qualities occur in which groups. (Single qualities can recur: shades of color, kinds of sounds, etc. have no unique space-time position and can occur in different bundles.) A person's total experience is thus a chain of unique but overlapping bundles of qualities (1940, pp. 337–8).

With this doctrine Russell can defend the principle, called the "identity of indiscernibles," that two things cannot possess the same qualities. If particulars are substances distinct from their qualities, different particulars *could* have all the same qualities, but if particulars are just bundles of qualities, they cannot have the same qualities and differ. If particulars are bundles of qualities, the identity of indiscernibles *must* be true. Moreover, his analysis shows that we no longer have to assume that particulars are a metaphysical category in addition to qualities. In "On the Relations of Universals and Particulars" (1912) he had argued on the basis of an analysis of perceived space relations that there must be particulars. He now rejects that argument. Finally, we need not regard "this" as a name for an unknowable substrate but we must accept names for classes of qualities, words for qualities, verbs like "compresent," and logical vocabulary.

17 Transcending experience

Since the 1920s, Russell has believed that we do not observe events directly. Experiences come at the end of a causal chain, what we experience are percepts "inside our heads." Even in a case as simple as "there is a dog," what verifies the sentence transcends our experience. That is, what verifies it cannot be identified, since we experience patches of color, not dogs. The question is what "verifier" corresponds to "there is a dog" and makes it true? To use Russell's jargon, what does a true sentence like this *indicate*?

Russell sees no reason to deny that there are verifiers in these cases. If we infer that someone is tall from the fact that Joe is tall, this is due to thinking that Joe's height verifies the existential sentence. And if we can make this assumption when the verifying fact is known, we can do so in the case where the verifying fact is unknown. Whether we perceive and can name a verifier has no bearing on whether there is a truth-relation. When a sentence has a verifier that lies outside experience, what it indicates is a fact that verifies some particular sentence that we cannot utter for want of the appropriate name. (Thus, a sentence that transcends experience must contain a variable.) This opens up the possibility that there are sentences that we know to be true even though we cannot perceive what verifies them. These can be quite ordinary sentences, such as "something fell."

The above has introduced one sense in which a sentence—and a premise—might transcend experience: we cannot perceive what verifies it. A harder question concerns whether there are truths that are not known. Metaphysics enters into Russell's discussion of this issue in several ways. He defends a logical correspondence theory of truth as correspondence with facts against an epistemic one where truth is correspondence with experience. This issue concerns only basic propositions (i.e. those that convey the kind of knowledge contained in a single experience), not complex ones formed from basic propositions.

The problem is that if we define the truth of basic sentences by their correspondence with experience, there will be propositions that are neither true nor false since there will be sentences for which we have no corresponding experience. Take the basic proposition "There was snow in Manhattan yesterday": it is either true or false. But the epistemic view does not guarantee that sentences formed from it by substitution of terms will be either true or false. For example, "There was snow in Manhattan in the year 1 A.D." (1940, p. 277) is neither true nor false on the epistemic account of truth since we have never had that experience. This is far too narrow and would imply that a great many very ordinary sentences (such as "all men are mortal") are neither true nor false. Russell therefore decides that it is better to define "truth" so that it means correspondence with fact, allowing a fact to lie outside our experience. This guarantees that sentences are either true or false but it puts us in the domain of metaphysics. It rests on the metaphysical assumption that the substitution of words of the right type in a basic proposition yields a sentence that indicates either a negative or a positive fact (p. 293). In short, it commits him to negative facts.

18 What there is

Russell's attempt to arrive at a minimum vocabulary is a step toward using that language to decide the metaphysical question of whether there is need to infer the existence of universals. The question whether there are universals turns on whether there can be meaningful sentences without them. Russell assumes that we can eliminate universals by using qualities and the relation of *similarity*. Instead of saying that a tulip is yellow, we can say that its color is similar to *this* and point to something yellow. As he noted decades earlier, this does not eliminate all universals but merely reduces them to the relation of *similar*, which cannot be eliminated. This is apparent when we consider the similarity of sentences asserting similarity. The sentences "A is similar to B" and "C is similar to D" both use the word "similar," and we do understand this to mean not that the meaning of "similar" is similar in these cases, but that it is the *same*. The word "similar" can have *one and the same* meaning on different occasions of its use and not merely a *similar* meaning only if what it means is a universal. Russell therefore argues that we cannot give meaning to sentences about what is similar without assuming the existence of at least one universal (1940, p. 347).

Russell explains language in terms of similar stimuli producing similar reactions. His theory assumes that sensations can be similar, since otherwise they would never have the effects they do. On the argument above, if reality has no general feature of *similarity*, we might still notice similar stimuli and respond in similar ways and we could even say that they are similar. What we could not say is that assertions of similarity are similar. This conclusion does not imply the existence of an entity that could be named or correspond to a noun. Admitting the need for universals does not commit Russell to a theory of Platonic ideas; he is not committed to a universal *similarity* corresponding to a noun, and he still holds the view expressed in 1918 that a predicate must occur as a predicate.

But his point is that we must treat *similar* as a general feature of the world, and once we do that, there is no good reason to deny that there are other universals. Russell concludes "that complete metaphysical agnosticism is not compatible with the maintenance of linguistic propositions" (1940, p. 347).

CHAPTER FIVE

Theory of knowledge

The theory of knowledge is the study of the forms, justification, origin, causes, and limits of knowledge. Except in his early work, where he maintains that one form of knowledge consists in relations to objects, Russell restricts the word "knowledge" to a certain class of true beliefs. Whether the study of knowledge is a study of a class of true beliefs or is more broadly defined, the questions that Russell raises come to these: What is it that justifies saying that a proposition (or belief) is true, and how is it that we come to think it is true? In raising these questions, he uses categories familiar to a mathematician and logician: he inquires into knowledge of conclusions and of premises. However, his theory of our knowledge of premises and consequences is foundational in a way not typical of a system of logic. That is, among the beliefs that constitute a body of knowledge, some are supposed by him to be more basic or primitive than others and to be those from which the others are derived. The premises are not all empirical; logical principles are included as well. A component of this foundational doctrine is a conviction that premises (at least the empirical ones) are true because of their relation to extralinguistic fact and not, say, because of cohering with other premises in a system.

Conceiving of knowledge in this way, Russell's strategy is to organize a body of beliefs in some science or discipline and show how certain beliefs are related to and follow from immediately given, un-inferred, premises. This practice highlights logical relations among propositions and focuses attention on the principles involved in deriving some from the initial beliefs, in particular, those premises and principles that are minimally necessary to the science in question. It also provides a context for talking about the difference between premises that are logically basic and those that are psychologically basic. The latter topic introduces issues about certainty and other characteristics of belief.

While Russell addresses the justification of beliefs by identifying premises and principles of inference, he is equally interested in the question of how we come to know. That inquiry plays an unusually prominent role especially in his middle and late period work—unusual, given that philosophers commonly regard questions about how we come to have a belief as falling within psychology, not within epistemology. But Russell does not share this view: For him, the study of knowledge may involve questions about stimuli, responses, association, interest, perception, feelings, and so on. Psychological matters, he thinks, are highly relevant to how we come to know what words mean and so to the theory of knowledge, which cannot avoid the problem of meaning. We cannot account for our primitive beliefs (beliefs not justified by inference from other beliefs) except by understanding how we grasp what is meant by the words in them. For this reason, Russell's study of knowledge is driven from inquiry into premises to an investigation into words and the link with experience that supplies them with meaning. Since there are different kinds of premises—some are factual, others are principles of inference—his twofold inquiry often considers what justifies logical principles, how we come to know them, and how the words that enter into them have meaning. Russell's epistemology changes considerably over his long career. The goal of this chapter is to identify the central doctrines in different periods of Russell's work on knowledge and to show how it overlaps and supports his logic and logical analyses.

I The Early Russell

1 Logical knowledge

Russell's work is largely an attempt to give a satisfactory account of logical, mathematical, and empirical knowledge and their relation to each other. Despite a youthful ambition to explain the relation between these two kinds of knowledge, in early work

Russell focuses on logical and mathematical knowledge. Issues of knowledge first appear in the context of his opposition to various idealist and empiricist arguments about the truth of logical and mathematical propositions and knowledge of their truth. Logical and mathematical propositions like "$2 + 2 = 4$" evidently differ from those like "geese fly with their necks extended," since we can know that the former are true independently of experience and we cannot find out the truth about geese and their necks except by observation. Immanuel Kant recognizes this distinction when he calls those propositions whose truth is known independently of experience a *priori* and those whose truth we know only through experience a *posteriori*.

What Russell objects to in the idealist or Kantian account is not the category of a *priori* knowledge but the manner in which Kant interprets it. Kant held that we experience things as in space because our understanding consists of categories that we bring to experience and which shape our experience. Since any condition of experience is independent of experience, it follows that propositions about space, that is, propositions of geometry, are known to be true a *priori*. But this is not a very satisfying notion of the a *priori* status of geometrical propositions: it seems to say that they are a *priori* only in the sense that we cannot help but believe them. In *Principles of Mathematics* (1903), Russell argues that by Kant's view, if human nature changed, geometrical truths would no longer be a *priori*, which is absurd. The same argument applies to arithmetic. On the Kantian approach, that $2 + 2 = 4$ is true only on condition that we believe it a *priori*. According to Russell, $2 + 2$ equals 4 even if no one thinks it—even if there is no one *to* think—but nothing in Kant's view ensures that what we believe a *priori* is true; it might be false (1903a, pp. 450–1). This is unacceptable since mathematical and logical truths must be true unconditionally.

In general, Russell objects to Kant's tendency to identify psychological facts about how we think with what is objectively true even if no one thinks it. Russell's account of mathematical and logical truth is metaphysical rather than psychological. In his early work, Russell regards propositions as complex entities, specifically identifying those in mathematical logic as complex entities consisting of formal relations (such as *or*) between indeterminate entities (*any x*). It is because the propositions of mathematics and logic subsist independently of time and space, and therefore independently of human minds, that they are always true and we can have *a priori* knowledge of their truth. Russell still needs to account for the process of cognition by means of which we have access to such entities but this doctrine at least establishes that the propositions of logic and pure mathematics are always objectively true.

How then do we know their truth? The answer has been given already. If propositions in mathematical logic are complex entities subsisting in space and time, they are not available to the senses. We rely on our senses to hear or see sentences that express them but not to know that they are true. Russell dismisses any empiricist theory of our knowledge of pure mathematics and logic. An empiricist attempt to use the resources of sense to explain mathematics fails, he says, because even if mathematical truths could be induced from sense experience (e.g. from counting), the use of induction rests on a principle of induction that cannot be validly induced from experience and so must be known independently of experience. Thus, mathematical and logical knowledge requires some other kind of awareness than sensation. His account of that kind of awareness is part of a larger account of knowledge of entities of different sorts.

2 Acquaintance

Following the *Principles*, questions of how we know are prominent in Russell's work and reflect his study of the Austrian philosopher Alexius Meinong, student of Franz Brentano and founder of a school of experimental psychology. From Meinong, Russell gets support for the notion, implicit in the *Principles*, that we cannot be aware without being aware of something. Russell regards awareness as a relation. As a relation, its existence depends logically on that of its terms, hence there must be something that is aware and something of which it is aware. Awareness is an external relation between a mind and an object, a relation that holds between a knower and an object but is not a property of them. The externality of the relation ensures that the knower remains distinct from what it knows. It also ensures that awareness of an entity is not mediated by an idea or image, though these might of course occur during awareness. Like a door that gives way directly to the outside, awareness is unimpeded access to what is known. Being direct, it cannot be in error: for example, if we experience a patch of color, we cannot be mistaken that we do.

The above remarks concern the logical form of the relation of awareness. In "Knowledge by Acquaintance and Knowledge by Description" (1911) Russell uses the word "acquaintance" to refer to what is common to *kinds* of awareness, including sensation, imagination, and conception. The reference to *sensation* might lead one to suppose that what is meant is the physical act of sensing, such as the mechanism of light rays hitting the retina, and so on. But in his use, the word "sensation" refers to a nonphysical act of awareness. For example, when we see a patch of color or hear a sound we are conscious of the color or sound and this consciousness is what he means by sensation. Thus, sensation—or any other form of acquaintance—does not facilitate knowledge of objects: it *is* that knowledge. Philosophers talk about knowing that something is the case, such as $2 + 2 = 4$, or about knowing how to do something, such as ride a bike. Russell's conception of acquaintance, his primary account of knowledge, is neither; it is a theory of the various kinds of consciousness.

Besides sensation, imagination is also a form of consciousness and so is conception. In these forms of awareness some simple or complex entity is known. Depending on the kind of acquaintance, the object of acquaintance can be a sense datum (sounds, a patch of colors), a memory, an image, or a universal.

It might seem that anything can be an object of acquaintance, but this would follow only if it were possible to know everything directly, and there are a great many cases in which we are not or cannot be directly conscious of a thing and only know *about* it. These cases constitute knowledge of objects by description. A description has meaning in virtue of things known by acquaintance. If you never tasted a pineapple, you could still know what was intended if it was described by qualities you have experienced, for example, sweet, large, and spiky. Knowledge by description further presupposes what Russell calls "knowledge of truths" or propositional knowledge. A description must be accurate or it does not identify or pick out the intended object. Thus, you must know some fact about a thing in order to form a description that applies. If you know nothing at all about a thing or nothing that is unique to it, then you cannot know it by description.

3 Introspection and conception

Sensation is a relation to sense-data occurring in the present moment—a loud bang, a certain color—but knowledge would be very limited if it consisted solely of data occurring right now. Other forms of consciousness, such as introspection and recollection, help to overcome this limitation. Russell addresses these issues at length in *Theory of Knowledge*, a text he began in 1913 and some parts of which were published in 1914 as "On The Nature of Acquaintance."

It is by introspection that we are conscious of the images occurring in memory, dreams, and hallucinations. Though the introspective data given in dreams and delusions are as real as sense data insofar as they are objects we directly experience, dreams and hallucinations do not add to our knowledge and must be distinguished from sense data and other sources of data, such as memories, that do add to it. One way to differentiate them from sense data or data given in memory is by their correlations. The data of dreams and delusions do not have the correlations with other qualities that sense data have: in a dream, houses may float above the ground. Compared to sense data, they are also more directly and obviously linked with desires and wishes. Introspective awareness of images given in memory is somewhat more useful in widening the scope of knowledge beyond the present moment, but the knowledge of the past obtained in this way is open to error. Notoriously, an image of something remembered may differ from the actual event or thing. Knowledge of the past therefore cannot be based solely on those memories that consist in images (1913, p. 22). Reliable knowledge of the past requires acquaintance with objects that are past. This is not introspection but recollection in the true sense and it occurs only with respect to the very recent past; for example, when we are conscious of the sounds of a clock striking after the striking has finished. It is this kind of "true" memory that explains why we know that there is a past.

Introspection therefore has some role in augmenting memory, and it is also the means by which we know our own feelings and other mental contents. There is no such knowledge of the self, however. In *Problems of Philosophy* (1912) Russell argues that we directly apprehend the self or subject, but he shows signs of doubt on the issue. By the *Theory of Knowledge* (1913) he argues that we know the self by inference, as one of the terms in the relation of acquaintance, for example, as the "I" in "I see the sun." The inferred subject need not persist for more than a fleeting moment and therefore is not the same as a mind. Like physical objects (tables and chairs and people), minds are constructed from data and are not themselves data. Russell's philosophy is called *mind/ matter dualism* not because he thinks there are entities called *minds* but because he accepts that there is a nonphysical (mental) domain that is related to the physical. Acquaintance is the relation between the two domains, and it connects an inferred logical subject (the fleeting self) with a datum.

The above remarks describe introspection and recollection and how they augment sensation. But knowledge is still very limited without consciousness of universals, the form of awareness called *conception*. It might seem that in sensing a quality, such as a patch of color, we apprehend the color as a universal. This is not the case, however. We become acquainted with these universals by a distinct act of mind. This is masked by the fact that we have to use a universal to describe what we sense. We speak of seeing a yellow flower, yet what we sensed was something particular—a patch of yellow in a certain shape—and we did not *sense* that it fell under the category *yellow* or *flower*. Though it is true that we may only come to apprehend a universal after having sensed particular instances and also true that the universal enables us to grasp the nature of what we have sensed, on Russell's theory, consciousness of universals is distinct from sense awareness, though in the ways just noted it may bear on what we know in sensation.

4 Belief or judgment

It is one thing to be aware and another to judge. The above data of sense, introspection, memory, and conception are the starting place for knowledge. They are data for the beliefs or judgments on which our knowledge rests. From 1906 to 1918, Russell develops what is called the "multiple relation theory of belief or judgment". On this theory, when a person believes that entities are combined in a certain way or have a certain property, there is a fact of belief that contains the believer and the entities believed in. Mental acts like supposing, desiring, and willing get similar treatment but belief is treated as most important. Beliefs are facts just as facts of sense are facts. Object A may in fact be a deeper blue than object B, and Jack may in fact believe that A is deeper blue than B. Russell's theory emphasizes that a fact of belief depends on the existence of the entities that enter into it: in a sense, the fact contains the entities. To represent a belief fact it is therefore necessary to represent the believer in relation to the various other entities that enter into the fact. To express Jack's belief, for example, it is necessary to have symbols for Jack (the subject), for the relation "believes," for the objects A and B and the relation *being deeper blue*. These must be arranged in the right order, to represent that A is deeper blue than B and not the other way around.

It might seem that a fact of belief ought to involve images or ideas rather than the actual entities that form the content of the belief. But Russell thinks that we are acquainted with data directly, not through images that represent them. He therefore argues that the data known by acquaintance enter into what we believe or judge and into the fact of belief. Early on, he tried to use images to explain judgment but abandoned the attempt, and in "Knowledge by Acquaintance and Knowledge by Description" he says of such an approach that "ideas become a veil between us and outside things." If we took judgments to be about ideas, we would never, "in knowledge, attain to the thing we are supposed to be knowing about, but only to the ideas of those things" (1911a, p. 155). In other words, if ideas or images represented things to us, and we had no other form of access to them, we could not be sure that there were any things at all or, if there were, how accurately our images depicted them. For reasons like these, Russell is persuaded that beliefs are complexes of entities, namely, sense data and universals (relations and properties), brought together in a meaningful way by the cognitive act of believing.

Judging (believing) is not a dual relation and can be in error, as when a person thinks that *A* is before *B* when *B* is actually before *A*. But when we judge or believe what we perceive while perceiving it, the room for error is very small. If you have acquaintance with the shining sun and judge that it is shining, your judgment is apt to be correct: it is an observational report of a present experience. There is room for error even here since we may be mistaken about whether a belief is actually derived flawlessly from a present experience. This happens in adding up columns of numbers, for example. Yet whether a judgment is formed without perception of the object judged or in the presence of the event or complex, acquaintance supplies the data that enters into it and forms a belief, which is the sort of thing that can be described by a sentence.

5 Data and premises

In *Our Knowledge of the External World* (1914), Russell tries to establish a connection between scientific knowledge and what we know in sensation. Though he refers to sensed objects, logical objects, and other entities as "data," in this text he also uses the word to refer to those facts of sense, logical propositions, facts of memory, and facts consisting of relations and properties that contain these objects. These facts are, or supply, the premises upon which rest the common beliefs we take for granted, such as that there is a past or that there are other minds. They are also the primitive premises from which the truths of physics follow.

Russell sometimes refers to the common beliefs which we begin with as "data", meaning that they are data for analysis: these beliefs rest, logically, on primitive premises, that is, on data in the above sense of primitive premises. To arrive at premises from the beliefs we take for granted involves several steps. To begin with, a premise must be expressible in words. The beliefs with which we begin do not have to involve words. They must thus be put into language to serve as premises. Moreover, these "data for analysis" are beliefs that seem indubitable when we start, but analysis often shows some of them to be more certain than others. Hard data are those beliefs that remain certain even on analysis and can therefore serve as premises. For example, no amount of critical reflection will cause you to feel doubt that you experience a datum of sense or did so in the last minute (1914a, p. 72). Similarly, that a whole is greater than its parts commands immediate assent, once we understand the words. But on reflection, whether there are other minds or an external world is not so certain. Such beliefs are called "soft data" since they dissolve on analysis. (Again, we are now speaking of the data of analysis.)

The distinction between hard and soft data is related to the difference between primitive and derived beliefs. A belief is logically primitive if is believed without the support of other beliefs.

Otherwise, a belief is deductively or inductively inferred from other beliefs. But beliefs may be logically primitive, because not known by inference, without being psychologically primitive. For example, we do not think that objects in our line of sight continue to exist when we close our eyes on the basis of an inference from other beliefs, but experience causes us to have this belief. The belief in objects is also not psychologically primitive; this is why it becomes less certain upon reflection and why it is a questionable premise from which to infer anything about the world. According to Russell, a premise must be logically as well as psychologically primitive. Beliefs that satisfy these criteria may serve as premises. Indeed, there must be some such beliefs, since without them knowledge is impossible: inferred beliefs must begin somewhere in beliefs that are given by experience and known to be true.

Russell emphasizes the distinction between hard and soft data of analysis in order to eliminate assumptions from the premises upon which knowledge is based. If the premises are not clear, that is, if they incorporate assumptions, the whole process is skewed. We must begin with "clean" data and premises whose relation to each other is clear. Only then it is possible to know what data are available for construction and in what sense physics "follows" from sense data and principles of logic.

6 Knowledge of science

Hard data do not provide much help if the goal is to demonstrate the existence of matter as an unseen underlying substrate of qualities. Russell has not found any way of inferring from hard data to the existence of matter understood in that way and he gives little weight to the fact that it may be psychologically impossible to shake the belief that sense data are signs of objects. The fact that we cannot infer from hard data to indestructible unseen atoms seems to imply that the hypothesis of matter as something permanent is too metaphysical, too unlike the fleeting nature of what we sense. In 1914–15, he therefore interprets the statements of physics as about classes of sense-data, arguing that these constructed objects account for all that is verifiable in physics. He justifies replacing inference to unseen objects by constructions from sense data by appealing to Occam's razor, the principle that we should not multiply entities unnecessarily. Since sense data are fleeting his procedure does not retain all of the properties physics traditionally attributes to matter. In particular, physics "always assumed that there is *something* indestructible which is capable of motion in space" (1914a, p. 103) and thus we "have still in physics, as we had in Newton's time, a set of indestructible entities which may be called particles, moving relatively to each other in a single space and a single time" (p. 104). (This point was made in 1914 when it was about to become an obsolete view of what physics takes as ultimate; these parts of the original text are revised in later editions.)

He concludes that physics can only be verified and the connection between sense experience and physics explained if we are agnostic about the existence of matter in this sense and instead construct objects from sense-data. To understand what this means, consider looking at a coin from two feet above it: you may see a silver color and a round shape of a certain size. The coin can be imagined as the center of points: North, South, East and West. Keeping your distance above it and moving your attention clockwise, between North and East, there are an infinite number of spatial positions, each slightly different than its immediate neighbors. You can also view the coin directly from the side: you will see a straight line. There are an infinite number of perspectives between the one that presents to us a straight line and the one that presents a perfectly circular shape. There is also the matter of distance: if, viewing from above or from any angle, you move closer, the shape gets larger in increments; if you move farther away it gets smaller. Moving away in any direction there is a vanishing point.

Since no one experiences all the data available from all of angles and distances, a construction of an object based on the sense data of a single person would be very incomplete. Yet it is possible to fill in each of the classes or series comprising the construction with hypothetical data continuous with those sensed and present at hypothetical perspectives. Above, we began with an actual perspective, our own, from which we experienced certain data, but we can easily imagine other perspectives that may or may not be occupied by perceivers but that constitute a system of perspectives. These perspectives or "private worlds" can be used in several ways. By the similarity in what is seen from them, we can establish their relations to each other and arrive at the inferred physical space containing them. And by assuming laws of perspective we may

introduce data occurring at these perspectives. When data perceived from some perspective line up in specified ways with what
is perceived in others, the resulting system of aspects or data can
be regarded as the (momentary) logically constructed thing. Where
these series of aspects converge or overlap is the place of a thing in
inferred space.

Thus, by employing hypothetical data from all possible perspectives, Russell is able to construct an object, and a physical space,
and locate the object and the position of the perceiver in that physical space. In this way, he is able to satisfy the statements of physics
that refer to the appearances of objects from places or times where
there is no observer. This allows him to define matter in a way that
can verify the propositions of applied physics.

What verifies physics is confirmation of predicted observations,
that is, sense data. To verify propositions of physics the hypothetical data need not be assumed to exist and a theory about the status of the unobserved aspects or perspectives is not needed. When
he is talking about constructions as a solution to the problem of
verifying physics Russell is agnostic on this point. But this agnosticism does not disbar him from asking whether there are reasons
to believe that the hypothetical aspects exist. He is only disbarred
from concluding that, if they are real, they make a difference to
verification. Thus, in discussions about the status of sense data
we also find Russell arguing that qualities might exist that are not
sensed and that, if we assume this is possible, inference to them is
more plausible than inference to entities utterly unlike anything we
sense. In such discussions, he is a realist even though in presenting
constructions as a solution to a problem of verification he remains
agnostic about the hypothetical data.

II The Middle Russell

7 Consciousness revisited

In his early period, Russell acknowledged neutral monism to be
a simpler theory than his own dualism, but he rejected it on the
grounds that it could not account for subjective experience. By
1918, he has come to think that his own arguments against its theory of sensation are invalid. In particular, Russell rejects his theory

of consciousness as a relation between a subject of sensation and something physical, a sense datum. He had thought that he could, by introspection, discern a difference between a noise that is heard and consciousness of it. He now denies this: for a noise to be heard by someone is for someone to be conscious of the noise (1918c, p. 255). The belief that we can separate the two is due to thinking that there is a subject standing in a nonphysical relation of consciousness to what it knows, a physical sense datum. It is this theory that Russell rejects: henceforth sensation is not a relation between entities, and there is no "subject" or fleeting particular. Rather, cognitive mental acts are to be explained by means of causal arrangements of "sensations," which are now a nonmental, nonphysical neutral "stuff." If a "sensation," that is, a particular, enters into causal series governed by physical laws, such as the law of gravitation, it is physical; if it enters into a causal series governed by psychological laws, such as association, it is psychological and may have effects that include those we call "being aware."

What had prevented him from adopting neutral monism before was the belief that it was, in a sense, too materialistic to explain the subjective experiences involved in belief and underlying our use of words like "I" and "here". He had also assumed that all words occurring in a meaningful sentence must have meaning. Russell now begins to think that we can account for the use of sentences like "I was here" causally: no mental domain is needed to account for the experiences. He also realizes that words like "this" need not have meanings just because they occur in meaningful sentences. Certain series of events cause someone to say "I was here," others cause someone to say "I am here," and the occurrence of these words and sentences can be explained without reference to anything but their causes. In much later work, Russell imagines a machine that utters sentences like these under different conditions: there is no temptation to think that it has inner experience. He does not make that point now, but he is not far from it.

8 Behaviorism and belief

Neutral monism often relies on behaviorism and pragmatism in order to avoid reference to putative mental states. Though Russell does not think behaviorism and its appeal to habit explains all knowledge, he thinks it explains some. For example, it explains our use of words, which is a kind of knowledge, or at least it can do so in certain cases. Using language often involves nothing other than using the right words on the right occasions. If someone shouts "Car!" we jump aside; we do not need to experience anything introspectively, such as an image, to give meaning to the word, which we have acquired by habit. But other cases of knowledge cannot be explained by in this way. This is already evident in "The Philosophy of Logical Atomism (1918) when Russell argues that habit directed to the satisfaction of some desire cannot explain abstract knowledge (1918a, pp. 194–5). For a dog to know that sitting on command is a means to a cookie is for the dog to desire the cookie and sit on command, and similarly, for a man to know that the train leaves at 10 is for him to begin running for the train at 9:55, but for a person to know a truth of mathematics—what activity is that? In a few years, Russell decides that logical and mathematical propositions are not about the world. At that time he concludes that knowledge of logic is *a priori* because what is conveyed is entirely linguistic: logical propositions are ways of showing that sets of symbols are equivalent. It is easier to use desire, habit, and activity to explain mathematical and logical propositions after he adopts this view, but in 1918 logic and mathematics appear to be forms of knowledge that cannot be explained in this manner.

At present, what Russell most dislikes is behaviorism's denial of images and of introspection, both of which have begun to play a prominent role in his theory of knowledge. He continues to accept introspection, and the introspection knowledge we have of images is the principle way he prevents belief and knowledge from collapsing into behavior. A theory of images allows him to retain something of the "contemplative" view of knowledge. It enables him to say that when we use words, we may call up images of what the words mean and that because these are part of what we know in using words, our word use is not merely a matter of learned behavior.

Without a relational theory of knowledge there is, however, no room left for knowledge of objects: all knowledge is "knowing *that*" or propositional. This applies to introspection and memory, too. He therefore construes introspection as knowledge consisting in uninferred beliefs about images. Memory is knowledge of the past consisting of feelings, like recognition toward images. This is an about-face from his earlier rejection of images as part of belief. Then, he thought that we could not completely trust that the image represented what it is supposed to. But images solve a number of problems about belief, especially what we believe when a belief is false. If Jane believes that B is before A, and A is before B, then *what* is involved in her belief? There is no fact consisting of A before B, so what is she believing?

In *Analysis of Mind* (1921), Russell answers this question by distinguishing between what a sentence *expresses* and what it *asserts* (or *denies*), which is the objective fact. What a sentence expresses is a feeling of rejection or assent (a belief feeling) toward a complex of images (or words). This is what a sentence means, and the images exist, as a fact, even if the belief is false and corresponds to nothing. Russell uses the notion of feelings toward images to explain belief as a psychological occurrence. It is still a multiple relation theory, but there is no subject, since this has been eliminated, but the feelings of belief are multiply related to different images, which are a whole.

9 Introspection and memory

Russell does not think it is possible to explain cognitive mental phenomena in behaviorist terms, but he is willing to use behaviorism to account for noncognitive mental phenomena. *Analysis of Mind* (1921) reflects this willingness by its emphasis on the continuity between human and animal behavior, progressing from phenomena like desire that can be accounted for organically, to cases requiring complex analyses involving habit, to events we regard as cognitive that require still different treatment. His account of complex behavior involving habits rests on analyzing a kind of psychological causality called "mnemic" causality. Mnemic causality involves a person's (or animal's) past. Falling is a response to a present stimulus, but pulling your hand away from a flame that you see but do not yet feel is caused by a present stimulus and past experience. Thus, the past event is a partial cause of your present behavior. There is no doubt that there are such phenomena. Language is an example. If you hear "Lake Superior" and think of a suspension bridge, this involves the stimulus of the word and past experiences.

Mnemic phenomena play a role in Russell's evolving account of introspection and knowledge of the past by means of images. Images are related with images and sensations by laws of association.

This is evident in our response to novel cases. We are surprised to discover that a certain cat has no tail because we associate cats with tails and had imagined this cat to have one. Hence, an image is caused by a present stimulus plus past experience and association (1921a, p. 150). This differs from a sensation, which only has a physical cause. But sensations and images do not differ intrinsically: given his adoption of neutral monism, they can only differ in their correlations and in how they are caused. Similarly, introspective knowledge cannot be intrinsically different from any other kind of knowledge.

In his earlier work, Russell worried that knowledge of the past by means of images would be open to skeptical doubt, since we could never compare the image to the original to make sure of its accuracy. He now thinks that a theory of knowledge need not refute such implausible worries and that skepticism presents an impossibly high standard of certainty. Still, he takes the matter seriously enough that he tries to explain why we experience images as of something past that is their prototype (pp. 161–2). This feeling of recognition is knowledge too and is among our primitive data. With respect to sensation, for example, when we see someone a second time and experience recognition, the prior event causes a feeling of familiarity that tells us that the feeling is due to a prior event. On his theory of acquaintance, a single instance might constitute knowledge. Now, knowledge consists of the effects events have on us, such as the association of images with sensations. Thus, knowledge is causally complex and never a single occurrence.

Yet the *Analysis of Mind* contains signs of a shift underway in Russell's thinking about introspection. Until now, "introspection" meant knowledge of images or thoughts, and he denied that it could be reduced to the observation of bodily sensations, as behaviorists do when they reduce thinking to tiny movements of the lips and tongue. Confirmation of Einstein's theory of relativity in the summer of 1919 causes him to broaden his conception of introspection. That event has shown him that the universe is "infected through and through with subjectivity" (1921a, p. 230). The kind of subjectivity he has in mind is not attributable to differences in perceptual apparatus or in the psychological state of the observer (which might be a camera). As he intends it, "subjectivity" has to do with the fact that aspects of the physical world previously thought to be constant, such as time, have been shown to relative to the place of the observer. The physical dependence on the standpoint of the observer is not a new idea but relativity theory has shown that this phenomenon goes deeper than had been supposed. To use an example from his later work, a camera placed close to a stage shows a larger image than one placed further away.

This suggests that *all* of the data available to a person is received at a unique vantage point under unique conditions. Thus, all of what we know is *private* in the sense that knowing is the result of a causal chain that is unique to each person, and this means that inquiry is always a form of self-observation. Behaviorism prides itself on objectivity by rejecting introspection, but physics has shown that the belief in objective data is a delusion.

10 Inference to an external world

The subjective nature of the data interests Russell as opening the way for a new philosophy of physics. His next steps are to build a case for inference from our "private" data to the external world. This is alluded to in *Analysis of Mind* and reaches full expression in *Analysis of Matter* (1927). In his early period, he engaged in constructing entities (particles, points, and instants) from sense data in order to show how to make statements in physics deducible from statements about classes of hard data. The constructions would not have the property of permanency that physicists in their metaphysical moments might attribute to things in the external world, but these properties are not verifiable anyway and so it did not matter. But physicists also make statements about how things might appear in a place where there is no perceiver or at times when there is no one to perceive, and even if these unverifiable hypotheses are merely ways of simplifying the statement of causal laws, they had to be accounted for by his constructions. For this reason, Russell hypothesized unperceived aspects or perspectives. For the purpose of addressing the verification of physics he put aside whether the unobserved aspects exist.

By the early 1920s, physics has developed in such a way that it does not assume anything like indestructible particles: it relies on fleeting events. On relativity theory, space and time are a continuum and events have replaced permanent things among its basic concepts. In the past, the world of physics had been so unlike the fleeting data of sense that there was little to justify the inference from sense data to material particles. This is no longer required, and even though physics points to the subjective nature of data, inference to unobserved physical causes is now easier to justify. Russell concedes that a solipsist will not be persuaded, but solipsism dismisses far too much of science and commonsense to hold any interest for him. He also rejects phenomenalism, which he regards as inconsistent because it accepts the testimony of other people while at the same time regarding all but hard data as a convenience in science. As he sees it, if we are to allow induction in order to accept testimony, then we ought to allow it in general, since there is no difference in principle between inferring the existence of other people and inferring the existence of an external world.

Russell's current position is therefore an indirect realism in which we infer from the private data we experience, which he calls *percepts*, to events in the physical world that are their causes. The link between events inside and outside the brain is a central concern of *Analysis of Matter*. It is bound up with the claim that "perceptions are *causally related* to antecedents which may not be perceptions" (p. 9). This new position does mean that he abandons constructions. What the new developments in physics mean is that it is easier to justify the inference from the data comprising the construction to the unobserved events that fill it out. Russell still thinks we cannot base physics on private phenomena alone and must include unobserved events, yet there is no longer any need to abstain from the question of the reality of this data. The hypothetical data can be treated as real events inferred on the basis of continuity with what we perceive.

The construction of objects is now joined to the task of explaining how perception can be the basis for inference to the external world. This task rests on his belief that our knowledge of the unobserved world is structural and that we must abstract from the conditions of sense organs, from the influence of the past on experience, and from physical facts about an observer's position, motion, and so on, so as to arrive at structural properties that are present in different perceptions. To explain how perception *can* be the basis for inference to the external world, what is needed is a philosophical account of perception, and of events, showing that it is not *a priori* impossible for any principle of inference to justify induction. These issues are discussed in the next two sections.

11 Structural knowledge

Though percepts are known subjectively and intrinsically, they can only be utilized publically by science in their objective features. Physics cannot talk about the subjective experience of sound but it can talk about the relationships between sound waves that result in experiences we call louder or softer. Thus it is the objective and structural features of our percepts that enter into scientific knowledge and it is they that are the basis for inference to events in the physical world. Yet Russell goes further and argues that physics provides only structural or mathematical knowledge. He therefore denies we can know anything intrinsic about unobserved events, such as that they are the same in quality as percepts. This idea is his *structural realism*.

It is a departure from the view he earlier defended, namely, that qualities that exist when they are not perceived are like what we would perceive if in the right position to do so. To presume knowledge of the qualities of unknown events is to presume to know more about the world than is compatible with physics and the causal theory. There is no basis for this but neither is there for the opposite mistake of assuming that *nothing at all* can be known about the inferred world. The world is not a *Ding an sich*. Physics gives us knowledge of structures, and if we accept it and the causal theory, we may legitimately infer relations or structures in the world from perceived relations, that is, from relations among our data.

Russell argues that a series of percepts occurring in a brain is causally connected with a series of unobserved entities external to the brain and that we can infer the latter from the former. We must of course be able to perceive some relation among our percepts since what we infer from relations among percepts is the existence of relations among unobserved events. When sounds appear softer as we move away from a central point, we infer that unobserved events (e.g. sound waves) radiate out from a central point on a similar pattern and that these are causing our percepts. We make this inference on the basis of postulates, which may be quite unconscious. A key assumption is that causes and effects are structurally similar. This allows us to infer from a relation among our percepts to a similar relation as cause.

In the *Analysis of Matter* the status of these assumptions is not yet clear. Russell does not treat them as *a priori* knowledge. He accepts that some *beliefs* are synthetic and *a priori*, that is, not derived from previous experience. If we stumble walking downstairs in the dark because our body was prepared for an extra step, our expectation of another step is an *a priori* belief because it is not inferred from experience (1927a, p. 185). Yet such cases do not constitute knowledge, he says, since they can be false. In the text, he therefore denies any knowledge that is both synthetic and *a priori*.

Beside these assumptions, other conditions are necessary if relations among percepts are to form a basis for the inference to structurally similar causes and give rise to knowledge. In particular, a series of percepts (say, the sounds of an approaching car) must form a causal series that is not jumbled up with another series of percepts occurring at the same time (perhaps the smell of burning toast). The series of percepts would have no identifiable structure if this could occur. If these conditions are satisfied, though we cannot say that the space-time relations that physics assumes are identical with those we perceive, we can assume a logical correspondence between them and that what we perceive "preserves their logical or mathematical properties" (p. 252).

12 Perception

Besides describing the kind of knowledge we can have of the physical world, Russell proposes a philosophical doctrine that is intended to explain how a causal theory of perception is possible. For physics, the causal theory of perception is simply the belief that events external to the brain give rise to events in the brain, our perceptions. The continuity between unobserved events and what we perceive is assumed, but what is not addressed is the philosophical question of what it is about events and percepts that makes their continuity possible. Russell's aim is to elaborate the nature of the continuity on which perception rests. In particular, he wants to avoid the notion that there is a chain of physical events—light waves, stimulation of the optic nerve, and the like—and then, miraculously, a mental event. Thus, percepts must be spatially continuous with other events in space-time and be able to be parts of physical causal series.

In *Analysis of Matter* (1927), Russell explains how that continuity is possible and how, in perception, "mental" percepts can be spatially and temporally related with chains of physical events.

On his account, percepts are events and therefore are no different than the unperceived events in the brain and in the external world. Series of events in space may terminate in a percept if they occur in a portion of space-time containing a brain. Thus, the word "percept" refers to the last in a series of events in the brain that began with events external to the brain. Percepts head a psychological causal series since, occurring in a brain, they have certain effects or call up certain responses.

Many different series of events are terminating in a brain at any one moment. When percepts occur at the same moment, they result in images, associations, habits, and other cognitive responses. For example, the sound of a bell and the smell of food, if conjoined often enough, is apt to cause an association of the two, so that the one recalls the other. The habits and responses initiated in this way are knowledge reactions; that is, they are what we mean by "knowledge". These images, habits, and other reactions are knowledge of the percepts initiating them.

What it means to know a percept qualitatively is to have a knowledge reaction to it. Since the reaction is a response to the percept, and knowledge of something *is* responsiveness to it, the knowledge, which is qualitative, is of the percept in question. A percept can be called *mental* in the sense that it is in a causal series with effects that we call mental. Yet knowledge reactions are the "mental" effects of a percept that is in a long chain of spatially continuous events. Given its continuity with that series of events, the percept also can be regarded as a physical event in the physical world. Because it is in a causal chain of events in the brain, it is in space—in the space of the brain. As Russell says, from the point of view of the physical world, "the whole of our perceptual world is, for physics, in our heads" (1927a, p. 336).

III The Late Russell

13 Experience

Russell's work after *Analysis of Matter* focuses on how the premises on which knowledge is based are grounded in experience and on the nature and justification of inferences that transcend experience. Russell promotes empiricism by emphasizing the connection between premises and experience, but he attacks and sets limits to empiricism in his examination of inference. Traditional empiricism denies that we have any *a priori* knowledge of the world: our knowledge is limited to what is derived from experience. Russell argues that *a priori* knowledge about the world is involved in inference and in any empirical knowledge that goes beyond immediate present experience. These themes become dominant in the late 1930s. In "On Verification," written in 1938, Russell asks, "How can an 'experience' afford a ground for a verbal proposition? And how can it be known to afford such a ground?" (1938a, p. 349).

The problem of inference is taken up in Sections 16–18 below. Turning to the first issue, Russell believes that empirical knowledge can be sorted into premises and propositions derived from premises. The former are certain and are made true or false by facts. Some logical positivist philosophers have abandoned that view. As Otto Neurath says in "On Protocol Sentences" (1932, pp. 202–3), no sentences are endowed with special certainty; moreover, a sentence is false when it fails to cohere with the other propositions in the edifice of a science, and any proposition can be made to cohere by sufficient adjustments to other sentences in the science (Neurath 1932, p. 203). This view undermines the connection of truth and falsity to nonlinguistic fact and overturns the idea that some propositions have a foundational role, a place at the basis of a system. Russell objects to the above position for both of these reasons.

First, he thinks that Neurath's position makes the truth and falsity of premises too linguistic. Sentences like "either that is a dog or that is not a dog" are true or false independently of the facts, but "that is a dog over there" is true only if that *is* a dog. (The premises supporting the body of knowledge cannot be propositions like "that is a dog"; they must report immediate experience and be on the order of "canoid features are occurring here now"). Second, epistemological premises must convey what an individual experiences and exclude any element of inference. For this reason, though science deals with the common and public aspects of sense experience, it is "built on the knowledge of individuals, and impossible except of this foundation" (1938a, p. 352). In sum, knowledge must be conceived foundationally, that is, as resting on premises, the premises must be true in virtue of fact, and they must express private experience.

For Russell, this means that the edifice of knowledge rests on the connection between a person's linguistic reports of experience and the nonlinguistic world. This is why he must explain the connection between language and extralinguistic fact. Other philosophers have viewed talking about how language relates to the world as unduly metaphysical, but Russell thinks it is necessary to an account of scientific knowledge since that knowledge occurs in words and sentences. A study of the logical basis for our other beliefs in propositions that we believe without inference and cannot doubt (so-called "basic propositions") requires studying how words come to have meaning rooted in a person's experience. Thus, the study of knowledge requires an inquiry into meaning. As Russell says in "The Relevance of Psychology to Logic" (1938): "We cannot consider the epistemological problem solved if we stop short of the verbal expression of what we know. We are thus involved in the problem of meaning . . . " (1938b, p. 368).

14 Words

The concept of an "object language" or "primary language" in which words report present experience is a means of exploring the connection between language and nonlinguistic experience. The point is to illustrate the kind of knowledge supplied by experience and the way that knowledge arises. An object language includes utterances like "doggie!," said by a child in the presence of a dog. Such utterances are defined by *ostension*, by pointing to what is meant. The understanding of words defined in this way presupposes being able to recognize the class of series of sounds that is a word and recognize the class of sensations that it is used for. Also, an association of the similar sounds and similar occurrences must take place for knowledge of such a word to occur.

The knowledge provided by such a language is extremely limited. Words or word-strings occur as mere responses to what is observed and without awareness that they are responses and have meaning. The deficiency is supplied by a secondary language, which conveys a different level and kind of knowledge. Syntactical and logical words and therefore ordinary sentences first occur in a secondary language. Sentences in a secondary language include words in a primary language but in a different way: in a secondary language words are mentioned and not merely uttered. It is therefore a secondary language that conveys knowledge about the cause of a word and whether it was used correctly. Russell thinks that in cases like hearing a bang and saying "what a bang!" we know that we said the words "what a bang!" and that it was because we heard a bang. The experience of causality is therefore expressed at the level of a secondary language.

Besides being able to be about language, sentences in a secondary language express the feelings of the speaker (along with whatever other content they convey). The feelings are the psychological meanings of logical and syntactical words. Words like "or" express experiences of hesitation or choice, words like "no" and "not" express and are learned from the inhibiting of an impulse, and other logical words are accounted for in similar ways.

This psychological and causal doctrine of logical words illustrates Russell's belief that the truth table analysis of the meaning of words like "or" and "all" is inadequate and leads to a misunderstanding of what can occur as premises to knowledge.

If we focus on what sentences indicate, if true, and explain logical words solely in terms of their contribution to the truth-values of sentences, we are apt to exclude molecular sentences from the list of factual premises, since they correspond to no single fact. This point can be extended to universal and existential sentences as well, and it is a doctrine of empiricism that our premises cannot be of the form "all F is G" or "Some F is G." Russell thinks that it is absurd and damaging to deny that general propositions like "there is no one here" are basic propositions. A causal and psychological account of logical words is valuable because it shows that sentences containing logical words like "all" must not always be interpreted as they are in logic. Many of the beliefs for which we require the use of such words can be interpreted by reference to psychological states. Giving this interpretation shows how they might occur as basic propositions and factual premises. And this shows that empiricists are wrong to reject all general and nonlogical basic propositions.

15 Premises

Basic propositions are defined psychologically as those we cannot doubt, but in the *Inquiry* Russell adds further constraints. He introduces basic propositions as those that are caused by or derived from an immediate perceptual experience and are logically independent, having no bearing on the probability or truth of any other basic proposition. He then expands the concept to include those logically independent propositions that are about dated events, immediate or not. This is the category of "factual premises." Factual premises and logical principles together are epistemological premises, the premises to knowledge. An account of knowledge requires various kinds of propositions among the factual premises. For example, understanding the notion of the past implies that some of our basic propositions are memories. Similar arguments are given to justify including other kinds of propositions among factual premises. Factual premises therefore include perceptual judgments like "this is hot," memories like "this was hot," negative and general propositions, such as "there is no one here," and propositions about emotional states, such as statements about belief or disbelief (1940, p. 153). It is from these premises that physical and psychological knowledge is derived.

The notion of a basic proposition is closely connected with a theory of truth. In early chapters of *The Inquiry into Meaning and Truth*, Russell accepts an epistemological form of a correspondence theory of truth, according to which basic propositions are those that can be derived from experience and observation, and whatever cannot be related to experience is neither true nor false (p. 289). A weakness of the theory is to leave no room for truth or falsity when there is and can be no experience. This is too strict and would leave us with only a handful of propositions that could be regarded as true. An alternative approach, which he adopts later in the text, is to define "truth" as correspondence with fact, making no reference to experience. On this "logical" theory, a definition of basic propositions retains those aspects that concern their form, for example, that they cannot contradict other basic propositions, but they are understood as whatever can be related to a fact. This definition includes all but not only the propositions considered basic on the epistemological definition but it allows truth to be wider than knowledge and basic propositions to include those that are true, though we have no means of knowing what makes them true.

An important feature of basic propositions is that they are logically independent. They cannot prove each other false, and their probability cannot be affected by any new evidence or by new premises or group of premises. There is no principle of deduction by which they can bear on each other in these ways, and yet we do adjust basic propositions in the light of new evidence. The fact that we do shows, Russell thinks, that we connect independent propositions to each because we operate under a principle of inductive inference (1940, p. 317). The relation of inductive principles of inference to the factual premises is made evident by his discussion, below, of the importance of knowledge learned from a single experience.

16 Single observations

Russell argues that a sentence like "metals conduct electricity" is a poor choice as a premise. It is too sophisticated and complex to sit at the basis of a theory of knowledge: to understand it we must analyze a complex percept like metal into components, such as shades of color, and judge that they are identical to those we remember (1940, p. 313). Such judgments cannot be certain and thus these premises are better off not assumed as the basis of an account of meaning and truth. Moreover, multiple observations about pieces of metal conducting electricity are relevant to the confirmation of such a sentence, and this seems to imply that an individual observation "this is metal . . . " can give us information. If so, then reports of such single observations ought to be our factual premises and not the general sentence.

However, propositions like "metals conduct electricity" also contain words that are derived from a process of repeated observations. These words are, as he says, condensed inductions. It is better, he thinks, to start with premises that contain no such words. His premises therefore exclude words for classes or words like "metal" or "dog." They are sentences such as "a canine patch is occurring here now." By using these as premises we show that no fact or a collection of facts logically implies any other fact. This is important because, if premises are logically independent and there is no deductive principle by which they bear on each other, in order for a one to affect our judgment of the probability of another, we have to employ some nondeductive principle. We may not see this if we use factual premises containing condensed inductions since we may think that we are avoiding such principles even while we are in fact relying on them. The fact that we *do* see factual premises as increasing or diminishing in probability relative to each other shows that we do employ such a principle.

The fact that evidence does cause us to reject or reevaluate a factual premise shows that we accept "*a priori* non-demonstrative forms of inference, which experience can neither confirm nor confute, but which we regard, in some circumstances, as more certain than the evidence of the senses" (1940, p. 317). Since such principles are known *a priori*, they are a point where empiricism breaks down.

17 Induction

In the *Inquiry*, Russell notes that when a gunshot occurs, events (airwaves) are thought to occur in the space between the gun and any percipient and to impact the structure of the ear in a way that gives rise to what we call a sound (1940, p. 303). He defends the need for *a priori* synthetic principles of inference with such cases in mind but without making an in-depth study of these principles, their status, and their role in science. These questions are taken up in 1948 in *Human Knowledge*, his last major work in philosophy. The work originated in a desire to clarify when it is legitimate to infer from the observed to the unobserved and what principles justify us in doing so. What he hopes to produce is a set of principles analogous to those in deductive logic and justifying the kinds of nondeductive inferences that occur in science.

In *Analysis of Matter*, Russell thought that induction was a legitimate postulate of science (1927a, p. 398) and that the probability of a proposition (particular or general) increases as favorable evidence increases, so long as there is no contrary evidence. For a while he continues to think this principle will be on his final list of probabilistic postulates, but in 1944 he begins to change his mind. He soon concludes that the principle of induction is not merely weak but actually false unless supplemented by other postulates and that it therefore cannot be used by itself to justify induction. This is because without further assumptions the principle of induction gives equal weight to any number of possible inferences supported by the same set of facts, even when they are what we regard as wildly improbable.

Scientists confronted by a set of facts do not and could not follow up every such potential inference but are evidently making choices about which inferences are reasonable to pursue, guided by what

Russell calls "scientific commonsense." This conclusion shifts the nature of Russell's inquiry in *Human Knowledge*. He still wants to isolate the minimum of assumptions able to account for the inferences we make from the observed to the unobserved. But now it is also important to discover what postulates tell the scientist, or the average person, what is worth investigating. In "Non-Deductive Inference," an unpublished paper probably from 1945, Russell asks "in what circumstances do we think it reasonable to look for a law connecting different phenomena?" (1945?, p. 123). That is, he seeks the postulates that confer prior probability on and legitimize inductive inferences.

These postulates justify inferences that confer probability on their conclusions and, in fact, give some probability to the inference even before it is even carried out. But what is meant by "probability"? "Probability" in the sense that occurs in the calculus of probability is important but not sufficient for Russell's ends. First, the calculus is a piece of pure mathematics and has to be interpreted or applied; also, it must be interpreted in a way that can be applied to the world in all the ways we normally apply it. Second, Russell thinks that "probability" has a broader meaning than it has on the mathematical theory. On the mathematical theory, to say "probably this dog has fleas" means that if n dogs are inspected and m have fleas, there is probability of m/n that a dog will have fleas. But we also use the word "probable" in cases where such information is missing, as in "probably I heard a faint sound." For such cases, Russell defends a nonmathematical theory of probability as degrees of credibility. All beliefs, including those asserting what is approximately and typically true of events, possess for an individual a degree of credibility (1948a, p. 416). This is not a subjective theory, for instance, not a theory about feelings of certainty, but a theory about the degree of rational conviction that a completely rational man would attach to a proposition, relative to the evidence he possesses.

18 Postulates

On the basis of an analysis of scientific reasoning, Russell proposes five postulates to justify probabilistic inferences. The first four concern the existence of structural properties of the world. The first is the *quasi-permanence* postulate, that an event, say, a cat appearance, at a certain time and place is frequently followed and preceded at neighboring moments by a similar appearance in neighboring places. This postulate warrants inferring that the cat persists for some time. It is meant to replace the commonsense notion of a substance that underlies things. Second, from one event we can infer what is occurring at neighboring times and places in the same *causal line*. That is, we infer that a cat, trotting before us, is a slowly changing unity (1948a, p. 508) and probably will not vanish in mid-trot or explode. This postulate establishes that certain observed relations are causal relations.

Third, we assume that there are contiguous events in the intervening space between the origin of a percept and ourselves, and, in general, that between noncontiguous events in a causal line there is an intervening series of causal events. This postulate of *spatiotemporal continuity* justifies our inference to sound waves and other unobserved entities. It assumes causality rather than explaining it. The fourth is the *structural postulate*: we assume the existence of a central originating cause for clusters of structurally similar complex events and that the more complex the structures are, the less likely they are to be coincidental (p. 484). When we see ripples in a pool, there is a strong likelihood that something occurred at the center—a fish striking the surface, an acorn falling—and that the innermost ripple is the first. On this postulate, the structure of percepts is structurally identical with the events causing them. It assumes causal laws relating events.

The fifth postulate, *analogy*, governs inferences from the observed correlation of two qualities that there is reason to believe are causally related to the belief in their continued correlation when only one is observed. It warrants inference, for example, to the existence of thoughts or feelings in another body from the observation of its speech, on the basis of a qualitative grasp on our own feelings (p. 503). As with other postulates, the principle of analogy is approximate and conditional. For example, Russell does not think that the postulate supports the probability of thought occurring given any occurrence of speech, since he imagines that there might be automata that speak (as there now are). But he thinks that the probability increases with the complexity of the behavior, as in an entire narrative versus a short sound (p. 505).

In addition to analyzing what makes inferences probable, an additional task is to explain the status of the principles as items of knowledge. Because these principles justify induction they cannot be justified by induction from experience. For example, the belief that a cat's head—seen poking through a doorway—is connected to a body is justified by a deeply rooted expectation of continuity. But that expectation is not inferred from past experiences of continuity. Rather, it is *caused* by it. In fact, Russell's five postulates are elaborate animal habits. In "Postulates of Scientific Inference" he says "knowledge of general connections between facts is unlike knowledge of particular facts and has a biological origin in animal expectations" (1948b, p. 137). Because they are not inferred, such beliefs amount to knowledge that is *a priori* but not analytic.

Such *a priori* knowledge need not be certain, exact, or even entirely true. To count as knowledge, beliefs of this kind need only be roughly correct; they need to be close enough to give an initial high probability to an inference. In this way, they help to determine that a hypothesis is worth investigating. But the fact that postulates are usually correct is not grounds for our believing it. That would suggest that they have an inductive basis. Russell thinks that some inferences are due to the connection of properties in the world and that this is why some connections *seem* likely. But this is not an argument as to why they *are* likely. Russell's point is that we already do accept the postulates and accept them without reasons, that is, *a priori*.

The existence of *a priori* knowledge of the world is hardly surprising, he thinks, since this knowledge is the end result of habitual expectations induced by the world on animals that try to survive in it. This is also not a reason for believing the postulates; it is an explanation of why we do believe them. If we accept that there is such knowledge, the empiricist dictum that "all synthetic knowledge is based on experience" is mistaken (1948a, p. 516), since empirical knowledge involves sensible evidence but is not possible unless it also rests on premises that are about the world and yet are known *a priori*.

CHAPTER SIX

Language and meaning

The last two chapters addressed Russell's views on the ultimate constituents of reality and the nature and limits of empirical and logical knowledge. A third and closely linked inquiry concerns the nature of meaning. A causal theory of meaning emerges from Russell's reflection on the relation of language to the extralinguistic world. This kind of inquiry into language begins to emerge around 1918. At this time, Russell begins to view words and sentences naturalistically, that is, as events in the physical world and therefore causally related to it. A word, he argues, is a set or class of the sounds or marks that are the spoken or written occurrences of the word. As a set of sensations, words come to have meaning, he thinks, by association with other sets of sensations. The repeated sight of a toy (a set of sensations) associated with the sound "toy" (another set) may cause a child to learn to say "toy". The meaning of "toy" is therefore explained causally, in terms of the effects and causes of its utterance. His account does not limit symbols to sets of sensations. Images are also regarded as symbols that have meaning. Images are copies of the sensations that cause them and they come to mean by a straightforward mechanism of resembling their causes. By frequent coincidence with sensations and the images that copy them, words become doubly associated: with images on the one hand and sensations on the other. Thus, "Mama" (a class of sensations) is associated with the mother (another set of sensations) and with an image.

The above theory of language and meaning does not occur in Russell's work before 1918. In his earlier work, we read nothing about words as physical occurrences in causal relations and nothing about the images or feelings that words call up. Having no interest in symbols as mental or physical events, Russell "idealizes" them by treating words as single entities (i.e. neither classes nor instances of classes) related to other single entities, usually universals. At the same time his interest in what is meant rather than in how words mean leads him to conclude that "meaning in the sense in which words have meaning is irrelevant to logic" (1903a, p. 47).

None of this is very remarkable considering the nature of his inquiry. A mathematician or logician has no reason to study the ink marks, sounds, and so on used to express a proposition, the particular emotions or images that occur in us while thinking, or the causes of these feelings or images or marks.

Also, Russell is a Platonist who is persuaded that mathematical and logical objects belong to a third realm that is neither physical nor psychological. To keep this realm in sight he must oppose any tendency to regard a mathematical object, such as a number, as something physical or psychological. On his view, we misunderstand mathematics and logic if we confuse its nonspatial and nontemporal objects with physical or psychological data. It is natural, then, for him to regard language—as he later says of his early work—as something "transparent" that could be "employed without paying attention to it" (1959, pp. 13–14) and to "look through" words and sentences to the entities and complexes of entities relevant to mathematics and logic. The result is that language as a physical and psychological phenomenon is hardly examined in his early work, and the study of meaning is limited to a theory of entities and how we apprehend them.

Yet his early work contains problems and ideas that anticipate and result in the emergence of his later theory of language meaning and therefore cannot be passed over. The following pages begin with his early work, focusing on issues relevant to that later development and to problems of meaning in general.

I The Early Russell

1 Language and meaning

There is nothing contentious in the observation, made above, that the causal theory of meaning and related analysis of language is absent from Russell's work before 1918. But does *any* theory of language and meaning occur in his early work? Without agreement as to what is meant by "language" and "meaning" this question is impossible to answer, but it is worth raising in order to explore what is, what does and what does not occur in Russell's early treatment of language.

It is Russell himself who says that in his early work he had regarded language as something that could be ignored. Writing in 1959 he says that his interest in language, particularly its relation to the nonlinguistic world, began to develop in 1917 and 1918. Because he had thought that language could be ignored (1959, pp. 13–14), he had "never examined what makes its relation to the non-linguistic world" (p. 145). Nevertheless, Russell does not say that this early neglect of language and its relation to the world was absolute. After describing an inquiry into language as involving issues of vocabulary and syntax or grammar, he says that the contradictions discovered in mathematical logic had forced him to consider grammar early in his career.

Russell's 1959 assertion that contradictions forced him, early on, to study syntax (grammar) is a reference to the theory of descriptions. It is an allusion to his discovery that the use of a word or phrase in a significant sentence does not imply the existence of an entity that is its meaning. Prior to 1905, sentences like "the F is G" were thought to contain "the F" as a subject. In 1905, Russell concludes that the subject of the sentence is not "the F" but "there is one and only thing F and that is G". The theory is relevant to the relation of language to the nonlinguistic world because it shows that we need to arrive at the genuine logical grammar of a sentence before drawing conclusions about the nonlinguistic world. Running throughout much of Russell's philosophical work is the conviction that, if used carefully, grammar is a key to what there is in the world (the physical world and the world of universals).

What is missing from Russell's pre-1918 study is really the second part of the problem of language: how symbols as physical or psychological entities come to have meaning. His early perspective is that of Platonist philosopher and logician for whom words and sentences are glass: to be looked through, not at, in order to see entities and relations among the entities. Thus, symbols as psychophysical events (classes of sounds or marks) hold little interest for Russell and he has no reason to ask what causes certain classes of sensations to be symbols of or mean other classes of sensations. It is in this sense that we can say that he does not have a theory of language until 1917 or 1918. In the absence of this inquiry, no causal theory of meaning occurs in his early work.

2 Reading Russell

In examining Russell's doctrines of language and meaning, several obstacles to reading his philosophy are important to keep in mind. First, Russell systematically and frequently uses shorthand expressions that can be confusing, such as using "verb" to mean relations and "predicate" to mean a property. In "On the Relations of Universals and Particulars" (1912), we are told that this usage is shorthand for more cumbersome expressions, but Russell does not always draw attention to his rather perverse shorthand, and even if we know this fact about his work, we may forget that it *is* shorthand. The result is that a reader may believe a discussion to be about words and sentences when it is about what is in the non-linguistic world.

Second, Russell often uses terms in ways that are so unusual and against common usage that a reader is apt to assume that he must mean something more conventional and ordinary. His penchant for using words in unusual ways has already been amply illustrated by his conception of *propositions* as entities that are the meanings of sentences. This sense of "proposition" is not entirely divorced from normal usage since we do identify a proposition with the meaning of a sentence. But in admitting this much about propositions, most people do not mean anything more specific and they certainly do not mean that a proposition is a complex object that contains what it is about. Thus the proposition that the cat is on the mat is not usually thought to contain and be about an actual cat, mat, and relation of *being on*. Other examples of words used in unusual ways could be given, such as the word "expression" for a property or propositional function.

Third, Russell sometimes talks about entities in ways that suggest they have a semantic role or denote meanings. For example, before 1905 denoting phrases are said to have concepts as their meanings and the concepts are said to denote entities. Thus "a man" means an entity, the concept *man*, and the entity *man* denotes (or has falling under it) individual humans. Because denoting is a property we associate with language and it is difficult to know what is meant by saying that a concept (entity) denotes other entities, it is easy to think that Russell has the phrase in mind when he says that a concept denotes. The notion that a proposition, an entity, is *about* the things it contains is another example of how apparently semantic properties get transferred to entities.

The above facts contribute to the difficulty of determining whether Russell is talking about a symbol or about what it means. In most of what we read or hear in our daily lives, there is no such difficulty. We can tell from context, for example, that "Boston has six letters" is about the name "Boston" and not about the city. Partly because the subject matter of logic and mathematics is abstract, and partly for reasons like those noted above, it can be difficult to tell whether Russell is talking about a symbol or its meaning. Given his Platonism in his early period, he often is talking about something extralinguistic, but this is not always the case, and Russell's early work is therefore open to different interpretations to an unusual degree on these points.

3 Understanding meaning

Russell does not have a causal theory of meaning in his early period but he has a theory of the entities that are the meanings or denotations of words and a doctrine of how we apprehend those entities. What is meant by *a word* is not explained, but he proceeds as though words were single entities whose meanings are other single entities, namely, universals or particulars. Russell invokes knowledge by acquaintance to account for our awareness of the objects that are the meanings or denotations of words. Most of our words are general, and on his view we understand them by being acquainted with universals. Most words therefore do not have sensed objects as their meanings and our understanding of them does not depend on sensation, since sensation is not acquaintance with universals. But in sensation we may be aware of a datum, such as a patch of color or sound, and this sensible object can be the meaning (or rather the denotation) of a word like "this," if "this" is used as a proper name for the datum.

The doctrine of acquaintance describes different ways of being conscious of objects (e.g. sense data, images, and universals). This account explains us awareness of objects that are the meanings of words, but it does not explain how we know that they are word meanings. Russell seems to assume that we grasp *that* the object is the word's meaning when we understand a word by acquaintance with an entity, but this aspect of awareness is difficult to square with acquaintance, which is not supposed to provide knowledge that something is the case. Moreover, an account of our consciousness of words as such is absent from his work in this period, and it does not seem that he can explain how we know that an object is the meaning of a word so long as he does not say how we recognize different occasions of the same word. Though he would not deny that the intelligent use of a word involves being aware of an entity *and* that the entity is the word's meaning, the nature of our awareness of entities as meanings is not yet very clear in his work.

Russell is aware of the need for words like "this" and "here" and "I." Words like these do not occur on descriptions of the world that abstract from the observer. Thus geography talks about latitude and longitude, not "where I, the geographer, am." No such words are needed if we consider the world objectively, as a collection of objects. But these words are needed if we wish to describe the perspective of consciousness, which is more than an insensible occupying of the world, but a view of the world from within the world." The awareness of that perspective requires words like "here" and "now" that might otherwise be eliminated. Russell's objection to neutral monism is that it cannot account for words like "this" because it denies consciousness as a nonphysical relation to the world. On his view, it suffers from the kind of problem attributed to materialism even though it is not materialist. It is, so to speak, like someone who counts up the contents of a room and forgets to include himself, or like someone who includes his body in the count but leaves out his mind.

4 Images, symbols, and vagueness

Russell is interested in what words denote and not with the images, ideas, or feelings that may be associated with a word. He does not deny that we form mental pictures and associate them with words, but he rejects the view that mental contents (such as images) are necessary elements in meaning. In particular, he denies that images and ideas are needed to represent objects. Though an image of a cat may accompany the use of the word "cat," the image is not the meaning of the word nor does the image have to represent the thing meant in order for us to understand the word. Thus he rejects a representational theory on which words mean images or ideas that represent objects. If the connection between words and things were always indirect in this way, then we could have no certainty that images and ideas represented things adequately or, indeed, that they represented anything at all. This argument arises from Russell's quarrel with Idealism and one reason is why he conceives of the knower as in a direct cognitive relation of acquaintance with the object known.

Despite deep aversion to the notion that ideas or images mediate knowledge or meaning, Russell toys with the idea from time to time. In "On the Nature of Truth" (1907), he suggests that a proposition is a complex of ideas that a person believes. In the case of a relation between two things, the objects of the belief are not things and a relation but the ideas of the things and the idea of a relation. In the same paper Russell says that the theory cannot account for the correspondence between a belief and the fact that makes it true (1907, pp. 46–7). The theory is therefore very short-lived. Images and ideas also play a secondary role in his account of memory. In the unfinished text *The Theory of Knowledge* (1913) the most important form of memory is that involving acquaintance with past objects. Yet Russell allows that remembering often is not direct but consists of images, judged to be *of* data. In these cases, we know the past because we have images that serve as symbols of some event previously experienced. They serve as symbols and "mean" the event because we have feelings of familiarity toward them.

Images as symbols also play a role in his early discussions of vagueness. In one kind of memory, a complex image is said to share its logical structure with the complex sense datum it represents. Its ability to represent turns on the fact that elements in the image correspond one-to-one with elements in the complex and are related by the same relation. Though images are able to represent because of this structural similarity, they are also vague: for example, the images we form of the height of a man are each "capable of 'representing' a number of different heights" (1913, p. 175). It is because of "the vagueness of the representative character of images" that knowledge of the past is uncertain (1913, p. 176). To use his example, it is not that the image of a man illustrates a certain height and we are uncertain about judging whether the man is the same height. Rather, our image of the man's height is indeterminate. These ideas are the leading edge of his middle period theory of images as symbols and of sentences as relational structures.

5 Logic and meaning

Russell uses the word "logic" in two senses. In one sense it refers to a body of propositions, that is, to mathematical logic. In another sense it refers to the activity that arrives at logical forms and classifies them, in short, philosophical logic. By the end of his early period, he faces difficulties concerning both senses of logic and especially concerning the nature of logical propositions. In "Necessity and Possibility," which is written at the beginning of his early period we read that "the subject of the proposition is felt as a *variable*: it is not felt as fully determinate, but as an indefinite member of some class" (1905b, p. 518). What this means is that mathematical and logical propositions express hypotheses that are true of any object: a number, a person, etc. In this, they differ from the propositions of other sciences, whose hypotheses apply to a particular thing or class of things. It is because they assert hypotheses of anything whatsoever that logical propositions contain variables: they vary over any object at all.

Besides containing variables, what is distinctive about such propositions is their connection to logical form. The reasoning in mathematical logic is deductive, and the validity of a particular deductive argument depends on its form and not on the particular subject matter it is about. This means that we can abstract from a particular valid argument about Socrates and his mortality by replacing these terms with variables, and we will arrive at a valid argument form. Such valid argument forms, written as conditional "if, then" propositions, are logical truths. Besides variables, they contain the constants of logic, which are terms (e.g. *is* and *or*) that cannot be eliminated from a logical proposition in the process of replacing particular terms with variables.

Russell acts as if the constants of logic are entities and constitute logical forms. He assumes that logical propositions are about logical constants or forms, that these entities are the subject matter of logic. In "What is Logic?" we read that logical propositions concern "those forms which yield complexes however the variables are determined" (1912d, p. 55). Soon after this, and largely through the work of his student, Ludwig Wittgenstein, Russell begins to think that this view of logical propositions is flawed, though he is not yet sure how to correct it. Wittgenstein argues that logical constants are not entities—there are no objects, relations, or properties special to logic—and so cannot occur as subjects of propositions or as the bearers of names. Russell acknowledges both points in the 1914 *Our Knowledge of the External World* (p. 208) in the course of discussing the elimination of classes. We read that these ideas are from Wittgenstein's unpublished work, which has "important bearing on all logic and philosophy, since it shows how they differ from the special sciences" (p. 208). If there are relations and properties special to logic, then logic is like other sciences, each of which has terms special to it that provide it with a subject. If there are no entities special to logic, that is, if we can do logic without using these concepts, then mathematical logic seems to be deprived of a subject matter and to be about nothing at all. It seems to "differ from the sciences" in a very undesirable way.

It is not only Russell's Platonist conception of logical propositions that is at risk. To say that logical constants cannot occur as subject terms in propositions is to say that we cannot talk about them (or cannot do so legitimately). But logical constants include *relation*, *complex*, *fact*, *object*, and what philosophical logic does is talk about these items, for example, when it says that a fact is not an object, or that a relation requires objects. If such talk is not permissible, then it is not clear how philosophical analysis is possible. And if philosophical analysis is the essence of philosophy, then what becomes of philosophy? In the 1920s Russell accepts that the propositions of logic are empty of content beyond that of representing that certain symbols are equivalent. As for philosophical logic, he decides that even if we cannot legitimately talk about relations, facts, and the like, we can talk about the symbols for them.

6 Structure and meaning

Until the 1920s, Russell does not have a satisfactory account of logical propositions, and despite the problems above he continues to suggest that they are about forms. He faces further issues associated with the definition of logical propositions as those consisting of variables and logical constants. In the *Introduction to Mathematical Philosophy* (1919), he acknowledges that reference to constants and variables is not enough to define a logical proposition. He notes that when we say that a proposition is a logical one, we mean that it is derived by means of logic alone. By this criterion, some of the axioms of *Principia* are extralogical even though their expression requires nothing but variables and logical constants. For example, the axiom of infinity says that there are an infinite number of things in the universe and this is an empirical proposition that is therefore not derivable from logic alone. Russell does not know what the property is that characterizes all and only logical propositions but he thinks that it has some affinity to the older idea of that which cannot be rejected without contradiction. Because he rejects Kant's view of analytic sentences, he is unwilling to use the word "analytic" for this idea. Following Wittgenstein's lead, he uses "tautology" as a label for the unknown property, hoping eventually to see what it is.

In the absence of a defining property, we are thrown back on how we know that logical propositions are true. Logical propositions are those whose truth is known when we know their syntax (p. 201). This does not mean that we know their truth when we grasp the meaning of their syntactical words (words like "or"). Syntactical words are not syntax. Syntax is the relation among symbols. Russell thinks that a logical language can make do without syntactical words and rely on the spatial or temporal relation among words. Thus, a language with no words for logical forms could express what we want to express in logic and mathematics by means of the form of a proposition. So the truth of a logical proposition is known when we know its syntax and not when we grasp logical vocabulary, that is, syntactical words.

This defines our knowledge of logical propositions and is not intended as a substitute for a proper definition. For this, a further property, called "tautology," is anticipated. Russell never discovers what the property is, but over time, the word "tautology" (which had meaning before he pressed into this use) has taken on a variety of meanings. Moreover, the characterization of logic in terms of how it is known has taken on greater significance than Russell probably intended.

II The Middle Russell

7 A theory of language and meaning

In the spring of 1918, Russell delivers the series of lectures that he later publishes as "The Philosophy of Logical Atomism". These lectures respond to the logical difficulties just noted, suggesting that we cannot legitimately talk what symbols mean without putting symbols to wrong uses. Though we can say "relation words are not names," we cannot say "relations are not objects" without using symbols in ways that are illegitimate. Apart from this issue, which is discussed in an earlier chapter of the present study, one of the many difficulties Russell faces concerns the meaning of relation words. He had thought that what we grasp when we understand a relation word is a relation, a universal. But just as he now doubts that syntactical words imply the existence of entities, their meanings, he also doubts that relation words like "loves" and "before" mean relations. Different kinds of words mean in different kinds of ways, he says, and therefore they contribute differently to the meaning of a sentence. In work emerging right after the lectures, relation words are said to create relations among words. For example, we use "loves" as a way of relating "a" and "b" so that the relation among words can be compared to the fact, as either true to it or not.

In the *Introduction to Mathematical Philosophy*, Russell gave the logical basis for this doctrine saying that when two structures are similar, we can infer from abstract properties of the one to those of the other. It is this situation that is exemplified by an accurate map: places in a region correlate to places on the map, and relations defined for places in the region correspond to relations between corresponding points on the map (1919a, pp. 52–3). Sentences, then, are like maps—an idea very like Wittgenstein's picture theory of meaning, the theory that language represents by means of linguistic facts that picture other facts.

In addition to this account of relation words and sentences, Russell begins to develop a theory of subjective and objective meaning. This begins to emerge after the 1918 lectures are completed in connection with an attempt to appropriate neutral monism. Russell has long thought that neutral monism is a more elegant analysis of mind and knowledge than his dualist doctrine of acquaintance. The obstacle to his adopting that philosophy has been discomfort with the behaviorist analysis of meaning conjoined to it. Neutral monism sees the distinction between physical and mental as a matter of classification or grouping, not an ultimate difference in what is grouped, and it therefore cannot admit any nonphysical act or relation of consciousness. This does not leave neutral monism without an account of meaning, which it can explain by reference to behavior, but from Russell's perspective, without awareness of meaning, language reduces to the utterances of a parrot or machine. As mentioned earlier, awareness of meaning seemed not quite explained by his theory of acquaintance, but it is nevertheless critical to his conception. His present goal, therefore, is to show how neutral monism and behaviorism can be adapted to an analysis of meaning as a subjective event.

By the summer of 1918, several core doctrines are in place. They constitute a causal theory of meaning. He writes: "the essence of a symbol is that it is, by association, a causal link between an object and what might be called the 'idea' of the object" (1918b, p. 313). Symbols "denote" something objective and "express" something subjective and thus "have an objective and a subjective meaning; . . . , the former is their cause, the latter their effect" (p. 313). By a "symbol" is meant words as well as sentences. It will help to discuss words first, beginning with names.

8 Words and meaning

It is wrong, Russell now thinks, to think of "*one* entity, the symbol, pointing to *one* entity, its denotation" (1918c, p. 267). We arrive at a name in the same way we construct any ordinary body, that is, by unconscious inferences that collect particular sensations into classes. Since both ordinary objects and ordinary names are classes, "the relation of a symbol to what is symbolized is that of a class to a class . . . " (p. 267). A theory of the association of sensations suffices to explain the learning and meaningful use of names. We thus come to associate the class of similar noises of a certain kind with the class of sensations of another kind, say, those that are the appearances of a person. The meaning of a name is the class or system of particulars that cause the name to be used. But a name comes to have the same effects as the thing it means and so he can also say that the meaning of a name consists in the effects it has on a hearer.

So far, this is largely a behaviorist theory, but it breaks from behaviorism by including a theory of images. To begin with, images or ideas are caused by and are copies of stimuli. By association, we link similar sensations (a dog) with similar sounds or marks ("dog") as well as with images (of a dog). Because we associate images with words, images have cause and effect relationships just as words do. Having the mental picture of a robber can cause us to check our pockets, for example. Images sometimes serve as the subjective meaning of the word, and in these cases to know the meaning of a word is to have an image. This is not true of all words; verbs call up no images.

The theory above conforms to neutral monism in the following way. That philosophy admits only particulars, which are called "mental" or "physical" depending on the causal chains they enter into. A particular is physical if it is part of causal series governed by gravitation (for example) and psychological if in a series governed by habit and association. On Russell's version of neutral monism, some particulars, called "sensations," may occur in either way. Other particulars, notably images, occur only under psychological laws, as the effects or copies of sensations. But this does not make images and sensations intrinsically different; like identical twins living in different countries, they differ only in their associations and the laws under which they fall. The admission of images is a departure from behaviorism, but it is crucial to his attempt to preserve the subjective dimension of meaning.

It is important that images have meaning and that we experience them as symbols. It is in this sense that images are "essential for the understanding of words" (1919a, p. 5). A word may come to have the same effects as the thing it copies. For example, we move aside when we hear "Car!" even before we see or hear the car. But to use words correctly we must, at least at first, think about what they mean. Indeed, "the images and unuttered words that occur in a person" is what we call *thought* and "a person is . . . *conscious* of a circumstance when he uses words, or images of words, to others or to himself, to assert the circumstance" (p. 15). By stressing that we experience images as being of something, Russell distinguishes his account from a behaviorist theory of meaning. Behaviorism can account for the meaningful use of language by talking about observable phenomenon—say, moving aside on hearing "Car!"—but because it denies images and therefore ignores the role of images as symbols, it is incomplete as a theory of language and fails to account for awareness of meaning.

Finally, a theory of image-symbols is key to Russell's account of general words, now that he has come to doubt the doctrine of acquaintance with universals. Images are copies of particular sensations but the meaning of an image is subject to the will. We may use an image to mean something universal by focusing on certain characteristics and ignoring others. (1919c, p. 292). Thus, the use of an image can be generic and universal even though the image is a particular, as when we mean any dog by an image of a dog. Since there is no sensation or set of sensations that is *any dog*, the generic use of the image is not a copy of a sensation, even though the image is.

9 Propositions and meaning

We have been looking at Russell's theory of the subjective and objective aspects of the meaning of words. He also has a doctrine of the objective *versus* subjective meaning of propositions. On the one hand, there is what a proposition *indicates*, which is the fact that makes it true if it is, and on the other hand, there is what it *expresses*, the belief feelings of the speaker. These kinds of meaning can be treated independently of each other to a certain extent; for example, we can talk about a proposition as a fact related to the fact that makes it true or false and put aside all mention of its subjective meaning: what it expresses. But an ultimate explanation has to bring in both elements. To be more exact, it is necessary to include the content believed, the feeling of belief toward the content, and the relation of the content to a fact. The content of a belief is a complex of images or imagined words, say, about putting money away for a rainy day. Feelings of belief are distinct from that content and may be expressed in various ways, such as differences in tense. Thus "I will . . . " express a person's state of expectation about some content and "I did . . . " expresses a memory belief about some content (1919c, p. 296). Similarly, the word "not" expresses a feeling of disbelief (p. 304). In later years this notion develops into a theory of the subjective meaning of logical and syntactical words.

A complex of images (an image proposition or content) is more fundamental than a complex of words, since we have to arrive at the latter from the former by substituting words for images. In the simplest case, then, the content of a belief is a complex of images. With regard to the relation of the content to a fact, an image complex or proposition is more likely than a string of words to match the structure of a fact. If true, the structure of an image proposition is the same as the structure of the fact that makes them true. This is because the verifying fact consists "of the same relation as that which holds between the constituent images in the proposition" (1919c, p. 303). The purity of this case is rare, however, and in propositions consisting of words it does not occur. Here, "the linguistic symbol for a relation is not itself a relation, but a term as solid as the other words of the sentence" and so "the linguistic statement of a fact is a more complex fact than that which it asserts" (p. 303). It is for this reason that word propositions are so misleading, since we may mistake the role of the relation word and think it means something, a relation.

Russell's account allows him to explain words and statements of belief without assuming any special mental stuff. A belief is a class of feelings (sensations) toward images. Note that the classes of sensations and images that are a person's beliefs are part of what make up the class of classes that is the person. When a person believes, there is a relation between the class of classes that is the belief and the class of classes that is the fact corresponding to the belief. Thus, a believer, her belief, and the verifier of that belief belong to one world and not two, since the classes in question consist of the same neutral stuff.

10 Logic, belief, and philosophical analysis

Russell and Wittgenstein reestablish contact after the end of World War I. Their subsequent conversations lead Russell to finally resolve his unsatisfactory stance on the nature of logical propositions. He now accepts that logical and mathematical propositions are merely ways of showing that sets of symbols are equivalent. In the context of the book review that is the first published reference to his new position, Russell says that the laws of thought associated with the science of logic "are concerned with symbols" and "give different ways of saying the same thing" (1920, p. 405). He adds that "only an understanding of language is necessary in order to know a proposition of logic" and that this is why they "can be known without studying the thing to which they apply" (p. 405).

In his introduction to Wittgenstein's *Tractatus Logico-Philosophicus*, Russell accepts the need to distinguish between the sense in which propositions occur in asserting truth functions and the sense in which they occur in statements about an assertion or about a belief. He continues to work on this in notes as he prepares a second edition of *Principia Mathematica*. Briefly, a proposition is a class, namely, a class of psycholinguistic occurrences such as beliefs, sounds, or marks (1923b, p. 157). When we assert or believe something, which may be a truth function, what occurs is not the proposition as a class but only a member: the instance used in making the assertion or having the belief. In contrast, when we talk about an assertion or talk about a belief, as in saying "Jones believes *p*," the proposition as a class enters in. Thus a proposition occurs in different senses in asserting or believing something and in talking about an assertion or belief: in the one case as an instance (a single fact), in the other as a class of facts. Clarifying the ambiguity of "proposition" helps to sort out what it means to regard a statement of belief as a "function of a proposition" and is therefore important to distinguishing them from truth functions.

Despite making concessions to Wittgenstein about the nature of logic and belief, Russell rejects Wittgenstein's related view that the linguistic forms must be shown by words and sentences of a language and cannot be talked about. Wittgenstein's showing/saying distinction requires abandoning philosophical analysis. Since Russell regards philosophical analysis as the essence of philosophy and as the only genuine method of arriving at solutions to philosophical problems, including those in philosophy of mathematics and his logicist program, he is unlikely to regard Wittgenstein's idea favorably. Nor does he see any reason to do so. Russell concedes that we cannot talk about the structure of a language in that language, but says that we can talk about a language from within a higher language (1921b, p. 111). Wittgenstein's claim that there are things that cannot be said but must be shown fails to persuade him, he says, since Wittgenstein's book has shown that it is possible "to say a great deal about what cannot be said" (p. 111). It is some years before the notion of a hierarchy of languages is further developed, but in the 1940s it plays an important role in Russell's work.

11 Vagueness and perception

After writing the introduction to the *Tractatus*, Russell begins to connect the doctrine that logic consists of tautologies with an emerging doctrine of perception. The first step takes place in "Physics and Perception" (1922). An instance of a tautology is, for example, a series of black marks on a white ground or a series of sounds. A tautology says that "this symbol and that have the same meaning" and our understanding of it is derived "from perceptions of geometrical (or quasigeometrical) relations among symbols" (1922, p. 129). The paper does not address the limitations of perception and the element of vagueness that attaches to any symbol as a result of these limitations. Nor does it address how logic employs ideally precise symbols that allow it bypass the problem of vagueness. In the paper titled "Vagueness" (1923), Russell explains why perception makes symbols inherently vague and to what extent this applies to symbols in a logical language.

A language is vague if its words may mean more than one thing and if its propositions may be verified by more than one fact. The meaning of words is always vague or "one-many," Russell says, since we never perceive so precisely that we possess words whose application is precise. This is obvious for color words: "red" applies to a set of phenomena with no clear boundary. But the same can be said of words like "true" and "false." Consider the sentence "this is red": it is verified by a series of shades of color. If people are asked to identify the shades that make the sentence true, there is likely to be disagreement on at least some cases. Thus the application of words like "true" and "false" is also vague in these cases. This in turn has implications for the vagueness of words like "not" and "or." The meaning of these words is given by how they affect the truth or falsehood of the sentences in which they occur. Since the application of "true" and "false" is vague, so too is the meaning of these logical words. For related reasons, there is no precision concerning what is a tautology. As Russell puts it, "logical propositions . . . become vague through the vagueness of 'truth' and 'falsehood'" (1923a, p. 151). In "Logical Atomism," Russell adds that our perceptual limitations make it impossible to know whether something is simple or conceals further complexity. It follows that we cannot know with certainty if we are justified in using a name instead of a proposition (1924, p. 174).

But logic remains indifferent to the vagueness of symbols because it conventionally assumes that words like "true," "false," and "or" are precise, just as it conventionally assumes that a proposition corresponds to a particular fact rather than a series of similar facts and just as it assumes by convention that beliefs are certainly true or certainly false. These are simplifying assumptions, and logicians can employ them since logic is about symbols, not things. Thus "ideal" symbols can be imagined and endowed with imaginary precise meanings. Apart from logic, we cannot employ a precise language since we lack the perceptual acuteness that might give the symbols precise application, yet "we are capable of imagining what a precise symbolism would be" (p. 151). Reflections like these are part of a growing sense of the artificiality of logic and its separation from psychology. In his later work, this results in an attempt to provide the psychological underpinnings of logic.

12 Physics and language

Russell was willing to make images the centerpiece of his account of meaning in 1918 and 1919. In fact, in these years behaviorism was presented as failing to provide a fully adequate account of meaning because it omits images as symbols that have meanings. He denied that images were in space or that they fell under physical laws but assumed that they were part of a scientific theory of meaning even so. His position shifts in *Analysis of Mind* (1921): the recent developments in physics suggest to him that all data is "introspective" or subjective. Perceptions are influenced by conditions of our sense organs, by the influence of the past on our experience, by physical facts about an observer's position, motion, and so on. This means that the scientific data is, and has to be, abstracted from private data. Behaviorism denies that science employs or observes private data, but relativity theory shows that this doctrine is mistaken.

Russell views physics as supporting the importance of introspection (self-observation; scrutiny of our data) and negating the behaviorist tendency to dismiss introspection. The idea that introspection is supported is evident when he writes that physics shows that we must trust "observations which are in an important sense private" (1921a, p. 230). At first he also seems to think that the support extends to images, which, after all, are the data of introspection. Thus we are told that we ought not to "minimize their [images'] function in our knowledge of what is remote in time or space" (p. 230). But behaviorism cannot be completely disregarded and Russell admits that words "could, theoretically, be explained without introducing images" (p. 206), by behaviorism. By 1926, these apparently opposing ideas have begun to balance: the privacy of our data is a central component of the theory of knowledge, but images are not regarded as having any bearing on knowledge or meaning and meaning is explained entirely physically, in terms of behavior. In "The Meaning of Meaning," we read that images "should not be introduced in explaining 'meaning'" (1926, p. 140). Russell does not deny that images exist, nor does he say that they play no role in our experience of meaning. Rather, he wants to show how meaning can be "fitted into natural science" and explained as a physical event occurring under physical laws (p. 140). To this end, meaning has to be regarded "as a property of words considered as physical phenomena" (p. 142). He therefore decides to construct a theory of meaning without images.

Despite this, images remain a subject of philosophical discussion and Russell refers to them in later work in many of the ways we have seen so far, for example, as similar to their prototypes. In the meantime, he proceeds with a physical and behavioral theory of meaning, having already determined that it could suffice to explain meaning. The 1926 paper proceeds to sketch a theory of meaning that stresses association: when words and objects are experienced together often enough, the word comes to have the same effects as the object. Leaping aside when we hear someone shout "Car!" is his example. A learned reaction is involved in our use of words, but this can be explained in terms of associating bodily movements and need not involve associating ideas. He concludes: "In short, the meaning of a [spoken] word is the phenomena most closely associated with it" (p. 143).

III The Late Russell

13 A primary language

The Analysis of Matter (1927) assumes that it is possible to infer from percepts to unobserved events in the physical world and tries to show how that is possible, that is, how percepts can be a basis for inference to the external world. It does not directly address the nature or justification of inductive inference. These issues require an examination of the premises upon which inference to the external world rests, and of how the truth of the premises is secured by experience. Russell's late work turns to these epistemological questions after first explaining how words come to have meaning, and sentences, significance. *An Inquiry into Meaning and Truth* (1940) describes a hierarchy of "languages" based on a primary or object language, each level being the subject of the next level and, therefore, providing it with words and phrases.

A hierarchy is necessary to avoid paradoxes, but Russell's concern here has less to do with that issue than with explaining and securing the connection between language and experience. If there is such a hierarchy, it must have a base consisting of words and phrases whose meaning is supplied by experience. Thus Russell supposes a level of language (an "object language") at the base of the hierarchy and consisting of words whose meanings are known by ostensive definition (by pointing to examples) and used to indicate the presence of what they mean—as when a child says "doggie!" at the sight of a dog. Such words are of different kinds; they may be names, words for qualities, words for relations, and even words for private experiences such as belief. Because each person learns different words by ostension and acquires others words by verbal definitions, there are in fact as many such object languages as there are language users.

A person's object language may consist of utterances like "dog!" but it can contain no logical or syntactical words. The object language does not consist merely of single word utterances; though it includes no syntactical words, it permits syntax, that is, combinations of words. Thus, utterances like "dog, cat, woof-woof, pffft!" can occur in the primary language. Russell has in mind a language in which words are used and not mentioned, that is, in which there are no references to language or meaning. Thus in the object language words or strings of words occur as responses, as noises or movements, but without the reflection on their meanings that can only occur in the secondary language. In a sense, there are assertions in the object language, but not with the implication that what is asserted might be denied. This is clearly a limited language. Anyone who possessed it and no other level of language would be able to state what he or she observed but would not be able to make or understand inferences (1940, p. 70). Such a person could, in theory, see all there is to see but not know or say what it meant to do so.

When Russell shifts from discussing the object language as it might arise in a child to the role of object words in the propositions and premises used by adults, he continues to refer to the sentences that result as "in" the object or primary language. This can be confusing. When he says that sentences like "this is hot" are in the object language what he means is that they could be translated into an object word sentence ("hot!") or into a string of object words. The class of premises called "judgments of perception" (roughly the same as observation reports) is in the primary language in the sense that they could be translated into it. It might seem that "this is hot" would fall into a higher language since it contains syntactical words and since we are told that syntactical words first occur in the secondary language. But the hierarchy of languages does not encompass all words. It excludes words that are defined verbally, for example, "dodecahedron," and it also excludes logical or syntactical words that are redundant to a logical language. Since "is" is not needed in symbolic languages (p. 64), it is an extra wheel, so to speak, that is not in the primary, secondary, or any higher language. Thus sentences like "this is a dog" are in (i.e. translatable into) the object language simply by omitting "is a" and "this."

14 Impersonal reports

But are the premises to knowledge conveyed by sentences of the form "this is a dog?" A dog is an inference from what we experience. Russell thinks genuine premises for knowledge must avoid words that are "condensed inductions." Premises of the right sort require the right sort of words, and a primary language does not ensure this without bringing in further constraints. If premises cannot contain words like "dog," we might conclude that they have to be like "this is a canine patch." The trouble here is the presence of the word "this." Words like "this" and "I" and "here" are egocentric; they convey the perspective of the subject. If we are to arrive at premises able to serve science, such words will not do, and getting rid of them is part of the task of arriving at a minimum vocabulary, a list of words or of kinds of words able to account for the phenomena. To begin with, it is important to note what happens to the egocentric element in the transition from the object language of a child to the sentences of an adult. A child's object language consists of implicitly egocentric utterances even when words like "I" do not occur. "Hot!" says what is later expressed by "I am hot" or "this is hot." Thus the child's object words are judgments of perception but without explicit egocentric words. When maturity brings greater language skill, words and phrases like "this is" are added to the originals, and the element of egocentricity detaches from the original object word and shifts to the new phrases. Russell writes: "in a developed language object-words such as 'hot', 'red', 'smooth', etc., are not egocentric" (1940, p. 127).

Despite the transference, the sentence "this is hot" remains egocentric. A science attempts to eliminate these references to the subject; physics does this, for example, by defining "blue" by reference to light waves. Russell has to show how it is possible to arrive at impersonal observational reports able to serve as basic propositions or premises in a science from sentences that convey an individual's percepts. He begins by arguing that judgments like "this is hot" can be expressed as "hotness belongs to this." Nothing seems to be gained by this locution, but the advantage comes from the additional idea that "this" denotes a bundle of qualities that could be given a name, say, "W." If "W" denotes all the qualities a person is experiencing at some moment—a squeaking sound, the smell of toast, excessive warmth, etc.—then "I am hot" can be rendered "hotness belongs to W." This rendering of a person's present experience erases the egocentric element and thus makes it "ready for incorporation in impersonal science" (p. 128).

As explained in earlier chapters, this treatment of egocentric words serves another function: Russell resists the idea that "this" or "I" or "now" or "here" are words that denote substances such as a subject or instant of time or point in space. Such entities are to be defined by bundles of qualities.

15 A secondary language

The last two sections have addressed the nature of the interface between certain words and extralinguistic experience as well as how words come to form sentences that, under further constraints, can function as premises. Russell's notion of a secondary language was mentioned only briefly, and yet to understand his conception of the premises to our knowledge, that language needs to be further explained. The secondary language consists of words that convey our feelings toward primary language utterances. For example, to believe "this is not sugar" is to have a feeling of rejection toward the proposition "this is sugar." Words like "not" and "false" are based on such experiences. Such words have meaning in a way that differs from the way primary words have meaning, since the experiences that give rise to primary language sentences are experiences of the world, while those that give rise to secondary sentences are experiences about language, such as expectations and beliefs (1940, p. 66). In the 1920s, Russell said that all of what we experience are events in ourselves and that emotions differ from sensations solely in the complexity of their causality (1927b, p. 226). His theory of the meaning of secondary language words as opposed to primary words is in some ways analogous: their meaning involves a complicated causal relationship to our "external" experiences.

But why does Russell want to explain the meaning of logical words by a doctrine that refers to our feelings? It seems a peculiar thing for a logician to do. The reason has to do with an attempt to protect the premises of knowledge from undue restriction based on an overly narrow and idealized approach to logical words. In logic, such words are viewed solely in terms of their contribution to truth-values. This tends to focus attention on what a sentence indicates. Since sentences of the form "p or q" evidently do not indicate disjunctive facts, and the same can be said of other molecular cases, it comes to seem that our basic propositions or factual premises ought not to include anything that might be conveyed by a molecular sentence—that atomic sentences suffice. The point can be extended to universal and existential sentences as well: it is thought that our premises cannot be of the form "all F is G" or "some F is G." Indeed, this restriction is a doctrine of empiricism.

The value of a psychological account of logical words is that it does *not* conform to the unduly artificial logical meanings assigned to such words. Russell thinks it is obvious that when a person believes "no cheese is in the larder" he does not refer to everything there is. Thus he wishes to show that sentences containing words like "all" must not always be interpreted as they are in logic. And if some other interpretation of them can be given, say, in terms of impulses or feelings, it becomes possible to see that certain general sentences might be premises and thus that empiricists are wrong to reject all general and nonlogical basic propositions. Besides, what a person expresses—states of feeling like hesitation, rejection, and so on—belong to immediate experience just as surely as do sensations like heat. There is no reason to exclude this kind of knowledge from our premises, and if we do not include them we make ourselves less able to explain knowledge. Thus, Russell argues that among basic propositions there must be some negative and general propositions, as well as some that are about belief. But the meaning of these sentences and the secondary words they contain is not what is given by a logical analysis; it is the meaning explained by his causal and psychological account.

16 Significance

A particularly thorny part of the *Inquiry* concerns the significance of sentences. The issue is complex. On the one hand, it involves showing that there is something, a proposition (a group of images, percepts, impulses, etc.) that *is* the significance of a sentence. If we are to say why a sentence is significant even when false, it is necessary that there be propositions apart from the facts that make them true or false. On the other hand, it is necessary to explain why significant sentences are significant, that is, why they are not gibberish. We might be tempted to say that rules of significance answer this question, except that this opens up the possibility that we could make up any rules we liked. Russell does not accept this possibility and therefore thinks that "it is not enough to form rules that ensure that any and only those forms of words that follow them are significant; we need to understand why that is" (1940, p. 182). He does not doubt that we can find rules that circumscribe the set of significant sentences, but from his perspective this is not enough.

So what is it that ensures that sentences make sense? It is in part due to the belief states of the sentence user but also due to the fact that the world contains natural kinds that can be described by certain categories. Putting aside how the world constrains sense, a sentence is significant because it bears a relation to the belief states of the sentence user. What a sentence *expresses* is its subjective meaning, and what it *indicates*, if it is true, is its objective meaning. A sentence is significant if what it expresses is a possible belief, that is, if we could form images or have percepts that could give rise to the sentence or its contradictory (p. 175). Not every spoken or written sentence can be caused by some percept or image or cause an image in the listener or reader. We can imagine and might at one time have perceived Socrates drinking the hemlock but we cannot imagine or perceive quadruplicity drinking procrastination (p. 177). Significance can therefore be explained causally: " . . . a spoken sentence is 'significant' if its causes are of a certain kind, and a heard sentence is 'significant' if its effects are of a certain kind" (p. 190).

It was noted above that Russell thinks that giving a list of rules is not enough to account for the phenomena of significance. That being said, it is important for him to describe those rules and a logical language containing them. The importance has to do with his desire to see whether logical rules of significance square with the causal conditions of significance he has described. In general, Russell always wishes his philosophical analysis outside of logic to square with logic and *vice versa*. But his concern here is also very specific. On the logical principle of atomicity, logical principle given a hierarchy of atomic, molecular, and general sentences constructed according to syntactical rules, any sentence in the hierarchy is significant and any significant sentence of any language can be translated into it. Russell wishes to see if this is true. He wishes to see whether the language he has described, consisting of object language words (names like "W," relation words, and the like) and basic propositions, squares with the kinds of sentences described by a logical language.

What is to be tested is the logical principle, not his psychological or causal language. Can the significance of the sentences he has explained psychologically be explained by logical rules of combination? Will only significant sentences arise from this initial group of sentences if we substitute words and generalize? It seems at first that the principle fails, since some sentences do not obviously fit anywhere in the logical series. For example, sentences of the form "A believes p" do not appear to be atomic, molecular, or general. However, this is from the perspective of the usual logical analysis of words like "or" and "believes." His psychological analysis opens up a way to see at least some of these sentences as on a par with atomic sentences. This means the principle above is not refuted, though he notes that it has also not been shown to be true.

17 Expressing, indicating, and verifying

In most cases, we do not have access to what a sentence indicates if it is true: we only have access to what we experience, which is what the sentence expresses. Russell often talks about what a sentence "expresses" in terms of feelings of hesitation and the like, but what a sentence expresses is not limited to emotion. If a person sees blue and says "this is blue," the sentence expresses that she experiences blue. In a case like "this is blue" or "this is hot," what the sentence expresses is what it indicates if it is true. These cases involve the least possibility of error because there is no gap between what is expressed and indicated. We can verify the sentence by the same event that caused us to assert it. But a sentence like "this is a dog" leaves a gap between what we experience (some shape or sound) and what verifies the sentence, since we experience sounds and patches of color but not dogs. There is no reason to despair, however, since there must be some justification for sentences of this sort and some way of connecting what we express with what we indicate.

In the *Inquiry*, Russell's long discussion of truth attempts to show how what a sentence expresses is connected with something in the unobserved world that makes it true. He concludes that we regard an assertion like "there is a dog" as true because we have a percept of a certain kind and because we assume certain *a priori* principles connecting what we experience with an external world. Truth at any level beyond that of immediate experience therefore requires the acceptance of *a priori* principles about the world. Russell's account of those principles was sketched in the last chapter. Standing in the way of accepting sentences whose truth or falsehood transcends experience are a number of doctrines, including the verifiability criterion of meaning. In its strongest form, this criterion identifies the significance of a proposition with its method of verification. A sentence cannot be true if it is not meaningful, and this doctrine therefore restricts truth as well as meaning. Russell denies that we know the meaning of a sentence if we know what could make it true and that it has no meaning if determination of truth or falsehood is impossible. His argument in defense of truth that transcends experience falls outside the scope of the present discussion, but it was touched on in the last chapter of this study when it was noted that "true" and "false" must be defined so that it is possible for sentences to be true even if we cannot verify them, since, in fact, a great many of very ordinary beliefs cannot be verified.

18 The external relation of language

Human Knowledge: Its Scope and Limits (1948) does not break new ground with regard to the theory of meaning, but it provides some clarity on details concerning the relation of language to non-linguistic fact. This issue is part of Russell's quarrel with the logical positivists who view inquiry into the relation of language to the world as unduly metaphysical. Russell dismisses their attempt to study language in abstraction from its relation to fact, arguing that language is about the world and that to ignore this aspect is to fail to address language in its most important feature. In *Human Knowledge*, this theme is in the background as he investigates how we acquire language habits. For example, a child who learns to say "mama" has formed a word habit by noticing certain similar percepts, but habit formation is impossible without the repetition of similar characteristics. Since the existence of language depends on reacting to similarities, we cannot explain similarity as a matter of language. The same point can be extended to the relation between language and the world.

In his middle period, Russell suggested that we experience images and ideas as symbols, that is, as "of" something. He makes a comparable claim now. Learning to say "mama" involves having sensations of a certain kind; these sensations give rise to images, which are thus part of the conditioning process. The presence of images explains why a child does not use "mama" merely as a reflex response to the sight of the mother but uses it in her absence to bring the mother close. Among other things, this fact demonstrates that images are instinctively felt to possess external reference (1948a, p. 123) To use another example, when we have an image of something in the past, we instinctively believe that the images comprising the memory are *of* something external to and prior our present experience and not that the *images* existed in the past (p. 124). This is a conditioned response, that is, a form of belief-like behavior. Part of the conditioned response is behaving as though sensations are *of* something. Humans are not alone in this; an animal that sniffs the air every time it smells water is demonstrating an impulse to treat stimuli as external to it. In humans, the response to a stimulus is more likely to involve our mouths (i.e. language) than our noses, but in either case the belief that sensations have external causes is a primitive expectation and one we cannot root out.

This does not prove that symbols have external reference, but it serves to explain the source and nature of our conviction. Put another way, whether or not language actually has an external relation, that is, whether or not it is actually "of" something, we are unable to avoid behaving as if there is such a relation: we cannot reduce *that* relation to a feature of language.

CHAPTER SEVEN

The infinite

As much as possible, *Principia Mathematica* was meant to be a *general* system of logic and mathematics—its principles were meant to apply both to finite and infinite sets and numbers indifferently. The set theory and arithmetic of the infinite (called "transfinite" arithmetic) in *Principia* came from the work of Dedekind, Cantor, and Peano, but especially from Cantor. Russell, along with Dedekind, Cantor, and Peano, considered set theory to be a part of logic. In this chapter, we describe the transfinite set theory and arithmetic of Russell's logicism.

The material in this chapter could have as well come at the end of Chapter 2, on naïve logicism. However, it seemed better to go straight from the development of the real numbers in Chapter 2 to Russell's mature restricted logicism, for by then the reader knew enough of the basics and was ready to tackle the mature logicism, with its apparatus of type theory, the theory of descriptions, axiom of reducibility, and the no-class theory. We turn now to the deferred subject of logicism and the infinite.

1 Cardinal numbers, finite, and infinite

Georg Cantor's set theory is radically different from the set theory that came before it. Prior to Cantor, mathematicians and logicians had used Boolean logic and set theory, as well as the logic and set theory of Charles Sanders Peirce and Ernst Schröder that were based on Boole's work.[1] Boolean logic and set theory was a limited affair, principally fashioned to formalize Aristotelian logic. Also, it did not carefully distinguish between set membership and class inclusion (where one class is a subset of another). For example, it did not distinguish between a class containing a single element and that element itself. Third, it did not adequately express existence. Fourth, it was inadequate for describing the logic of relations. (Boole had none; Peirce and Schröder had one that was impractical.) Fifth, it did not consider infinite sets at all.

Cantor began solving these problems by precisely defining infinity and treating it as a finished totality rather than, as those before him did, as only a potentially infinite value of a series of finite numbers indefinitely increasing in magnitude. Cantor was the first to successfully define infinity. Then, taking the notion of a set with an infinite totality of members, he defined numbers to describe infinite sets, which he called "transfinite numbers." Not all infinite sets are equal. Some are larger than others (have a greater infinity of members). So some infinite numbers are larger than others. He then described the arithmetic of these infinite numbers, which he called "transfinite arithmetic." And with these concepts, he was able to precisely define the ideas of a limit and of continuity for the first time.

At the time Russell was developing his logicist philosophy, Cantor's set theory was just becoming known and was at odds with the earlier set theory of Boolean algebra. Russell rejected much of Boolean algebra and set theory and was a champion of Cantor's work. In particular, Russell took Cantor to have to have given the first adequate definitions of infinity and continuity, though Peano is credited with first clearly distinguishing between class membership and class inclusion for unit sets. This last was a distinction of great importance to Russell.

Russell was thus an early advocate of Cantor's new set theory with its precise definitions of infinite sets, infinite numbers, continuity, and limits, and he included as much of Cantor's set theory and transfinite arithmetic in his own set theory and in his logicist account of mathematics as possible.[2] However, Cantor's definition of the most basic concept of set theory, namely, a set, was vague, and it was Peano who first clearly defined the concept with his distinction between the relations of set membership and of class inclusion. Cantor, however, did not have a logic of relations, nor did Peano. Russell corrected this problem by using Peano's logical notation to create for the first time a clear and usable logic of relations.

Regardless of these last two shortcomings (no clear concept of a set and no good logic of relations), Cantor did invent the theory of infinite classes and infinite numbers. With infinite numbers, Cantor can be said to have introduced a new type of number into mathematics. In fact, he introduced several new numbers, though it was hardly the first time this had happened. Earlier "new numbers" include zero, negative numbers, irrational numbers, and complex numbers. While irrational numbers had been described by the ancient Greeks and negative numbers by the Hindus in the seventh-century A.D., neither was fully accepted by mathematicians until the nineteenth century. Complex numbers were likewise fully accepted only in the nineteenth century. Cantor's new numbers were just the most recent in a long line of new numbers added to mathematics.

Besides infinite numbers, Cantor introduced cardinal numbers and ordinal numbers. Both cardinal and ordinal numbers, like infinite numbers, are whole numbers. (There are no fractions or square roots of infinity.) Cardinal numbers are either natural numbers or infinite numbers considered independently of their order in the series of numbers. Specifically, they are the numbers defined by the Frege-Russell definition of number—as a set of sets similar (the same in number) with one another. This definition works for both finite and infinite sets, thus defining both finite and infinite cardinals.

Once cardinal numbers are identified and named (0 is the set containing the null set, 1 is the set of all singletons, 2 the set of all couples, $\aleph_0$—aleph null—is the smallest infinite number and the number of finite numbers, etc.), we can use them to say how many members a set has, and so to say there are 50 united states, 4 years of college, and 14 stations of the cross. But cardinal numbers do not have any particular order: they are defined without reference to order. Similarly, classes, unless specified otherwise, are collections of things without any particular order to their members, because they are similarly defined without reference to order.

What defines the order of a set of objects is an ordering relation. To order objects, a relation must be asymmetrical, transitive, and closed for its field. A relation R is asymmetrical if, when x has the relation R to y, y cannot have relation R to x; R is transitive if, when x has relation R to y, and y has R to z, x has R to z; R is closed for its field if for any two objects x and y in its field, either x has R to y or y has R to x. And the field of a relation is the set of all objects that have that relation to something or are what something has that relation to. The relation *less than*, for example, is an ordering relation; it can be used to arrange any set of numbers by order of magnitude, for example, to order the natural numbers in a series by magnitude. It can similarly be used to order the rational numbers or real numbers by order of magnitude.

An ordinal number is the number of a set of things considered in some particular order. Anything considered in a particular order is called a "series." A relation defines a series and each series has what may be called a "length." An ordinal number is the number of every series that has the same particular length. A finite ordinal number names a series with a finite length.

In the case of finite series, their length is just the number of members in the series. So the ordinal number 7 applies to any series with 7 members in it. No matter how you arrange a finite number of things, it will have the same length. The ordinal number of any series with a finite number of things in it is thus the cardinal number saying how many things are in the series. There is not much difference between finite cardinal and finite ordinal numbers. However, the situation is quite different for infinite cardinals and ordinals. But before considering those, let us consider, without metaphor, what we mean by the "length" of a series an ordinal number indicates.

A series is defined by a relation: we can speak of a series simply by referring to the relation that defines it. An ordinal number is the set of all series similar to one another. Two relations are similar when they can be correlated 1-1. The field of a relation R is the set of all things x such that x has relation R to y, or y has R to x. Finally, two relations R and S can be correlated 1-1 when each member of the field of R is correlated with a member of the field of S, and vice versa, so when two members x and y of the field of R are such that x has the relation R to y, the corresponding two members of S, namely, x' and y', will be such that $x'Sy'$. Two series are then said to have the same "length" when they are similar.

This is really the same as saying that two series have the same length when they contain the same number of things, as long as it is understood that a set of an infinite number of things can be put in different orders and the two resulting infinite series can have a different number of things in them, and so be different lengths. Note that this requires a series to be counted in a particular order. So we can say that two series are of different lengths, when they have a different number of members, as long as we count the elements in their specified order.

But what exactly does *this* mean? It means that the shorter series can be put in a 1-to-1 relation with part of the longer series, but the longer series cannot be put in a 1-to-1 relation with any part of the shorter series. Before going further with this, let us first consider the cardinal numbers, in particular, the infinite cardinal numbers.

Each natural number is finite, yet the total number of natural numbers is infinite: they are defined so that they go on "forever," so there are an infinite number of them, yet each by itself is a finite number. The finite *cardinal* numbers are just the natural numbers considered without reference to any order. And since the natural numbers are infinite in number yet each is finite, the number of cardinal natural numbers cannot itself be a natural number. Cantor thus assigned it an infinite number using the Hebrew symbol $\aleph$ (called an *aleph*), calling the number of cardinal natural numbers $\aleph_0$ (aleph null).

Cantor argued that $\aleph_0$, the number of cardinal natural numbers, is the smallest infinite number, but that there are larger ones. He assigned the numeral $\aleph_1$ to the next largest cardinal infinite number and $\aleph_2$ to the one after that (aleph 1 and aleph 2, respectively). He then proved that the number of cardinal real numbers is greater than the number of cardinal natural numbers, and hypothesized that they were the next largest infinite number in size, $\aleph_1$. These infinite numbers are cardinal numbers too, because each is just the set of all sets of a particular infinite size without regard to order, with $\aleph_0$ being the set of all sets that are the same size as (i.e. similar to) the set of cardinal natural numbers. $\aleph_1$ is then the set of all sets similar to the cardinal real numbers, and so on.

The difference between a finite and infinite cardinal number is this: if one takes any proper subset of a class with a finite number of members, the number of members of the proper subset will be less than the number of members of the original set. This is not always the case for infinite classes. Any class with an infinite number of members can be correlated 1-1 with *some* subsets of it—namely, those which also contain an infinite number of members. The even numbers, for example, are a subset of the natural numbers that can be put in 1-1 correspondence with them, like this:

$$1, 2, 3, 4, \ldots, n, \ldots$$
$$2, 4, 6, 8, \ldots, 2n, \ldots$$

And each series will go on forever.

Not all subsets of the natural numbers can be put in a 1-1 correspondence with the natural numbers themselves. Clearly, the finite set $\{1, 2, 3, 4, 5\}$ cannot be put 1-1 with all the natural numbers. But any subset of the natural numbers with no last term can be. For example, we could begin with any enormously large natural number n, take the nth power of n, then the nth power of the nth power of n and so on to get $\{n, n^n, n^{n^n}, \ldots\}$, and it could still be put 1-1 with all the natural numbers. This in fact is the property that Cantor used to define an infinite set: a set that can be put 1-1 with some subset of itself is an infinite set.

This property of infinite sets to be correlated 1-1 with proper subsets of themselves has been known for centuries, in fact, millennia, but it has always been taken as self-contradictoty. A subset of the natural numbers like the even numbers are clearly less in number than the natural numbers, being a proper subset of them, but they can be correlated 1-1 with them, and so are, at the same time, equal to them. But a set cannot be both equal and unequal to another set. This was taken as a proof that infinite sets cannot exist. It was Cantor's genius to see that it is not self-contradictory for an infinite subset of an infinite set to be equal in size to the original set, but in fact is a property that defines infinity. On the basis of this, he developed the theory of infinite sets as well as infinite numbers and their arithmetic.

Briefly, the arithmetic of infinite cardinal numbers is this: the familiar properties of commutativity, association, additive identity, inequality, and distribution all hold for addition and multiplication of infinite cardinal numbers. That is, for any infinite cardinal numbers a, b, and w:

$$a + b = b + a$$
$$a + (b + c) = (a + b) + c$$
$$\text{if } a \leq b, \text{ then } a + w \leq b + w$$

$$ab = ba$$
$$w(ab) = (wa)b$$
if $a \leq b$, then $aw \leq bw$
$$w \times (a + b) = wa + wb$$

However, addition and multiplication themselves are much different for infinite cardinal numbers than they are for finite cardinal numbers. Where n is a finite natural number, they are:

$$1 + \aleph_0 = \aleph_0$$
$$n + \aleph_0 = \aleph_0$$
$$\aleph_0 + \aleph_0 = \aleph_0$$
$$n \times \aleph_0 = \aleph_0$$
$$\aleph_0 \times \aleph_0 = \aleph_0, \text{ but}$$
$$\aleph_0 < 2^{\aleph_0}$$

In other words, the sum of the smallest infinite cardinal number, $\aleph_0$, and any other number less than or equal to $\aleph_0$ is equal to $\aleph_0$. However, let $\aleph$ be equal to any infinite cardinal number greater than $\aleph_0$ (e.g. $\aleph_1$ or $\aleph_2$ or $\aleph_3$) and $\aleph_0 + \aleph = \aleph$, $\aleph_0 \times \aleph = \aleph$, and $\aleph \times \aleph = \aleph$. The rules for infinite cardinal numbers are fairly intuitive. The rules for infinite ordinal numbers are different.

2 Infinite series and infinite ordinal numbers

Infinite cardinal numbers are not the only new numbers that Cantor introduced. He also introduced *ordinal* numbers. As with cardinal numbers, ordinal numbers are both finite and infinite. Finite ordinal numbers were described in the previous section. They are really not much different from finite cardinal numbers in practice. But infinite ordinal numbers, which we discuss in this section, are very different from infinite cardinals.

All series having ordinal numbers—in particular, infinite series with infinite ordinals—are well-ordered series, and a well-ordered series is one for which every sub-class except the null set has a first member. Ordinal numbers are numbers indicating the "length" (as we have metaphorically called it) of a well-ordered series. Two well-ordered series with the same "length" (the same number of elements when taken in a specific order) have the same ordinal number. A series is determined by a relation, which not only defines the order of a set of things, but also defines what those things are by determining what kind of thing can have that relation to what other kind of thing. The relation is thus equivalent to the series of ordered objects, so we can speak of the ordering relation in place of the series it orders.

Cardinal numbers are sets of similar sets; ordinal numbers are sets of similar relations. Let us call the similarity that ordinal numbers have *ordinal similarity*. For two relations R and S to be ordinally similar there must first be a 1-1 relation between the members of each series, that is, between the fields of R and S, just as with two similar sets. But for two series to be similar, the two fields must also have a similar order. And two fields have a similar order when the 1-1 correlation between them is such that for any two objects x and y of series R, x has relation R to y whenever w and z, the two objects they are correlated with in the series S, are such that w has relation S to z. To say that two relations have the same length, and thus are of the same ordinality, is just to say that they are ordinally similar. Again, we are primarily talking about infinite series here.

But what is it for one *infinite* series to be longer than another infinite series and thus to have a greater number of elements? Again, it is this: if part of one infinite series is ordinally similar to all of the second infinite series, but no part of the second series is ordinally similar to the first, we say that the first series is greater than the second series. To see this, consider the following two infinite series:

(a) $1, 2, 3, 4, \ldots, n, \ldots$

(b) $1, 3, 4, 5, \ldots, n+1, \ldots 2$

Notice that they each contain all of the natural numbers—they are cardinally similar. However, they are not ordinally similar: the second is greater ("longer") than the first, for a part of it, everything before 2, can be put in a 1-1 relation with the first, but not even the whole of the first can be (ordinally) correlated 1-1 with the second.

The second series is longer than the first, even though they each contain the same infinite number of objects. Order matters.

Or consider the third infinite series below that results from putting the 2 at the beginning of it. Then we have:

(c) $2, 1, 3, 4, \ldots n, n + 1, \ldots$

It should be obvious that series (c) can be correlated 1-1 with series (a), and vice versa. The two relations are ordinally similar. Again, order matters when considering the length of an infinite series.

Now we give the ordinal numbers themselves for series of different length. The ordinal length of any finite series is just the cardinal number of its members. For infinite ordinal numbers, the smallest is the series of natural numbers ordered by magnitude, as in series (a) above. Its ordinal number is ω, the Greek letter omega. If you add one element at the end of an ω series, as in series (b) it is called $\omega + 1$. The 1 comes after the ω because, again, with ordinals, order matters. If, instead of putting 2 after all the other natural numbers, you put it at the beginning of that series, as in series (c), its ordinal number is $1 + \omega$. But series (a) is ordinally similar to series (c) so they have the same ordinality, and the ordinal number of series (a) is ω. Thus, $1 + \omega = \omega$, while $\omega + 1 > \omega$.

Because order matters in determining the size of an ordinal number, the law of commutativity does not hold for ordinals: for any two ordinals, a and b, it will *not* in general be true that $a + b = b + a$. Other laws of arithmetic change for ordinals as well. But first, back to naming the ordinals.

If you add n to the end of an ω series, it is $\omega + n$. For the series

(d) $1, 3, 5, 7, \ldots, 2, 4, 6, 8, \ldots$

the ordinal number is 2ω, whereas $\omega 2$ is simply a series with two elements for every natural number, as in:

(e) $0, 0', 1, 1', 2, 2', 3, 3', \ldots$

where a number with a prime simply means that the number is something other than a natural number, say, a fraction or a square root. (Contemporary set theoreticians usually write the two in the other order; this is Russell's way of writing them.) While 2ω means a couple of progressions, $\omega2$ means a progression of couples. It should be clear that $\omega2 = \omega$, while $2\omega > \omega$, although 2ω, $\omega2$, and ω each have a cardinality of $\aleph_0$. Order matters for ordinality, but not cardinality.

As stated above, commutativity for both addition and multiplication does not hold for ordinal numbers. However, the associative law and one version of the distributive law do hold. They are:

$a + (b + c) = (a + b) + c$, and $a \times (b \times c) = (a \times b) \times c$
(associative law)

$(b + c)a = ba + ca$, but $a(b + c) \neq ab + ac$
(distributive law)

3 An infinity of things and the axiom of infinity

There are two other modifications that Russell makes to the naïve logicism of his 1903 *Principles of Mathematics* that are prominent in the restricted logicism of *Principia Mathematica*. The first is the introduction of the axiom of infinity to logicism, which obviously is about infinity, and the second is the introduction of the multiplicative axiom, which also is about infinity. These axioms are not assumed in order to avoid the paradoxes of self-reference, but more simply because, in the first case, Russell had believed that he could easily prove that there were an infinite number of things in the universe when he wrote the *Principles*, but by the time he wrote *Principia*, he had realized that he could not prove it. Yet the existence of an infinite number of objects is assumed by logicism, and in fact throughout much of mathematics and especially by the Peano axioms and Cantorian transfinite arithmetic. As for the multiplicative axiom, Russell's 1903 logicism assumes it, but Russell did not realize that he had assumed it until 1904. In the 1910 *Principia*, he states this assumption explicitly as an axiom. We will consider the first axiom in this section and the second in the next.

In 1903, Russell believed that he could prove that an infinite number of entities existed by purely logical means. The proposition that there are an infinite number of things is needed for the Peano axioms to be true—specifically, it is needed to prove axiom 3 of the Peano axioms, which asserts:

3 no two natural numbers have the same successor

This axiom presupposes infinity: if there were only a finite number of things in the universe, Peano axiom 3 would not be true. To see this, consider the following argument:

Axiom 3 says that no two numbers have the same successor. Given that assumption, it follows that when $m + 1$ is the successor of m and $n + 1$ is the successor of n, if $m + 1 = n + 1$, it must be the case that $m = n$. Now suppose there are only a finite number of things in the universe, for example, suppose there are 10 things. Then, 0 (the set containing the null set) would have a successor, namely, 1, and 1 would have a successor, namely 2, and so on, until we got to 10. 10 is the successor of 9, but what is the successor of 10?

We have a numeral for the successor of ten, namely 11. But in this case, where we are assuming that there are only ten things in the universe, how many is eleven? Ten is the set of all sets with 10 members. But if there are not 11 things in the world, the set of all sets with 11 members would be empty—11 would be the set containing the null set, that is, zero. Similarly, the numeral 12 would be the set of all sets with 12 members, and since in the case there not 12 things in the universe, the set of all sets with 12 members would also be the set containing the empty set. Then, $11 = 12$, because both are sets containing just the empty set, but then Peano's axiom 3, that no two numbers have the same successor, will be false because $10 + 1$ will equal $11 + 1$, yet $10 \neq 11$! The same would be true for a universe containing any number of things as long as the number was finite.

To prevent this from occurring, we must assume that for any number n, $n \neq n + 1$; this assumption is the axiom of infinity. Russell expresses the axiom of infinity this way at times, for example, on p. 77 of his *Introduction to Mathematical Philosophy* (Dover edition). But at other times, he expresses it in other ways. For example, on p. 131 of *IMP*, he expresses this by saying: for any number n, there is at least one class of individuals having n terms. This guarantees axiom 3, because only 0 will be the null set, so we will never arrive the conclusion $m + 1 = n + 1$ when $m \neq n$ for natural numbers m and n.

In *Principia Mathematica*, Russell states the axiom of infinity in both of the above forms (at *120.03 and *120.33). He first defines it as saying that for any number n, n things exist. (Actually, he says that for any number n, n things *of the same type* exist. We will get to this point in a moment.) And he later states it by saying that for any natural number n, $n \neq n + 1$. By assuming one or the other of these two formulations of the axiom of infinity, Peano's axiom 3, that no two numbers have the same successor, will be true. But without that assumption, it will not be true. Notice that in either formulation, it asserts that something *exists*, in this case, an infinite number of things. For this reason, the axiom is what is called an *existence assumption*.

In 1903, in the *Principles*, Russell thought that he could prove this assumption as follows: Even if the universe is empty, there is a null set. The number zero is the class of all classes with no members, and the class with no members is the null class. If sets A and B have the same members, they are the same set. Every set with no members has the same members as every other such set. They are thus all the same set, which means there is only one null set. And zero is the class containing the null class. Zero thus exists. It is a class containing one thing.

The number one is the class of all classes with one member. Because zero is such a class, it belongs in the class that is the number one. Thus, there is at least one member in the class that is the number one, so the number one exists. For any number n, there are $n + 1$ numbers between zero and n, inclusive of zero and n. Thus, the finite numbers exist and there are an infinite number of them, which is aleph null ($\aleph_0$). And from these, higher orders of infinite numbers can be created, as one creates the rational numbers from the integers and the real numbers from the rationals. (pp. 497–8)

By the time Russell wrote *Principia Mathematica*, he did not think the above argument was sound, for by then he had accepted the theory of types as part of his logic, and with type theory, the above argument cannot be made. For example, while zero is a class containing the null set, one is a class containing the class containing the null set. Thus, zero and one are of different logical types. Thus, the sets that are the numbers zero and one cannot be members of the same set, and the number two cannot be formed. With type theory, we cannot add different numbers together to get ever greater numbers, as Russell did in his 1903 argument. Russell thus no longer thought he could prove the existence of an infinite number of things by the time he wrote *Principia*, but because much of mathematics presupposes this and especially Peano's axiom 3, Russell was obliged to assume it as an axiom.

4 The multiplicative axiom, a.k.a. the axiom of choice

There is one final axiom of logic (or really, of set theory) that Russell added to the 1910 logicism of *Principia* that was not a part of the 1903 logicism of *Principles*. This last one Russell called the "multiplicative" axiom, which is now more commonly known as the axiom of choice. Russell's multiplicative axiom, like the axiom of infinity, is an existence theorem about infinity. The axiom of infinity claims that an infinite number of objects exist. The multiplicative axiom says that particular ways of ordering infinite classes of objects always exist. One version claims that it is always possible to select one member from every set in an infinite collection of non-empty sets. An important alternative version of the multiplicative axiom says that every set can be well-ordered, that is, arranged so that every subset of it has a first member. One must make some such assumption to know the product of an infinite number of factors, hence the name multiplicative axiom.

Russell had not realized in 1903 that he had assumed this axiom in the arithmetic of infinity of his early logicism. In 1904, Ernst Zermelo first explicitly stated the axiom of choice '(i.e., the multiplicative axiom) and used it to prove the well-ordering theorem, that every set can be well-ordered.[3] In addition to proving that every set can be well-ordered by assuming the axiom of choice, one can prove the axiom of choice by assuming that every set can be well-ordered. This shows that the two theorems are equivalent. Russell quickly saw that the axiom of choice was equivalent to his multiplicative axiom, and that it must be assumed for many proofs about infinity. In the 1910 *Principia*, Russell utilizes it explicitly.

Let's start with the definition of multiplication to see what the problem is with multiplying an infinite number of factors together. Russell says that whenever you define some mathematical operation such as multiplication, you must be able prove that there is a number produced by that operation. The proof of this is an existence theorem. Russell defines arithmetic operations in logicism using set theory. For example, addition of m and n is defined "constructively," that is, with instructions for finding ("constructing") the sum $m + n$. They are: take a set A with m number of members and another set B with n number of members, and with the set theoretic operation of class union form the union of A and B ($A \cup B$), The sum $m + n$ is then the number of members of the set $A \cup B$.

Similarly, Russell defines the product of m and n by producing a class having the number of members that is $m \times n$. To multiply m by n and find their product, we take a set A having m members and a set B with n members, and form a class of all possible ordered pairs of one member of A followed by one member of B. The number of ordered pairs is the product $m \times n$. Specifically, for the m members of A, $x_1, x_2, \ldots, x_m$, and the n members of B, $y_1, y_2, \ldots, y_n$, the set of all ordered pairs you can form from one member of A and one member of B is $\{ <x_1,y_1>, <x_1,y_2>, <x_1,y_3>, \ldots, <x_2,y_1>, <x_2,y_2>, <x_2,y_3>, \ldots, <x_m,y_n> \}$. The number of these ordered pairs is $m \times n$. This can always be proved for a finite number of factors, as in the case of $m \times n$ where there are just two factors. However, for an infinite number of factors, one cannot prove that a set whose number is the product of those factors exists without assuming the multiplicative axiom.

Notice, it is not that we cannot show how to construct the product of *two* infinite numbers. We know how to do this. For example, it can be shown that $\aleph_0 \times \aleph_0 = \aleph_0$. The problem occurs when we have an *infinite* number of factors to multiply, *even when each factor itself is finite*. But what is this multiplicative axiom that we supposedly need and yet cannot prove, you no doubt wonder. To state the multiplicative axiom, we first introduce the concept of a selection, which is a set constructed by selecting exactly one member from a group of sets: for a set k with a number of other sets as members, a selection of k will be a set constructed by selecting exactly one member from each set that is a member of k.

Again, we multiply *m* by *n* using a set *A* with *m* members and a set *B* with *n* members by constructing a third set of all ordered pairs consisting of one member of *A* and one of *B*. Each ordered pair is a *selection* from *A* and *B*. The number of all such selections is the product *m* × *n*. To find the product of two factors, *m* and *n*, we make selections from *A* and *B*. To define the product of *n* factors, we make selections from *n* sets, *A*, *B*, . . . , *N*. When multiplying a finite number of factors, we can always do this. But when *n* is infinite, so that there are an infinite number of classes and we must select one member from each to create a selection, it is not certain that this can be done. Even when we know that each of the sets is nonempty, we cannot be sure there is a selection. The multiplicative axiom says that a selection from a set of nonempty classes always exists, even when the set has an infinite number of members. This claim cannot be proved.

Why can't we *know* that there is a selection from an infinite number of nonempty sets? Why do we need to *assume* this? Why can't we prove it instead? The answer is controversial, that is, disputed. For now, we simply support this claim inductively by pointing out that so far no mathematician has proved the multiplicative axiom from more basic assumptions. There have been a number of purported proofs, but in each case the proof is found to assume a proposition that is equivalent to the multiplicative axiom: you can prove the multiplicative axiom if you assume some other proposition, but to prove the new proposition you must assume the multiplicative axiom. Still, these arguments are useful for finding propositions that are equivalent to the multiplicative axiom and that shed some light on explaining the problem.

In some special cases, you *can* know that a selection exists from an infinite number of classes. For example, for a set *k* containing an infinite number of sets, if you know that one of the sets is the null set, you know that no selection can be made from *k*. (If one of the factors is zero, the product is zero, just as with finite multiplication.) Or if you know that each member of *k* has exactly one member, you know that a selection can be made. Then, exactly one selection can be made: an infinite number of ones multiplied together still equal one. And if you know that each class contains exactly two *natural* numbers, you know that in each class one member is greater than the other. You can then stipulate the rule to take the least member to construct a selection, and thus know that a selection exists for that particular set of infinite sets.

On the other hand, if k contains an infinite number of couples (sets with two members) that we do not know anything about, for example, if we do not know whether or not the members of these couples are natural numbers and so cannot be sure that they can be ordered in terms of greater and lesser, we cannot know that a selection can be made from the couples. For a finite number of couples we can go from one to another, determining what the members of each are by enumeration. By ordering them in that way, we know which we are taking when we select a member from each couple. However, for an infinite number of couples, we cannot use enumeration, but must know enough about their members to define a rule saying which to select.

Similarly, we can make a selection from an infinite number of sets when each set contains any finite number of members that we know enough about to put in some order. We can then define a rule for picking exactly one from each set. But when we do not know anything more than that there are an infinite number of sets each containing a finite number of members, we do not know enough to define a rule to pick exactly one from each and form a selection.

In addition to knowing that one cannot make a selection from an infinite number of sets when one is the null set, or knowing that one can make a selection when each set has one member, or each has two members that are natural numbers, we can also make a selection when each of an infinite number of sets consists of a subset of the *natural numbers,* even when each consists of an infinite subset of the natural numbers. Here too we know enough to order each set so that we can specify a rule for making a selection from them.

When we have an infinite number of sets each consisting of an infinite subset of the natural numbers, we can make a selection from them because we know that any subset of natural numbers can be ordered so it has a least member, and when this member is taken away it has a new least member. We also know enough so we know that we can order them and any subset of them with the relation of *less than.* And knowing this much, we can construct a rule for selecting a member of each of these infinite subsets. It is because we know enough about the members of each infinite subset that we can organize them and create a rule for selecting exactly one from each subset. Specifically, for any infinite number of sets whose members can be arranged so that it has a least member and each of its subsets does too (so that when the least member is removed from the set, there will always be a new least member), we can construct a rule for selecting one member from each set, even though there are an infinite number of them.

Here is a new definition: Any set of objects ordered in this way is said to be a *well-ordered set*. That is, any set that can be arranged so that it has a least member and every subset of it does too is called a *well-ordered set*. So if we have an infinite number of sets, and the members of each can be well-ordered, we can make a selection from them. It is because the natural numbers can be well-ordered so that every subset of them is well-ordered that we know there exists a selection from an infinite number of subsets of the natural numbers, even when every one of these infinite subsets itself is infinite. More generally, we can make a selection from any set consisting of an infinite number of well-ordered sets.

We know, then, that we can make a selection from any set containing an infinite number of well-ordered sets. But are all sets well-ordered? No. Even the natural numbers can be arranged so that they are *not* well-ordered. The issue is not whether all sets *are* well-ordered but whether they *can* be well-ordered. If so, there is a selection from every infinite collection of (nonempty) sets. But it is not known whether all sets can be well-ordered, though many people think they can be. But since it cannot be known (cannot be proved), to treat any arbitrary infinite set of objects as capable of being well-ordered, we must *assume* that it can be done.

The axiom of well-ordering is equivalent to the multiplicative axiom. If all sets can be well-ordered, there is a selection from any one of them, even from an infinite number of sets each with an infinite number of members. It can be similarly proved that if there is a selection from such a set of sets, the sets can all be well-ordered. The two axioms are equivalent. But can a selection be made from any infinite set of sets. There are many special cases of infinite sets of sets from which we can make a selection. But in general, we do not know. We can only *assume* that it is possible.

We originally decided that we needed the multiplicative axiom to define multiplication. That definition is a very general one: to multiply two factors, u and v, we take a set with u members and another with v members and create another set of all possible selections we can make from the first two sets. The number of selections will be the product of u and v. In this definition, we do not know what kinds of objects these sets contain. Similarly, when we define the product of an infinite number of factors, we must start with a collection of an infinite number of sets, each with the number of members that is the number of the factor it represents, and seek to create a set of all possible selections from them. But because this definition is general—it does not tell us what sorts of objects are in these infinite sets—we cannot know whether or not they can be well-ordered, and so cannot know if we can make a selection from them or how.

Beyond this we will not go in our introduction to the infinite in Russell's logicism. Suffice it to say, the multiplicative axiom and its equivalent propositions are of great interest—in fact, they are among the most interesting propositions of set theory—and further study of them would be rewarding to anyone making it, no matter what the results.

5 Logicism: Logic or mathematics?

Here is one last problem with the multiplicative axiom: though the axiom can be stated in completely logical concepts, Russell viewed it as a mathematical proposition, perhaps because it cannot be proved from simpler logical propositions. This would mean that his logicist program is not a complete success. In the same vein, one might wonder if the axiom of infinity is truly a logical axiom, or if it too belongs to mathematics. Again, it can be stated in purely logical terms, but Russell thought that that is not in itself enough in itself to make it a logical principle. In fact, Russell thought that it is neither, but that it is an empirical question as to whether or not there are an infinite number of things in the universe. But empirical or not, it is one that both logic (as used in logicism) and mathematics (as used in transfinite arithmetic) need, so it is still either an axiom of logic or mathematics.

Finally, it will be remembered that Russell had to assume an axiom of reducibility to make the logicism work when it includes the theory of types. Russell thought that this too is not a logical axiom, but here one might take exception with him. It can be described in purely logical terms, but more than this, every instance of it in logic is known to be true. This seems to give it inductive support, with all of the evidence for it coming from logic itself, and to thus make it a logical axiom in the authors' eyes. Here too, as with the multiplicative axiom, the reader is commended to his or her own study of what counts as logic and what counts as mathematics and whether logicism is one or the either or neither or both.

NOTES

Chapter 2

1 Frege, *Foundations of Arithmetic* (1884); *Basic Laws of Arithmetic* (vol. 1 1893, vol. 2 1903); Dedekind, *Essays on the Theory of Numbers* (1888).

2 For Russell's letter and Frege's reply, see van Heijenoort, *From Frege to Gödel*, pp. 124–8.

3 For Frege's definition of number, see Frege, *Foundations of Arithmetic*, chapter 4, p.195,ln.9.

4 *Introduction to Mathematical Philosophy*, p. 9.

5 *Principia Mathematica*, vol. 2, 1st ed., section c summary, *120 summary, pp. 187, 207.

Chapter 3

1 Example due to Bill Barthelemy.

2 *Principia Mathematica*, first edition, p. 70.

Chapter 7

1 Texts by Boole and Peirce on set theory and logic are in Ewald, *From Kant to Hilbert*, vol. 1, chapters 11 and 15.

2 For Cantor on set theory and transfinite arithmetic see Cantor, *Contributions to the Founding of the Theory of Transfinite Numbers*, 1915. The statement about how much of Cantor's set theory Russell incorporated is due to Gregory Landini.

3 In, "Beweis, dass jede Menge wohlgeordnet werden kann," *Mathematische Annalen*, 59, 514–16. English trans. in van Heijenoort 1967, pp. 139–41.

FURTHER READING

For Russell's logicism read *Introduction to Mathematical Philosophy* then *Principia Mathematica*. Useful modern accounts of logicism to read along with these are Elliott Mendelson, *Number Systems and the Foundations of Analysis*, and Robert Stoll, *Set Theory and Logic*.

Accessible accounts of Russell's early and middle period philosophies are, respectively, *Problems of Philosophy* and *Outline of Philosophy*. Russell's principal works on metaphysics, knowledge, and language are *Our Knowledge of the External World*, "Philosophy of Logical Atomism," *Analysis of Mind, Analysis of Matter, Inquiry into Meaning and Truth*, and *Human Knowledge*.

Russell's own accounts of his changing philosophy are "My Mental Development" and *My Philosophical Development*. Other good surveys of his thought are A. J. Ayer, *Bertrand Russell*, and Peter Hylton, *Russell, Idealism, and the Emergence of Analytic Philosophy*.

For Russell on religion, war, education, sexual morality, science and society, his political activism, and history of philosophy, see, respectively, *Why I Am Not a Christian, Justice in War-Time, Education and the Social Order, Marriage and Morals, The Scientific Outlook, Yours Faithfully, Bertrand Russell*, and *History of Western Philosophy*. Russell's three-volume *Autobiography* is a literary classic.

REFERENCES

Abbreviations: *CPBR* is *Collected Papers of Bertrand Russell*. The number after it denotes the volume number. Thus *CPBR6* is volume 6 of the *Collected Papers of Bertrand Russell*. The first date in an entry is the original date of publication. Later dates in the same entry are to later editions. All page references are to the later editions.

Collected papers of Bertrand Russell

Vol. 4. *Foundations of Logic, 1903–05*, Alasdair Urquhart (ed.). Routledge, 1994.

Vol. 6. *Logical and Philosophical Papers, 1909–13*, John Slater (ed.). Routledge, 1992.

Vol. 7. *Theory of Knowledge: The 1913 Manuscript*, Elizabeth Ramsden Eames (ed.). Allen and Unwin, 1984.

Vol. 8. *The Philosophy of Logical Atomism and Other Essays, 1914–19*, John Slater (ed.). Allen and Unwin, 1986.

Vol. 9. *Essays on Language, Mind, and Matter, 1919–1926*, John Slater (ed.). Unwin Hyman, 1988.

Vol. 10. *A Fresh Look at Empiricism, 1927–1942*, John Slater (ed.). Routledge, 1996.

Vol. 11. *Last Philosophical Testament, 1943–1968*, John Slater (ed.). Routledge, 1997.

Other references

Cantor, Georg, 1895–7, "Beiträge sur Begründung der transfiniten Mengenlehre," *Mathematische Annalen* 46, 481–512; 49, 206–46. English tr. Cantor 1915.

—, 1915, *Contributions to the Founding of the Theory of Transfinite Numbers*, La Salle IL, Open Court. Repr. Dover, 1955.

Dedekind, Richard, 1872, *Stetigkeit und irrationale Zahlen*, Braunschweig, Vieweg. English tr. Dedekind 1901.

—, 1888, *Was sind und was sollen die Zahlen?* Braunschweig, Vieweg. English tr. Dedekind 1901.

—, 1901, *Essays on the Theory of Numbers*, Chicago, Open Court. Repr. Dover, 1963.

Ewald, William, 1996, *From Kant to Hilbert*, vol. 1, Oxford, Oxford University Press.

Frege, Gottlob, 1884, *Die Grundlagen der Arithmetik, eine logisch-mathematische Untersuchung über den Begriff der Zahl*, Breslau, Köbner. English tr. Frege 1950.

—, 1893, *Grundgesetze der Arithmetik, begriffsschriftlich abgeleitet*, vol. 1, Jena, Pohle. Partial English tr. Frege 1964.

—, 1903, *Grundgesetze der Arithmetik, begriffsschriftlich abgeleitet*, vol. 2, Jena, Pohle.

—, 1950, *The Foundations of Arithmetic*, tr. J. L. Austin, Oxford, Blackwell. 2nd rev. ed. 1953.

—, 1964, *Basic Laws of Arithmetic*, tr. M. Furth, Berkeley, University of California Press.

van Heijenoort, Jean, 1967, *From Frege to Gödel*, Cambridge, MA, Harvard University Press.

Kant, Immanuel, 1783, *Prolegomena zu einer jeden künftigen Metaphysik*, Riga, Hartsnoch. English tr. Kant 1988.

—, 1988, *Prolegomena to Any Future Metaphysics*, tr. James W. Ellington, Indianapolis, IN, Hackett.

—, 1781/1787, *Kritik der reinen Vernunft*, Riga, Hartsnoch. English tr. Kant 1965.

—, 1965, *Critique of Pure Reason*, tr. Norman Kemp Smith, Boston, Bedford/St. Martin's, 1965.

Neurath, Otto, 1932/1933, "Protokollsätze," *Erkenntnis* 3, 204–14. English tr. Neurath 1959.

—, 1959, "On Protocol Sentences," tr. George Schlick, in *Logical Positivism*, ed. A. J. Ayer, Glencoe, IL, Free Press, pp.199–208.

Peano, Giuseppe, 1889, *Arithmetices principia, nova methodo exposita*, Torino, Bocca. English tr. Peano 1973.

—, 1973, *Principles of Arithmetic, Presented by a New Method*, in *Selected Works of Giuseppe Peano*, tr. Hubert Kennedy, Toronto, University of Toronto Press, pp. 101–34.

Russell, Bertrand, 1903a, *Principles of Mathematics*, Cambridge, Cambridge University Press. 2nd ed., W. W. Norton, 1937.

—, 1903b, "Points about Denoting," *CPBR4*, pp. 306–13.

—, 1905a, "On Denoting," *Mind* 14, 479–93. Repr. *CPBR4*, pp. 415–27.

—, 1905b, "Necessity and Possibility," *CPBR4*, pp. 508–20.

—, 1907, "On the Nature of Truth," *Proceedings of the Aristotelian Society* 7, pp. 28–49.

—, 1908, "Mathematical Logic as Based on the Theory of Types," *American Journal of Mathematics* 30, 222–62. Repr. Russell 1956.

—, 1911a, "Knowledge by Acquaintance and Knowledge by Description," *Proceedings of the Aristotelian Society* 11, 108–28. Repr. *CPBR6*, pp. 148–61.

—, 1911b, "Le réalisme analytique," *Bulletin de la société française de philosophie* 11, 53–82. English tr. "Analytic Realism," *CPBR6*, pp. 133–46.

—, 1911c, "L'importance philosophique de la logistique," *Revue de métaphysique et de morale* 19, 282–91. English tr. "The Philosophical Importance of Mathematical Logic," *CPBR6*, pp. 33–40.

—, 1912a, *Problems of Philosophy*, London, Williams and Norgate. Repr. Oxford University Press, 1976.

—, 1912b, "On the Relations of Universals and Particulars," *Proceedings of the Aristotelian Society* 12, 1–24. Repr. *CPBR6*, pp. 167–82.

—, 1912c, "On Matter," *CPBR6*, pp. 80–95.

—, 1912d, "What is Logic?" *CPBR6*, pp. 55–6.

—, 1913, *Theory of Knowledge*, *CPBR7*.

—, 1914a, *Our Knowledge of the External World*, Chicago, Open Court.

—, 1914b, "On the Nature of Acquaintance," *Monist* 24, 1–16, 161–87, 435–53.

—, 1918a, "The Philosophy of Logical Atomism," *Monist* 28, 495–527; 29, 33–63, 190–222, 345–80. Repr. *CPBR8*, pp. 160–244.

—, 1918b, "Bertrand Russell's Notes on the New Work He Intends to Undertake," *CPBR8*, pp. 313–14.

—, 1918c, "Manuscript Notes," *CPBR8*, pp. 247–71.

—, 1919a, "Analysis of Mind," *CPBR9*, pp. 4–15.

—, 1919b, *Introduction to Mathematical Philosophy*, London, Allen and Unwin. Second impression 1922.

—, 1919c, "On Propositions," *Aristotelian Society Supplementary Volume* 2, 1–43. Repr. *CPBR8*, pp. 278–306.

—, 1920, "The Wisdom of Our Ancestors," *Athenaeum* no. 4,680, 43. Repr. *CPBR9*, pp. 403–6.

—, 1921a, *Analysis of Mind*, London, Allen and Unwin. Repr. Routledge, 1997.

—, 1921b, "Introduction to Wittgenstein's *Tractatus Logico-Philosophicus*," *CPBR9*, pp. 101–12.

—, 1922, "Physics and Perception," *CPBR9*, pp. 125–33.

—, 1923a, "Vagueness," *Australasian Journal of Psychology and Philosophy* 1, 84–92. Repr. *CPBR9*, pp. 147–54.

—, 1923b, "Truth Functions and Meaning Functions," *CPBR9*, pp. 156–8.

—, 1924, "Logical Atomism," *Contemporary British Philosophy*, first series, ed. J. H. Muirhead, London, Allen and Unwin, pp. 357–83. Repr. *CPBR9*, pp. 162–79.

—, 1926, "The Meaning of Meaning," *The Dial* 81, 114–21. Repr. *CPBR9*, pp. 138–44.

—, 1927a, *Analysis of Matter*, London, Kegan Paul, Trench, Trubner. Repr. Spokesman Books, 2007.

—, 1927b, *Outline of Philosophy*, London, Allen and Unwin. Repr. Routledge, 1995.

—, 1938a, "On Verification," *Proceedings of the Aristotelian Society* 38, 1–20. Repr. *CPBR10*, pp. 345–59.

—, 1938b, "The Relevance of Psychology to Logic," *Aristotelian Society, Supplementary Volume: Action, Perception, and Measurement* 17, 42–53. Repr. *CPBR10*, pp. 362–70.

—, 1940, *Inquiry into Meaning and Truth*, New York, W. W. Norton. Repr. Routledge, 1995.

—, 1945? "Non-Deductive Inference," *CPBR11*, pp. 121–9.

—, 1948a, *Human Knowledge: Its Scope and Limits*, London, Allen and Unwin. Repr. Routledge, 2003.

—, 1948b, "Postulates of Scientific Inference," *CPBR11*, pp. 129–38.

—, 1956, *Logic and Knowledge*, Robert Marsh (ed.), London, Allen and Unwin.

—, 1959, *My Philosophical Development*, New York, Simon & Schuster.

Whitehead, Alfred North and Bertrand Russell, 1910–13, *Principia Mathematica*, 3 vols., 1st ed., Cambridge, Cambridge University Press. 2nd ed., Cambridge University Press, 1925–27.

Wittgenstein, Ludwig, 1921, *Tractatus Logico-Philosophicus*. English tr. London, Routledge & Kegan Paul, 1922.

Zermelo, Ernst, 1904, "Beweis, dass jede Menge wohlgeordnet werden kann," *Mathematische Annalen*, 59, 514–16. English tr. van Heijenoort 1967, pp. 139–41.

INDEX